"CHURCH AND AGE UNITE!"

NOTRE DAME STUDIES IN AMERICAN CATHOLICISM
Sponsored by the
Charles and Margaret Hall Cushwa Center
for the Study of American Catholicism

The Brownson-Hecker Correspondence
Joseph Grower and Richard Leliaert, editors

The Survival of American Innocence:
Catholicism in an Era of Disillusionment, 1920–1940
William M. Halsey

Faith and Fatherland: The Polish Church War in Wisconsin, 1896–1918
Anthony J. Kuzniewski

Chicago's Catholics: The Evolution of an American Identity
Charles Shanabruch

A Priest in Public Service: Francis J. Haas and the New Deal
Thomas E. Blantz, C.S.C.

Corporation Sole: Cardinal Mundelein and Chicago Catholicism
Edward R. Kantowicz

The Household of Faith:
Roman Catholic Devotions in Mid-Nineteenth-Century America
Ann Taves

People, Priests, and Prelates:
Ecclesiastical Democracy and the Tensions of Trusteeism
Patrick W. Carey

The Grail Movement and American Catholicism, 1940–1975
Alden V. Brown

The Diocesan Seminary in the United States:
A History from the 1780s to the Present
Joseph M. White

"Church and Age Unite!"

THE MODERNIST IMPULSE IN AMERICAN CATHOLICISM

R. Scott Appleby

University of Notre Dame Press
Notre Dame   London

Library of Congress Catalog-in-Publication Data

Appleby, R. Scott, 1956–
    Church and age unite : the modernist impulse in American
Catholicism / R. Scott Appleby.
        p.   cm. — (Notre Dame in American Catholicism)
    Includes bibliographical references and index.
    ISBN 0-268-00782-9
    1. Modernism—Catholic Church.   I. Title.   II. Series
BX1396.A77   1992
282'.73'09041—dc20   90-50976
                                                                            CIP

282.73
App

CONTENTS

ACKNOWLEDGMENTS

"Nothing we do, however virtuous, can be accomplished alone," Reinhold Niebuhr wrote, "therefore, we are saved by love." And by attentive mentors, generous colleagues, and dedicated friends and family. Martin E. Marty has been mentor, colleague, and friend during the years in which this project originated and developed from doctoral thesis to monograph. His enthusiastic support made the challenge of meeting his exacting standards liberating rather than burdensome. I feel very fortunate to have worked with him. In the early stages of thesis formulation David Tracy guided me through the bibliographical thicket of philosophical and theological modernism. Arthur Mann brought his extensive knowledge of American social and intellectual history to bear upon the thesis and offered several insightful suggestions concerning the organization and style of the narrative. John Root took apart the chapter on Zahm paragraph by paragraph, but was kind enough to guide me in putting it back together. David Schultenover offered many helpful suggestions and corrections to chapter 2. Jay Dolan invited me to present an earlier form of chapter 4 at the Cushwa Center for the Study of American Catholicism and continually encouraged me to complete the revisions of the manuscript. Without his persistence I would not have finished the project.

Joseph M. White, Christopher Kauffman, William S. Dolan, and William Portier contributed archival information, notes, and interpretations. Portier was especially generous with his important discovery of the "biography" of John Slattery. John Bowen hosted a week at St. Mary's Seminary in Baltimore and oriented me to the Sulpician archives housed nearby. James Connelly provided convenient access to the Holy Cross archives at Notre Dame. The late Robert G. Kleinhans provided useful criticism of an earlier version of the manuscript. Joseph McShane offered moral support, advice, and warm friendship over the years. Kathleen Mullaney guided me in the translations of the

Slattery manuscript. Patricia Mitchell and David Spesia spent hours proofing and copying the manuscript in its various versions. Barbara Lockwood, a cherished friend and colleague, demonstrated considerable grace under pressure in typing and helping to edit various versions of the manuscript. Ann Rice of Notre Dame Press skillfully steered the manuscript through the publication process.

The book is dedicated to Peggy Appleby, whose forbearance and encouragement enabled me to initiate and complete this project even as our home filled with four children.

All these people saved me through their love, but none of them are responsible for any errors in what follows.

INTRODUCTION:

The Trajectory of Modernism in American Catholic Thought, 1895–1910

In 1895 American Catholic priest John Zahm of Notre Dame began work on a book entitled *Evolution and Dogma*. A scientist as well as an apologist for Catholicism, Zahm felt obliged to confront the implications of Darwinism and the general theory of evolution for Christian theism. When, within four years, his efforts brought him to the brink of public censure in Rome, he obediently withdrew his book from publication and renounced whatever theological errors it contained.[1]

Fifteen years after Zahm began *Evolution and Dogma,* another American Catholic and a former priest, William Laurence Sullivan, published in book form a series of *Letters to His Holiness Pope Pius X.* Therein he repudiated papal claims to religious authority and castigated the Roman system of theology articulated by Jesuits "whose reputation for scholarship," he charged, "is one of the most extraordinary delusions of the pious."[2] Due to the continued confinement of Catholic theology and philosophy within that system, Sullivan concluded, he was compelled, as a patriotic American and a modern Christian, to end his communion with the Roman church. His parting shot served as an epitaph to fifteen years of American Catholic intellectual activity: "The very air and soil of America are favorable to Modernism, as to all other movements that make for intelligence, strength, sincerity and independence."[3]

In his seminal 1976 study of the modernist impulse in American Protestantism, William R. Hutchison identified a cluster of beliefs—in cultural immanentism, religiously based progressivism, and the adaptation of religious ideas to modern culture held—by liberal Protestants

1

from 1870 to 1930. These modernists differed from other liberals by the level of self-awareness with which they appropriated the modern. They accomplished deliberately what others had attempted without self-conscious and sustained reference to modernity, namely, the recasting of the gospel in terms of what was then modern thought. Modernists were fully aware that they were modernists.[4] In what follows I have identified a similar impulse among an influential group of American Catholic priests—mainly, progressive scientists, seminary professors, litterateurs, and missionaries—who absorbed and attempted to integrate into their teaching, writing, and self-understanding, the theological, philosophical, and methodological insights of the "movement" that came to be known as modernism.[5]

Pulling together threads of European Catholic modernism, American Protestant liberalism, and American Catholic progressivism, the American Catholic expression of modernist thought was, given this varied intellectual pedigree, unique both in content and idiom. In the decade-and-a-half between *Evolution and Dogma* and *Letters to His Holiness*, the Catholic Church in the United States experienced a flurry of activity distinct from prior Americanizing and liberalizing efforts of priests and prelates, and resolutely opposed to the neo-scholastic theological orthodoxy which reasserted itself with a vengeance in America, as elsewhere, after 1907. This era of intellectual vitality was inaugurated by Zahm's early work on evolution; raised to a level of self-awareness by priest-professors of St. Joseph's Seminary, Dunwoodie (in Yonkers, New York), who addressed themselves to the theological problems attendant upon the rise of historical consciousness, the notion of vital immanence, developmentalism, and critical methods of inquiry; and radicalized by Sullivan and by Josephite priest John R. Slattery, both of whom eventually renounced the priesthood and the Roman Catholic Church.

The priests who are the subject of this study were few in number and did not produce a single *magnum opus* that could withstand the withering intellectual and ecclesial tests of their generation. Their work was largely derivative in that they drew upon, and developed for their own audiences, the insights of European Catholic modernists such as Alfred Loisy, George Tyrrell, and St. George Jackson Mivart. And, once the papal condemnation of modernism unleashed a torrent of criticism upon their European mentors and initiated procedures of repression throughout the Catholic intellectual world, the influence and momentum these American priests had begun to enjoy was abruptly stifled.

Yet this period of modernist influence became an important and explicit episode in the larger, ongoing process by which the American Catholic church came to know the modern world. These priests were the first American Catholics to perceive and to fully confront the range of intellectual challenges posed to religion by nineteenth-century scientific, historical, and literary-critical scholarship—and the first to appropriate the new terminologies and methodologies in order to comprehend them and bring them "into conformity with Christ." They were, in this sense, the first modern American Catholics.[6] Their story, beginning in 1895 with Zahm's attempt to reconcile post-Darwinian theories of evolution with Catholic theism, and ending with Sullivan's radical Americanism in 1910, is one of an increasing awareness among certain progressive Catholic apologists that a radically different, surpassingly modern worldview lay behind the new methods of reading and interpreting creation, history, and the Bible; that the religious sensibilities possible within this worldview must be developed and articulated in dialogue with post-Kantian epistemological and philosophical systems; and that such a religious worldview stood the best chance of providing a reliable and lasting foundation for twentieth-century Catholic identity. These levels of awareness, embodied by the entire group of priests rather than by any one of them, were expressed in their enunciation of a simple dictum: the ancient faith must be wed to modern thought.[7]

Associated with this dictum were certain implications for American Catholic intellectual and religious life. Because the nature of the relationship between God and the human community—revealed in nature, in sacred texts and traditions, and in personal and communal history—required fresh examination in the light of "modern thought," the traditional apologetics, abounding in refutations of modernity and grounded in a pre-modern philosophical theology, would no longer suffice. The enemy, they came to believe, was not modernity as such but the virulent forms of atheism thriving within the modern religio-cultural environment—and thriving, in large part, because theism in America had provided no modern counterforce. The mounting of such a counterforce required that priests be educated in the new methods and ideas and thereby become competent to supervise their application in matters of faith.[8]

At first, these American priests did not fully perceive the need for a new synthesis between the claims of faith and science, dogma and history. Before 1895 Zahm was occupied primarily with absorbing the details of the new theories of evolution, popularizing them for a

Catholic audience, and discerning their implications for the understanding of divine providence. His early treatises on the topic argued for the acceptance of the general theory of biological evolution but did not indicate the ways in which such acceptance necessitated a reconceptualization of theological categories such as divine providence and human freedom under God. With *Evolution and Dogma*, however, the Notre Dame priest-scientist explicitly addressed the constructive theological task. He did so by demonstrating the possibility, within the Catholic tradition, of holding to some version of "theistic evolution" and thereby harmonizing, and even unifying, the claims of science and faith.

Within a decade, the professors at St. Joseph's Seminary in Dunwoodie, New York, were presenting the concept of theistic evolution to their students as but one among many new possibilities for Catholics seeking to express the traditional faith in contemporary terms. These men became aware of, and engaged seriously, a variety of new possibilities, including the notion that religious creeds are in large part formulas owing as much in conception to historical exigencies as to divine inspiration; the importance of pre-notional religious experience in the life of the believer; and the need to replace discursive, quasi-scientific ways of speaking about the divine with more imaginative, intuitionist religious language.

These American Catholics eventually discovered that the European modernist program of theological updating, spiritual renewal, and institutional reform was imbued with a spirit of radical self-criticism that demanded a revising of the very categories and concepts of religious thought. They came to this discovery gradually, in fits and starts, over a span of fifteen years. One may speak of a "trajectory of modernism" in the critical thought of certain American Catholic scholars of this period, of a growing self-awareness affecting their understanding of the significance of their work as well as their changing relationship to the institutional church. This sense of identity grew particularly acute as it became obvious at the turn of the century that Rome looked with suspicion upon the efforts of their European counterparts. As they grappled with the specters of evolution and scientific criticism, vital immanence and developmentalism, American priests recognized, with increasing clarity as the new century dawned, that Rome's unswerving ecclesiopolitical commitment to the philosophical-theological system of neo-scholasticism precluded the possibility of a fair hearing for loyal dissenters. When the Vatican's condemnation of modernism came in 1907, these men faced a stark dilemma: respect the strictures imposed upon them by authority, or reject those strictures and thereby repudiate the institution and its exclusive claim of authority to mediate the religious tradition to the faithful.

Sullivan and Slattery chose the latter course. Each man allowed his personal vision of a renewed, restructured Catholicism to overwhelm his sense of loyalty to the contemporary institutional face of the tradition. Ironically perhaps, given their relatively sophisticated historical sense of the tradition, both of these men made their repudiation of Roman Catholicism a point of honor, thereby accepting the Vatican's identification of the religious tradition with its institutional embodiment. Each felt that the institution had corrupted the tradition beyond recognition or hope of redemption. Although Sullivan, for example, did in fact lend a "catholicizing" emphasis to Unitarianism, he did not self-consciously attempt to conform "vital religion" to the requirements of a Catholic sacramentality, anthropology, or worldview.[9] After experiencing what he described as the fickle personalities of the elites who controlled the future of the church in the United States, Slattery concluded that turn-of-the-century Roman Catholicism would not break free of the racism, authoritarianism, and theological exclusivism stifling its vital religious impulses. Both men moved outside of the tradition.

Thus, they moved beyond Catholic modernism as well. Common to the figures prominent in this study, and to many European Catholic modernists, was a thoroughgoing commitment to the task of preserving theological continuity with the fullness of the Catholic tradition as it had unfolded in history. They rejected the term "modernism" as a description of their efforts to the extent that it connoted something wholly unprecedented and new. To the contrary, they saw themselves as defenders, developers, and expositors of those essential themes and insights of Catholic religious experience, philosophy, theology, and even ecclesiology, that had been neglected or disdained by nineteenth century neo-scholasticism. Echoing European Catholic modernists such as Tyrrell and von Hügel, the American priests who dabbled in modernism—including Sullivan and Slattery during their "Catholic periods"—pointed to "reformers" who had arisen periodically in Catholic history to retrieve the fullness of possibilities inherent in the tradition and to prevent its identification with any one system of thought. The models for the European and American modernists were those who had served as advocates for, and defenders of, the rich catholicity of the tradition—"intellectual mavericks" such as Duns Scotus, Erasmus, Pascal, and Newman.

For example, Zahm argued forcefully that the theistic evolution discussed in *Evolution and Dogma* was part and parcel of orthodox Catholic teaching reaching back through Aquinas to Augustine—a claim which his neo-scholastic detractors adamantly rejected.[10] The editors of the *New York Review* reserved a prominent place in their journal for articles locating the seeds of "modernist" epistemology and ecclesiology in the writings of a line of great Catholic thinkers, their influence unduly displaced by the rise of Catholic integralism. At the head of this class stood Augustine, Duns Scotus, Pascal, and Newman. The latter was considered by many of the *Review's* contributors to be the father of the contemporary reawakening.[11] During his Catholic period, Sullivan described the notion of vital immanence as a biblical and an apostolic theme which informed the thought of Pascal, Newman, and the great mystics, among others. Progressive priests at the Catholic University of America were in contact with Zahm, Sullivan, and the Dunwoodians, and took up the general theme of the neo-apostolic character of modern religious thought in articles published in the *Catholic University Bulletin* demonstrating, to take one example, that the principle of development had been recognized by Catholic theologians since the apostolic age.[12] In sum, these American Catholic priests wedded the new scholarship to apologetics in an effort to delineate a firm historical foundation for the modern religious worldview they found appealing.

In addition to this emphasis on reclaiming and reappropriating neglected traditional elements of Catholic thought, the American modernists came eventually to share another impulse present in the work of their colleagues in Europe, namely, the tendency to attempt a synthesis of "ancient faith and modern thought." As their comprehension of the process of the historical development of religion grew more sophisticated, they began to see it as their right and responsibility to guide and direct the course of Catholic development in their own era. This entailed something more than open recognition of the need for a fresh apologetical tack and a greater familiarity with the established results of critical sciences. With varying degrees of self-reflection and adopting different strategies of approach, each of the figures and groups profiled here made at least a modest beginning at the task of reconceptualizing and rearticulating religious faith so that it might speak a vital word to modern men and women.

On the other hand, these American Catholic priests did not, by and large, approximate the sophistication and range of their mentors in England, France, and Germany. Zahm and some members of the staff at Dunwoodie never publicly addressed certain intricate and controversial questions suggested by their main body of work, including its implications for the concept of religious authority. These questions are not absent in their writings, but neither are they explored with the same directness and unflinching honesty which characterized the approach of their European colleagues. However, a small number of the Americans, most notably Sullivan, Slattery, and certain contributors to the *New York Review*, did engage directly the larger issues involved in their enterprise. But they did so after 1905 and, in the wake of the 1907 condemnation, the tone of these writings grew shrill and polemical, and any attempts at a complete "Catholic synthesis" were abandoned. [13]

The fact that these American Catholic modernists did not match their European counterparts in boldness of vision and sophistication of argument can be attributed to a number of factors: the absence of a consistently articulated theological tradition in their national background; the lack of institutional support for intellectual inquiry in the American church; and, consequently, the Americans' direct dependence on the European modernists (Zahm on Mivart, Driscoll on Loisy, Sullivan on Tyrrell). It is therefore not surprising that the American modernists were known primarily as the translators, commentators, and disseminators of the original work of Loisy, Tyrrell, von Hügel, Mivart, and their predecessors, such as Newman.[14] However, the priests who are the subject of this study also contributed to the elaboration of the new religious worldview by presenting modernism as the theological and philosophical expression of Americanism, a late nineteenth century ecclesiopolitical movement of clerics in France and America who believed that the unique ecclesial, religious, and political circumstances of the United States provided a suitable environment for the growth of genuine religious freedom and hence for genuine Catholicism in the twentieth century.

Americanism was embraced by bishops and priests who knew little of modernist thought but were initially supportive of it. Indeed, the American priests who dabbled in modernism were influenced and encouraged by a generation of liberal churchmen, including the prelates John Ireland, John J. Keane, and John Lancaster Spalding, who called for the Roman Catholic Church in the United States to adapt itself to the values of the modern American republic, including separation of church and state, and liberty of conscience and religious belief. "I preach the new, the most glorious crusade," the archbishop of St. Paul announced in 1893, "Church and Age! Unite them in the name of humanity, in the name of God!"[15] Although concerned primarily with the relationship between the church and the republic, this type of rhetoric, which included a ringing endorsement of intellectual freedom, seemed to Zahm, Sullivan, Slattery, and Driscoll to provide episcopal mandate for the complicated task of reconciling Catholic faith with the best of modern philosophy and science. Yet Archbishop Ireland did not perceive the radical implications of Americanism for the questions of authority and theological method—and later rejected the implications drawn by modernists. However, others such as Zahm, who traveled in Ireland's company and shared his enthusiasms for a unity between church and age, recognized that the achievement of the desired unity might require a bold adaptation of philosophical and religious thought. This presentation of Americanism and modernism as but two aspects of the same inchoate worldview was explicit in the writing of Sullivan and Slattery. [16]

Furthermore, these American priests believed in the importance of their role as the reporters and proponents of the new religious worldview, and thus set out to "convert" influential brother priests and a larger lay audience. It was precisely in their attempts to reach a larger public that they met sustained resistance from their religious superiors. Zahm merited the scrutiny of the hierarchy once he took to the summer chautauqua circuit to lecture on theistic evolution; the professors at Dunwoodie were likewise scrutinized once they began to publish the treatises of European modernists; and William Sullivan came under suspicion when he returned from missionary work in the rural South and began to develop a new apologetic for that audience. In the aftermath of *Pascendi Dominici Gregis*, Pius X's encyclical naming modernism "the synthesis of all heresies," even the most tolerant and indulgent of hierarchs, Farley of New York, could no longer deny the truth of the situation: these American scientists, theologians, apologists, and Scripture scholars posed a clear threat to the anti-modernists. Reprisals were swift and sure, and modernism in the American Catholic Church was crushed long before it came to full flower.[17]

The story of this short-lived episode within an otherwise meager intellectual history does indicate an openness to critical thought in the

American Catholic church at the turn of the century—and the limits to such openness. At some point in his priesthood each of the men profiled in this study—John Gmeiner, John Zahm, Francis Gigot, James Driscoll, William Sullivan, and John Slattery—attempted to integrate the thinking of European modernists and/or of American Protestant modernists into his own teaching and writing. The impact that these modernists and their writings made on their coreligionists is the subject of the concluding chapter examining the themes most prevalent in the Catholic periodicals of the day. From such a survey it is difficult even to speculate about the possible lines of development in the American Catholic assimilation of modernism had *Pascendi* not intervened. It is, of course, an interesting question. Could the Catholic community in the United States have produced, in the next generation, a thinker or thinkers of the stature of Tyrrell or Loisy? Would modernism in America, as in Europe, have taken on a sociopolitical cast? How might have the influence of mature modernist reflection shaped the social and intellectual agenda of the twentieth-century Catholic community? The sixth chapter does not attempt to provide direct answers to these questions, but it does examine the response of the Catholic community's intellectual leaders to the initiatives undertaken by their modernist colleagues.

In a study such as this, the use of terms and labels is always problematic. Even the standard labels "liberal" and "conservative" mislead, for they assume various shades of meaning when invoked by the historian, the political scientist, or the theologian. The term "modernism" is perhaps the most elusive of these, for its first and enduring definition was provided by its enemies. Obviously, given the anathemas hurled at them by Pius X, very few of the Catholic thinkers committed to the type of scholarship described in the broad and often inaccurate strokes of *Pascendi* answered to the name "modernist" which it imposed upon them. Even one who devoted a significant portion of his writing to an accurate description of modernism, George Tyrrell, preferred to refer to himself as a "liberal Catholic" to avoid the confused sense of the term "modernist"— but this only added to the confusion of naming. On the other hand, Americanist William Sullivan accepted for himself the term "modernist" unapologetically, even proudly—once he had separated himself from the ecclesiastical community which defined it originally. Because *Pascendi* did not make the necessary distinctions and thus incompletely comprehended the phenomenon of modernism, the actual modernists rejected the document and its terminology outright, or redefined the term completely. However, the historian may neither disregard the encyclical nor overlook the motivations behind it. *Pascendi* may not have been an accurate portrayal of the thought of Alfred Loisy—much less of the "movement"—but it was the articulation of the Vatican's perception that the new religious worldview at the heart of modernism threatened to topple every traditional belief, including the efficacy of the sacraments, the supernatural character of the church, and the divinity of Christ. It is beside the point to argue here that "tradition" was identified concretely and exclusively with the neo-scholastic version thereof: modernism threatened, above all else, the neo-scholastic synthesis, and the apostolic authority of the institution, and of the papacy itself, was not understood apart from that synthesis. Thus an understanding of anti-modernism does provide insight into those that they named "modernist."

To solve this problem of naming, some historians have avoided the term "modernist" altogether, or have replaced it with "developmentalist," a broader, more inclusive label descriptive of a "paradigm shift" in modern thought away from a classicist mentality to one informed by historical consciousness.[18] Because the events of the period in question, 1895 to 1910, form a distinct episode within the American church's gradual explication and application of developmentalist thought, I have retained the term "modernism" without relying exclusively on the definition of it provided by the encyclical. During this period the Roman church responded to the central institutional question raised by historical consciousness—the question of its implications for religious authority—by invoking the neo-scholastic habit of mind which had informed the decrees of the First Vatican Council. This response to historical consciousness was deemed to be inadequate and was challenged openly by developmentalist thinkers in biblical studies, philosophy, and theology. In turn the institutional church perceived and named the *full range* of challenges posed by developmentalist thought. Rather than harness the developmentalist genie to its own ends, the officers of the institution tried to force the genie back into the bottle, to repeal the discoveries and understandings of a generation of scholars. The modernists were the ones who first provoked a comprehensive response by the curia. Although they were not directly implicated by the encyclical, the Americans felt the sting of this counteroffensive no less sharply than did certain European modernists: they, too, were commanded by their religious superiors to suspend original research, to shut down presses, to abandon seminary curriculum reform, to renounce theistic evolution, to take an anti-modernist oath.

Second, although the magisterium actually singled out for condemnation a small number of modernists, it became clear, from the scope of the vigilance and repression which ensued, that it intended to inhibit or abort the projects of a far greater number of scholars. Perhaps it is hyperbole to claim that "everyone who was not dead" was under suspicion, but it is certainly true that dozens of European and American Catholic priests and laymen were plagued for the rest of their careers by the insinuation of modernism. They, too, were caught in the insulting and embarrassing atmosphere of heresy-hunting. Often misunderstood by their adversaries, their efforts were often repudiated by the church they sought to serve.

This is primarily a work of intellectual rather than institutional history. However, as Lester Kurtz demonstrated in a sociological study of the modernist conflict, both sides in the conflict were motivated at least in part by concern for their own status and power within the institutional church. Thus the integralists evinced an "elective affinity" for the neo-scholastic model because it legitimated their status within the institution. In this interpretation the modernists acted as "bureaucratic insurgents" attempting to overturn that model.[19]

Modernism was indeed defined by its enemies, variously described in these pages as "integralists," "neo-scholastics," or, simply, "anti-modernists." And it was in some measure a reaction against overweening ecclesiastical authority and the intellectual system which legitimated that authority. In recognition of this dynamic, I have included, especially in the treatment of Zahm, Sullivan, and Slattery, some of the details of the ecclesiastical interactions (and intrigue) that formed the month-to-month context within which these priests developed and refined their thought. Drawing on my own research and on a history of the Sulpicians by Christopher J. Kauffman and a survey of American Catholic biblical scholarship by Gerald P. Fogarty, I have summarized the now more familiar story of the priests at St. Joseph's Seminary, Dunwoodie.[20] In each of the chapters to follow, however, I am concerned less with covering every aspect of the narrative history and more with tracing what I take to be a coherent, if complex, line of thought that unfolded in the American church over a period of fifteen years. It did not, however, unfold systematically and in neat chronological sequence. The priests at Dunwoodie, for example, were just beginning their own efforts at a synthesis of ancient faith and modern thought as Slattery entered his radical phase and abandoned the endeavor altogether. The book is ordered according to this sequence of ideas. The chapter on Slattery, for example, follows those on Dunwoodie, for Slattery embodied the more radicalized position, and believed that "the trajectory of modernism," if traveled unflinchingly, propelled its adherents beyond the confines of Roman Catholicism.

A comprehensive definition of the phenomenon known as Roman Catholic modernism awaits the completion of critical historical research by a company of scholars now so engaged. But certain elements of this definition have already emerged and are useful indicators of modernist activity. On this basis I argue that "modernism" was for a time present in the work of certain American churchmen. In locating it, however, one must consider not only the example of the European modernists but also the specific cultural and religious context of the United States at the turn of the century.

1. John Zahm and the Case for Theistic Evolution

"Romanism and Evolution. Remarkable Advance. No Special Creation." "Father Zahm on the Six Days of Creation." "Father Zahm on Inspiration." "Father Zahm Honored with a Private Audience by His Holiness."[1] During the final decade of the nineteenth century, religious periodicals and secular newspapers in the United States chronicled the growing fascination of the American Catholic community with the public debate over the latest theories regarding the evolution of species. One figure in particular, John Augustine Zahm, a Holy Cross priest and professor of chemistry and physics in the University of Notre Dame, captured many of the headlines and captivated Catholic audiences with his clear and sophisticated explanation of the post-Darwinian controversies and his repeated assurances that the *idea* of evolution, properly understood, posed no obstacle to the faith of the Catholic.

In this regard Zahm played an unprecedented role in the religious history of the United States, for he combined in his person the seemingly diverse perspectives of the American citizen, the Catholic priest, and the evolutionist. Among the few American priest-scientists at the turn of the century, Zahm was the most competent, articulate, accomplished and the most prominent. Thus he was uniquely situated to contribute significantly to the process by which the American Catholic community came to know the modern world. For it was in the ongoing and bitter debate over evolution, and Darwin's theory thereof, that many American Catholics first encountered a scientific worldview buttressed by historical consciousness and developmentalist thought.[2] Zahm was the first well-known American Catholic scholar to provide positive scientific and theological commentary on the emergent theories of evolution.[3] As a prolific author, frequent lecturer before scientific congresses, and popular speaker on the Catholic summer-school circuit, Zahm reached a sizeable audience, especially from 1892 to 1896. His message was the ultimate compatibility of an evolutionary worldview and the central tenets of Catholic teaching on human nature, creation, and divine providence.

This public prominence also brought Zahm to the attention of the Roman Catholic curia. Curial officials moved to silence him when, like American Protestant and European Catholic scientists before him, Zahm suggested that certain traditional Christian doctrines could be interpreted as being compatible with the general theory of evolution. In many ways "the Zahm affair" epitomized the Roman Catholic crisis over evolution. It reinforced in the minds of conservative churchmen the suspicion that the application of critical methods of scientific inquiry to matters of revealed truth would lead Catholics astray. Zahm's opponents in the Vatican and in the American church linked his advocacy of evolution theory and modern science to the uncritical acceptance of American values that seemed to characterize the statements of certain "liberal" members of the clergy and hierarchy. Zahm's detractors worried that in addition to promoting what came to be called "Americanism," his approach to the question of evolution would seem to lend the authority of the church to a reinterpretation of patristic and scholastic terms and categories according to the inductive methods of science.

THE AMERICAN DEBATE OVER EVOLUTION

The theory of evolution by means of natural selection reached mainstream American thought through the writings of Herbert Spencer. His presentation of the new science was a subtle blend of Lamarckian and Darwinian hypotheses on evolution with the physicist Hermann Helmholtz's principle of the conservation of energy as set forth in his *Die Erhaltung der Kraft* (1847). Coupled with the notion that energy is never lost, the theory of natural selection as the point of continuity from survivor to survivor in each age and species led to a view of the universe as a self-contained dynamo constantly changing form, never surrendering matter or energy to extinction, ever producing intelligible varieties of organic life on earth. This vision Spencer endeavored to impart to the social sciences in the United States.[4]

In so doing, the British philosopher put the best face possible on Darwinism. The conservation of energy—Spencer referred to it as the "persistence of force"—played itself out in the incessant redistribution of matter and motion through new life, eventual dissolution, and rebirth. For Spencer the process was not simply random but progressive: in each moment of the progressive integration of matter (evolution) and its subsequent disorganization (dissolution), the entire life process moved incrementally forward. In short, the inner movement in each new interplay of environment and organism was toward specialization from a state of "incoherent homogeneity" to one of "coherent heterogeneity" and was a microcosm of the larger epochal progress of species from amoeba to human being. This ineluctable progress from homogeneity to heterogeneity, from monism to differentiation, is the story of the universe and a pattern that human societies emulate. Spencer's presentation of evolution softened the full impact of Darwin's theories as elaborated in *On the Origin of Species by Means of Natural Selection* (1859) and in *The Descent of Man* (1871).[5] Spencer insisted on mental as well as physical evolution, with the stated implication that the intellectual powers of the species would also become cumulatively more superb and lead, in the not-too-distant future, to the emergence of the ideal man. Spencer grounded this contention not on Darwin but on the older Lamarckian theory that the inheritance of acquired characteristics is the means by which species advance and, indeed, spawn new species. Whereas Darwin's newer theory was somewhat more fatalistic in underscoring the priority of the *environment* in selecting the organisms that had happened *by chance* to develop traits adaptable to its demands, Lamarck had placed the emphasis on the organism's use, development, and consignment to posterity of those traits which aided its survival in the environment. The latter's notion that acquired characteristics abetting adaptation were inheritable made the interplay between environment and organism appear directed to a goal and thus amenable to the providential design of God.[6]

To American Protestantism, the mainstream religious faith of the country, fell the immediate task of responding to the implications of Darwinism, neo-Darwinism, and Spencerian Darwinism for the relationship between science and religion. On the fringes of traditional theism, however, there were figures such as Francis Ellingwood Abbot, one of the first American theologians to develop a system of religious thought in complete consonance with Darwinian evolution.[7] He participated in the founding of the Free Religious Association and lent it a distinctively scientific character; he required, for example, that doctrinal and ethical expressions of faith be amenable to experimental testing.[8]

Abbot was the first in a line of Christian thinkers who attempted to refashion theological understanding in the light of science. Octavius Brooks Frothingham, who became president of the Free Religious Association in 1867, attempted to chart a *via media* between the scientism of Abbot and religious traditionalism. As did many of his fellow scientist-theists at this time, Frothingham betrayed an elementary and somewhat naive grasp of science. He made the common mistake, for example, of reading Darwin through Lamarckian lenses; his accommodation of evolutionary theory to religion was accordingly facile.[9] But he was one of the first to attempt to find a viable place for scientific method in a religious sensibility and to retain theological language and symbolism even while divesting that language and symbolism of traditional meanings.[10]

This effort at the conciliation of science and religion continued inside the evangelical churches in the 1860s and 1870s in the preaching and writing of Congregationalist Horace Bushnell and Presbyterians Henry Boynton Smith and Albert Barnes.[11] However, although these men did integrate some scientific data into their preaching—Bushnell, for example, incorporated into his sermons the geological discoveries of Charles Lyell—they were not scientifically competent enough to avoid the error of the free religionists of underestimating the possible threat of the new sciences to the religious worldview. What Frank Hugh Foster said of Boynton Smith applied as well to the others: "That an age of *exact observation of facts*, such as had never been known, had been ushered in, and that all reasoning was to take on new forms in consequence, had entirely escaped him."[12]

The full implications of the modern age did not escape the proponents of the "New Theology" which emerged in the Protestant churches in the 1880s and 1890s. Although the New Theology did not corner the market on appeals to scientific method, its proponents could with some justification boast of a solid pedigree of scientist-theists. In addition to popularizers like John Fiske, scientists anchored to Christian orthodoxy had embraced Darwinism from the beginning. Harvard botanist Asa Gray published numerous essays on his conviction that Darwinian theory did not contradict Christian doctrine. He criticized the churches' repudiation of evolutionary theory on dogmatic bases, and predicted that further scientific investigation built upon Darwin's empirical lead would confirm the optimistic view that God's purpose in creating the world could be best apprehended in evolutionary terms.[13] Edward Livingston Youmans, a chemist and, like Fiske, a popularizer of scientific research, served as a literary agent for Spencer in America and an advocate of the scientific worldview. The new science did not threaten his theism, he announced frequently.[14] A former Congregationalist minister, John Bascom, echoed Spencer's affirmation that the mind as well as the body evolved, and tied both to an ongoing spiritual evolution of the human race. Like many who studied scientific theory and remained ardently Christian, Bascom was quite selective in his appreciation of Darwin; he disagreed with the biologist's depiction of natural selection as a random, perhaps meaningless, process. While it was still possible to do so, University of California geologist Joseph Le Conte embraced Lamarck's notion of the ordered progress of evolution and saw God as its guiding master.[15]

While scientists dabbled in theology, liberal theologians spoke in scientific terminology and spent time in the laboratory. In *Theology of an Evolutionist* (1897) and *The Evolution of Christianity* (1892), Lyman Abbott, Congregationalist minister and ally of Henry Ward Beecher, shared the early liberal optimism that the harsher elements in Darwin's theory would be eliminated by the march of science, leaving evolutionary theory safe for Christian apologists. God's place as overseer of the harmonious and orderly progress of species did not allow for the repulsive and base struggles for survival sketched by Darwin.[16] Abbott's fellow Congregationalist pastor, Newell Dwight Hillis, was also a disciple of theistic evolution. He construed the salient points of evolution as commentary on ends rather than origins, on the ascent of man to God rather than a descent from apes:

> Man's descent from animals has been displaced by the ascent of the human body. This is not degradation but an unspeakable exaltation. Man is "fearfully and wonderfully made." God ordained the long upward march for making his body exquisitively sensitive and fitted to be the home of a divine mind. How marvelously does this view enhance the dignity of man, and clothe God with majesty and glory.[17]

Meanwhile, New Haven minister Newman Smyth was so fascinated with the developments in biological science that he took time off from his pastorate to experiment in his laboratory at Yale. His *Old Faiths in New Light* (1879) was an attempt to adjust theology to both Darwin and biblical criticism. In *Through Science to Faith* (1902) he contended that effective theology in the future would employ the insights into the physical constitution of the world uncovered by modern science.[18]

Conservatives dominated the early phases of the debate within the American Catholic community. Those who wrote or spoke forcefully on the topic seldom made the necessary distinction between evolutionism and Darwinism, in part because the latter, an easier target, was a means to discredit the former. Led by Jesuit neo-scholastics, the anti-evolutionists of the 1870s and 1880s played upon the general distaste for Darwin's theory of natural selection, and blurred the line between the idea of evolution and the possible means by which it could proceed. Furthermore, they linked Darwin's biological theory directly to the interpretations of its radical proponents such as Herbert Spencer and Thomas Huxley. Catholic anti-evolutionists pointed to these corollary patterns of thought to prove that Darwinism was not only an objectionable scientific hypothesis, but also a philosophical interpretation of the entire evolutionary process, one that advocated materialism and, by implication, atheism. By excluding direct creation and design, Darwin's hypothesis had, they insisted, provided the materialists with a completely naturalistic explanation for the development of the universe to render untenable the supernatural explanation provided by Scripture.

For example, Father F. P. Garesche of St. Louis University warned that the theory of evolution threatened not only the account of creation given in Genesis, but the basic truths of Christianity as well. He saw scientists as conspirators against revealed religion, heretics who worshipped matter as their God.[19] John Draper's pro-Darwin *History of the Conflict between Religion and Science* provoked from Garesche a response characteristic of his tribe: he excoriated the notions of evolution contained therein, dismissing them as a "farrago of falsehoods . . . all held together by the slender thread of a spurious philosophy."[20] Father Camillus Mazella of Woodstock College, Maryland, put the matter succinctly in his 1877 work *De Deo Creante*: the idea of human evolution is directly contrary to divine revelation. Among the arguments advanced to support this assertion was, significantly, the contention that the church fathers had disapproved of all principles that might be compatible with evolution. St. Augustine did not entertain evolutionary notions, Mazella insisted; despite his problems with the interpretation of Genesis, the bishop of Hippo had definitely taught the direct and immediate formation of Adam's body by God.[21]

This ongoing offensive against evolutionism and Darwinism, which continued in the 1880s even as an opposing party formed within American Catholicism, was not without a touch of irony. The traditionalists sought vindication wherever it lay, even in the thought of St. George Mivart, the English biologist who rejected Darwinism but replaced its explanation of evolution with his own. Several of these conservative opponents of evolutionary theory invoked Mivart against Darwin without acknowledging that he, too, was a thoroughgoing evolutionist—one who sought to reconcile developmentalist thought and Catholic doctrine. Mazella, an opponent of general evolutionary theory, cited Mivart, an evolutionist, to discredit Darwin.[22] A critic who had judged Darwinism scientifically, philosophically, and theologically false quoted Mivart to support his illogical conclusion that only the Bible prevented the acceptance of the hypothesis of the evolution of Adam's body.[23] Garesche, perhaps perceiving the contradiction, used Mivart against Darwin, but admitted along with the English biologist that "there may be a kind of evolution or development"—as long as it was restricted to lower forms of life.[24]

This confusion of tactics resulted in part from the desire of clerical apologists before 1890 to avoid a damaging public debate on the issue. Few sought controversy on this issue unless provoked; for a time the apologists hoped to chart a safe *via media* between the doctrines of creationism and evolutionism, "granting the probability of evolution without fully accepting it and rejecting it without fully condemning it."[25]

But this proved well-nigh impossible. The issue provoked polarization. When the *Catholic World* attempted, in 1873, to endorse Mivart's *On the Genesis of Species*, with its claim that the theory of evolution might stand "consistent with the strictest and most orthodox Christian theology" once Darwinism fell, anti-evolutionist Orestes Brownson called its bluff. The author of the favorable review, Brownson pointed out, had refrained from committing himself or fellow Catholics to the theory of evolution, and had, in fact, correctly repudiated Mivart's tenet that Adam's body had been formed over a period of time by purely natural causes. Why, then, had that same author recommended Mivart's book? Like other opponents of evolution, Brownson rejected the claim, advanced by Mivart, that venerable church theologians such as Augustine and Suarez had favored evolutionary explanations of human origins. He criticized the editors of *Catholic World* for printing the opinion that Catholics are free to accept every scientific theory that was not opposed to what the church had expressly defined as dogmatic. Mivart's view, Brownson continued, "smacks of Gallicanism" because it made science independent of the church's authority.[26]

As the debate continued into the last decade of the nineteenth century, the Catholic opponents of evolutionary theory became more precise and unyielding in reaction to the new science, in part because of the general Protestant acceptance of evolutionism. During the 1890s a spate of articles in the *Ecclesiastical Review*, the *American Catholic Quarterly Review*, and even the Paulist *Catholic World* exposed the dangerous mistakes of those liberal apologists who would defend evolution. They pointed to Protestant Lyman Abbott's *Evolution of Christianity* for a demonstration of the truly deleterious effects of a developmentalist mentality. By his revision or outright elimination of traditional doctrines concerning heaven and hell, the Fall, and the divinity of Christ, Abbott personified the ultimate threat of evolutionary theory: it fostered a worldview and an approach to religious faith that undermined the essentials of Christian truth.[27]

Now the true face of evolutionism had been unmasked, and one would do best not to argue the subtleties of the theory itself, but to silence its proponents altogether. Jesuit professor Joseph Selinger advanced the argument by stating that Vatican I had condemned evolutionary theory implicitly, if not by name, in its condemnation of materialism. Contrary to what the liberals contended, the Catholic was not free to embrace the theory of evolution simply because it had not been mentioned by name. Selinger represented those American Catholic anti-evolutionists who invoked the argument from authority, and presumed the matter settled.[28] Arthur Preuss even claimed that Darwinism could not admit of one eminent defender among the world's great scientists—a claim which did not stand up to scrutiny.[29]

On the other side of the argument stood a small but persistent assemblage of Catholics who considered openly the possibility of accepting the general theory of evolution and who asked: Is Darwinism and/or evolutionism tenable on strictly scientific grounds? If so, should the theory of the evolution of species be restricted to nonhuman species and forms of life? Could this restricted version of evolution pass dogmatic tests? Could the theory of human evolution be held scientifically? Was it in contradiction to scriptural accounts of human creation? As might be expected, the individual answers to each of these central questions ranged along a spectrum, from those who rejected any version of evolutionary theory as both unscientific and un-Christian to those who accepted even human evolution as both scientifically tenable and in keeping with Catholic dogma. Few clerics adopted either of these two extremes, while the majority of participants opted for a broad middle ground. With only one exception the accommodationists stopped short of embracing Darwin and natural selection in its unqualified expression. The divisive issue, instead, was a modified rendering that held that Adam's body was a product of evolution, but that his soul had been created immediately by God. Conservatives depicted this theory as scientific nonsense and Christian heresy. Father Selinger deemed it so patently contrary to the explicit text of the Bible that no reading of Genesis, however controverted, could justify it. To suggest that humans had evolved from lower forms of animal life was to deny the doctrine that God had created man in His image.[30] The craftiest of the anti-evolutionists linked Darwinism with Spencerian survival of the fittest, which Francis Howard, writing in the *Catholic World* in 1895, equated with Marxism and atheism. The type of morality fostered by the evolutionists would lead to the decay of civilization, he insisted.[31]

Among the accommodationists there was a variety of opinions regarding the appropriate limits to which the apologist might extend evolutionary theory and developmentalist thought in general, but they shared a preference for a new methodological, data-oriented approach to the question and a disdain for those who would rely excessively on the syllogisms of traditional scholasticism. "Medieval armor will not turn a bullet from a modern rifle," one wrote, "nor will the authority of a Medieval philosopher be secure behind which to fight a modern evolutionist."[32] The general idea of evolution would not fade away nor retreat in the face of scholastic pieties; it must be tolerated, understood, and recognized as the important idea it had become. Moreover, the *idea* of evolution, at the root of acceptable and unacceptable theories alike, was not inimical to the Christian faith.[33]

Paulist Augustine F. Hewit was among the first to take up the cause of evolutionism. He devoted a series of articles in the *Catholic*

World to his conviction that the acceptance of a qualified general theory of evolution posed no problems for faith and in fact bespoke God's wisdom and omnipotence in a way that special creation did not. He refused to admit that evolution was identical with either materialism or atheism, and insisted on maintaining the important distinction between the scientific theory and the various dangerous philosophies that had grown up around it. Hewit also stressed the distinction between matters of truth revealed by God and matters of science. Scripture said nothing about the means by which God created the world; the church fathers entertained no opinion one way or the other about evolution as a means of creation. Thus, science was free to proceed in its hypotheses concerning the ways in which creation unfolded, for revelation did not touch upon the question.[34]

In acknowledging the autonomy of science, and in distinguishing between evolution as a scientific hypothesis and as a philosophy, Hewit rejected the tactics of the conservatives and anticipated the approach of later liberals. However, he did not embrace wholeheartedly the full theory of evolution. He refused to consider the possibility, logical though it was, that humans too participated in the evolutionary spiral. He was consistent with his earlier limited endorsement of evolution in lower species, he insisted, because in this case of human evolution, Scripture *did* speak clearly against it in the Genesis account of Adam and Eve. Those evolutionists, Mivart included, who extended evolution to humanity gave support to atheists who would use science to subvert religion. They replaced the creature sublime in the image of God with "a stupid and vicious beast." Because Hewit believed that the human soul determined the species, he would not accept the notion that the human body developed apart from the soul. His was a moderate, selective appreciation of the new science.[35]

Fellow Paulist George M. Searle, an astronomer of some repute, inched closer toward accepting human evolution, but apparently did not cross the line. In the *Catholic World* he lauded evolution as a theory based on facts, not speculation, and maintained that the church would welcome the valid conclusions of scientists. Even if human evolution were one day unanimously accepted, Searle opined, it would not endanger the principles of the Catholic faith.[36] Six years later, in 1887, Thomas Dwight, a Roman Catholic professor of anatomy at Harvard, echoed that sentiment in an article for the *American Catholic Quarterly Review*, adding that the general idea of scientific evolution had been accepted by the majority of scientists, including Catholics. "No

Catholic need have any quarrel with evolution," he wrote, ". . . seen in the light of a sound philosophy . . . a large proportion of Catholic scientists believe in it to a greater or less extent."[37]

To this point in the debate, liberals and conservatives alike relied on the old style of apologetics—arguments from a defensive position. Conservatives were out to defend the faith from evolution; liberals employed a negative argument to demonstrate that evolution was not inimical to faith. But with the entrance onto the scene of Rev. John Gmeiner, the strategy of the liberals received a needed boost. Gmeiner, the most progressive of the liberals before Zahm, anticipated several of that priest's ideas and moved the liberals closer to a modernistic evaluation of the evolution controversy. He did this, in part, by relying not only on negative apologetics, but by construing positive arguments for evolution. In so doing he implied that the belief of Catholics required revision—not that the faith be impugned, but that the notions of divinity and creation be enhanced through renewed understanding. Let us be grateful to Darwin if only because he has provoked us to re-examine our concepts of God, Gmeiner suggested.

He published these views while still a professor of theology at St. Francis de Sales Seminary in Milwaukee. Sympathetic to the Americanism of John Ireland, Gmeiner welcomed an appointment to the archbishop's seminary in St. Paul in 1887. In the first pages of his treatise *Modern Scientific Views and Christian Doctrines Compared*, Gmeiner extolled modern science in language which would later appear in the speeches of Ireland: "the doctrine the Church has always held as to the relations between Science and Divine Revelation . . . may be expressed in these few words: *No truth of Science does, or ever can, contradict any truth of Divine Revelation.*"[38]

Gmeiner thought it unwise to abandon the study of evolutionary theory prematurely simply because conservative critics associated it with materialism. This theory might contain portions of truth and, by denouncing it now, he argued, we give it over entirely to the atheists and materialists to interpret as they will. The Catholic procedure has always been to give human knowledge the benefit of the doubt. Besides, Gmeiner continued, Catholics are free to hold the theory of evolution because figures such as Mivart hold it and are not condemned. Gmeiner held to a minimalist interpretation of ecclesial authority in such questions. Taking the case of Galileo as his model, he limited the reach of infallibility to extra-scientific matters:

It is true that Galileo was to some extent persecuted by authorities of the Church; as also, that his theory was for a short time condemned. But this was not done by any general Council or by any solemn definition *ex cathedra,* to which alone members of the Church are found to assent in matters of faith . . . no Catholic is bound to consider it as a definition ex cathedra (although it seems to have had the sanction of the Pope). Moreover, in as far as the decision on Galileo's theory was a decision on a purely scientific question . . . it did not properly come within the sphere of faith and morals, wherein alone the Church, or her visible head, defining ex cathedra, claims infallibility.[39]

Furthermore, Gmeiner's reasoning continued, the general theory does not contradict the Mosaic account of creation which, although lacking any evolutionary theory, contains nothing repugnant to that theory. The Mosaic account "teaches that the existing kinds of plants and animals *were brought forth by the Earth and water at the command of God,*" but whether this happened at once, at the command of God, or gradually, "on these points the Mosaic account gives us no information." On this issue "there may be permitted, without danger of contradicting Divine Revelation, a great latitude of opinion among Christians."[40]

Thus far Gmeiner's argument resembled that of Hewit, Searle, and other accommodationists. But he went on to call for a theistic interpretation of Darwinism, and in so doing acknowledged the ideas of liberal Protestant theologians and scientists, especially Joseph LeConte, upon whose book *Religion and Science* (1873) Gmeiner based his own.[41]

Evolutionary theory demanded a reformulation of the Christian notion of God's creative providence, extending it throughout human history rather than isolating it at a particular moment. Gmeiner thought such a reformulation consistent with a traditional belief in the ongoing activity of an immanent divine spirit:

Also the guiding providence of the Creator, in bringing forth, from quite simple forms of life, the countless now existing species—has not been made superfluous by Darwin's theory. On the contrary, assuming the Darwinian theory to be correct, one will have to exclaim, as Prof. John *[sic]* LeConte did . . . "How simple the means—how multiform the effects—how far-reaching and grand the design! How deeply they impress us with the wisdom, power, and glory of the Creator and Governor of the Universe!"[42]

Whereas Gmeiner invoked Protestant liberals in this argument, he adopted the stance of European Catholic modernists, especially St. George Mivart, by contending that evolutionary theory enjoyed a long, and much neglected, history in the writings of the great theologians of the Church. Gmeiner went even further than Mivart. The English biologist claimed, for example, that Augustine had, in works like *De Genesi ad Literam*, articulated a view of nature expansive enough to allow for evolution. Gmeiner insisted that Augustine actually *taught* evolutionary theory. In this interpretation Darwin simply lent the weight of empirical evidence to the teachings of the great theologian:

> We, therefore, need not be surprised to learn that St. Augustine, the perhaps most profound and philosophic of the ancient doctors of the Church . . . expressed views decidedly favoring the theory of evolution. If one compares the views of St. Augustine with the speculations of Darwin, one might be tempted to look upon St. Augustine as the venerable teacher who advanced some grand comprehensive ideas, which his disciple Darwin has explained more in detail. . . .

> These views of St. Augustine have by no means been repudiated as inconsistent with the Mosaic Account by the great Catholic theologians of the Middle Ages. St. Thomas, commenting on Genesis . . . observes: "In the day, when God created Heaven and Earth, he created also every herb of the field, not actually, but before it grew upon Earth, that is, potentially."[43]

Gmeiner concluded his book by advancing a distinction between the short-term results of scientific investigation and its ultimate contributions to knowledge. After sifting, revising, and carefully reflecting upon their investigations, scientists had and would continue to produce

> truth or facts which . . . are in perfect harmony with the truths of Divine Revelation, or the Doctrines of Christianity. Although, now and then, *at first sight* this does not seem to be the case, yet *thorough investigation* invariably reveals the harmonies existing between the truths which God teaches in the book of Nature and in the book of supernatural revelation. . . . It is never true Science that is dangerous to Religion, but only superficial

knowledge as now-a-days puffs up many a one who has not yet learned enough to see how little he really knows. . . . Whatever Science may discover, in the midst of human theories that continually succeed each other and change like the billows of the ocean—one thing is certain: the Rock of God's Word will never be shaken.[44]

Gmeiner's book was a type of *preparatio evangelicae* for the great proclamation of theistic evolution to come. The seminary professor did not, perhaps, feel fully qualified to attempt the detailed review and critique of neo-Darwinism necessary in preparing an adequate synthesis of its estimable points with the truths proclaimed in Catholic dogma. He was content to establish the ideological principles upon which such a synthesis could be built. Whereas LeConte opened his book with an endorsement of the general theory, Gmeiner merely presented scientific evidence in favor of the theory—similarity in human and anthropoid skeletal structure, and paleontological evidence linking the two, for example—alongside a discussion of problems associated with it, such as the absence of a missing link between the two species. He concluded from this that "the Darwinian theory may, and probably does, contain some valuable grains of truth—yet, as commonly understood, it is far from being a well-founded theory; it is no more than a bold hypothesis."[45]

What seemed to be a failure of nerve might be explained from the perspective of science as the caution of a layman in matters of technical difficulty under debate by the professional community; or, from the perspective of religion, as the prudence of a Catholic priest who recognized that he was drifting close to dangerous waters.[46] In an article submitted four years later to the *Catholic World*, he admitted that both considerations inspired his cautiousness. He chose to wait until his ecclesiastical opponents admitted the inevitability of the evolutionary views of creation, just as other archaic views had yielded to scientific evidence. "Perhaps (due to indisputable proofs establishing their contradictories) some other views widely held among theologians and educated men generally," he wrote, "will gradually be given up, and that even before this century closes."[47]

The task of attempting such a synthesis fell to a man bolder than Gmeiner who would accept evolutionary theory and seek to refashion Christian understanding of creation according to it. Toward the end of his teaching career, Gmeiner recalled: "Years ago I already held and still do hold the views [on evolution] now advocated by Dr. Zahm."[48]

MODERNIST THEMES IN THE APOLOGETICS OF JOHN ZAHM

During the course of his twenty-year career as an American Catholic apologist and scientist, John Zahm embraced at one time or another each of the various liberal-accommodationist positions on evolution outlined above. In the early 1880s he refused to accept evolution, discrediting it as an insubstantial and unprovable hypothesis. Yet by the time that controversy ended prematurely his career as reconciler of religion and science, he had come so far in assimilating Darwin that one observer concluded, "More than any other American Catholic, [Zahm] translated Darwin's theory into terms understandable and at least partially acceptable to his American and European Catholic audiences."[49]

Born in Ohio in 1851 to immigrant parents, Zahm entered the seminary at Notre Dame at the age of fifteen. Gifted with a natural aptitude for science, he rose rapidly in the ranks of the Congregation of Holy Cross, and by the age of twenty-three was a professor of chemistry and physics, codirector of the science department, director of the library, curator of the museum, and a member of the Board of Trustees of the fledgling university![50]

From 1875 to 1883 Zahm concentrated on building the science department at Notre Dame into a first-rate facility for, as he wrote to Orestes Brownson, Catholics lagged far behind American Protestants in experimental capabilities.[51] Accordingly, Zahm traveled to Europe to investigate and purchase the latest equipment necessary for up-to-date experimentation, including a galvanometer and a dynamo electric machine. Largely through his efforts, Notre Dame became the first American campus lighted by electricity.[52] During this period the young priest-scientist gained invaluable experience in translating technical information and analyses into concepts and language accessible to the general populace. His public lectures at Notre Dame, covering topics such as chemical affinity and the operations of electromagnetism, were well attended and provided the opportunity for the young orator to develop a distinctive style. During this period Zahm also grew in erudition and scientific sophistication, helped by his exposure to the research of leading European scientists during his intermittent trips abroad.[53]

In 1883 Zahm, secure in his position at Notre Dame, entered the public controversy over evolution. In doing so he established a personal pattern of exhausting all means of publicizing his ideas: he published articles and books, preached guest sermons, delivered public lectures, and debated prominent Protestant scientists and theologians. He expressed his strategy to his brother Albert, destined to become a credible scientist in his own right: "Keep yourself before the public always—if you wish the public to remember you or do anything for you."[54] Listeners reported enthusiastically that "unlike many a Protestant minister, Father Zahm knew what he believed, where he got his belief, and how to sustain himself in the same."[55] Response of this type bolstered Zahm's confidence and in time he fancied himself quite talented in defending both the church and science from false impressions.

This first phase in Zahm's apologetic career lasted for about a decade, until late 1893. His written and spoken words during this decade reflected a tentative, somewhat cautious, approach to the general theory of evolution. His presentation typically included an insistence on the ultimate harmony between the established results of scientific experimentation and Roman Catholicism, as well as a hesitant and incomplete articulation of theistic evolution. Paradoxically, he reserved his most strident criticisms not only for those agnostics, materialists, and atheists who transformed a scientific theory into a philosophical system, but also for the general notion of evolution itself and for Darwin in particular. What arguments he did muster in favor of theistic evolution emerged in anticipation that they might be needed in the unlikely eventuality that evolutionary theory would become a tenable hypothesis.

The basic pattern of this early approach was present in an 1886 lecture published later as "The Catholic Church and Modern Science." Beginning with the claim that the Roman Catholic Church "is the sole possessor of the sceptre of Science in the whole of Christendom," Zahm judged that "only those who get their information at second hand" were convinced that modern science demands that the church modify many of her dogmas and abandon some altogether. Others are misled, he continued, into thinking that the church is the declared enemy of true progress. Although the church "needs not apologists," he would undo these false impressions, and avoid any temptation to "minimize, even in the slightest degree, any doctrine the church proposes for our belief, or assert anything that is inconsistent with the strictest orthodoxy, or if you will, with the most pronounced

Ultramontanism."[56] Zahm asserted the priority of dogma over any claims of science, for "no liberalism in matters of doctrine can be tolerated. . . . What the Church teaches must be accepted as divine truth."[57]

Having laid to rest any doubts about his orthodoxy, the young priest proceeded to identify broad areas of freedom for scientific research, areas exempt from church teaching. On these matters, he warned, one must distinguish between official teaching of the magisterium and the private opinions of theologians and commentators. Thus the church had never and would never define the exact age of the world or of the human species, for such matters "have nothing to do" with faith and morals. Similarly, the church permitted an understanding of biblical inspiration that allowed for errors on the part of the authors in matters of history, biology, geology, and other scientific disciplines. Competent exegesis recognized, for example, that the six days of creation recounted in Genesis are to be taken allegorically as epochs rather than as twenty-four-hour days. Both Augustine and Aquinas, among others, confirmed this reading. Finally, the church had never taught the universality of the deluge; Zahm was free, or so he claimed, to accept it as a geographically limited phenomenon on the evidence of history and science. Zahm repeated these positions throughout his career as interpreter of church teaching.[58]

But on the matter of evolution, Zahm was ambivalent. On one hand, he rejected evolution because it was based on a number of highly questionable assumptions: the spontaneous generation of life from inorganic matter, against which stood "conclusive scientific evidence"; the "nebular hypothesis" that the earth and all heavenly bodies were originally in a state of incandescent vapor—"mere speculation"; and, the "unprovable" notion that one species evolved from another by a process of transmutation. Zahm concluded:

> Not a single fact in the whole range of natural science can be adduced favoring the truth of the transmutation of Species. . . . What, then, is our conclusion as regards evolution and faith? Evidently, to say the least, that evolution has proven nothing against the teachings of faith, from the simple fact that evolution, so far, at best, is a conjecture, a theory, not only unproven, but as now taught, apparently unprovable.[59]

A decade later Zahm would reverse himself on each of these judgments as scientific opinion consolidated behind these notions and his own knowledge and self-confidence increased.

Yet even in this early phase of his efforts, Zahm did not rule out evolution altogether. Having argued that it likely would fade into obscurity, he proceeded in the same lecture to plot out a position supporting a particular understanding of evolution. There are basically three types of evolutionists, he stated: the atheist, who denies the existence of a divine creator; the agnostic, who neither admits nor denies God's existence, and the theist, who believes in a personal God. Catholics could, of course, belong only to the third group—but could they hold to theistic evolution and keep the faith?

Zahm offered an affirmative answer to this question by first expanding the definition of creation to include derivative creation "when God, after having created matter directly, gives it the power of evolving under certain conditions all the various forms it may subsequently assume."[60] He went on to deny that either church teaching or Scripture stood in the way of this understanding of creation; in fact "according to the words of Genesis, God did not create animals and plants in the primary sense of the word, but caused them to be produced from preexisting material."[61] Furthermore, Zahm continued, even if popular belief assumed an instantaneous creation, the evolutionist simply maintained that "God did potentially, what the ordinary Scripture interpreter believes he did by a distinct, immediate exercise of infinite power."[62]

Concluding that "there is nothing in evolution contrary to Scripture," Zahm proceeded to plumb traditional teachings for opinions on evolution. Far from discovering objections to it, he found eminent theologians implying it or teaching it outright. St. Augustine, in his great work on Genesis, professed belief that animals and plants were brought into existence by the operation of natural causes: "He tells us explicitly that they were created potentially, and that they were afterwards developed into the manifold forms we now behold."[63] On the question of human evolution Zahm followed Mivart, who taught that "theistic evolution may embrace man's body, considered as separate from, and independent of, the soul, which was, Catholics must affirm, created immediately by God."[64] This theory, Zahm admitted, "may be rash, and even dangerous, but I do not think that, considering it simply in its bearing on dogma, any one could pronounce it as certainly and positively false." He concluded his careful discussion of evolution by stating that "as matters now stand, evolution is not contrary to Catholic faith; and anyone is at liberty to hold the theory, if he is satisfied with the evidence adduced in its support."[65] At this point

Zahm was adopting a stance towards the topic not unlike Gmeiner's: demonstrate the congeniality of theistic evolution to Christian doctrine, but stop short of acknowledging the validity of the theory on scientific and philosophical grounds.

Zahm's caution in this matter, uncharacteristic of his later campaigns, was due in part to science's limited understanding of evolution and the relative lack, in the early 1880s, of substantial evidence in support of it. Also, Zahm seemed unclear as to the proper relationship between metaphysical truths and scientific, empirically based truths. Is the Catholic priest-scientist primarily one who employs the deductive reasoning of traditional philosophy and theology, or one who approaches the challenge of evolutionary theory as would any empiricist, from a method of induction? Zahm's early and vehement rejection of Darwin stemmed in part from his identification of scientific inductionism with atheism. In the final work of this period, *Catholic Science and Scientists* (1893), Zahm struggled for clarity on this issue.[66]

In that book he described two opposing and equally erroneous extremes in the various attempts to reconcile science and religion. The "Scylla," in his words, of those who "ignore the principles of metaphysics, and who reject the teachings of revelation . . . [and] employ [the inductive method] to the exclusion of all other aids and methods," stood opposed by the "Charybdis" of those who still give metaphysics a place in their sciences, but who fail to distinguish properly between the functions of metaphysical principles and the office of simple induction . . . confound[ing] the former with the latter."[67] Zahm rejected both alternatives. "One class sins by exclusiveness," he wrote, "—by accepting only the empirical method, rejecting metaphysics entirely; the other, by giving it an exaggerated importance."[68] The philosopher erred, as did Spencer and Huxley, when he sought to judge affirmations of faith by empirical criteria; the religionist, when he sought to validate faith claims by induction.

Darwin, of course, fell into this classification; he too had "sinned" in presuming that science might act independently of metaphysics in drawing a picture of human design and purpose.

> What has been said of Tyndall and Huxley can, in great measure, be repeated respecting Darwin. As a close, patient observer of facts and phenomena in the various forms of animal and vegetable life he has had few, if any, superiors. . . . But here his merit ends . . . he is all along directing his energies not so much

to increase our knowledge of nature as to establish and corroborate a pet theory. . . . Facts are presented, assumptions made,
and conclusions drawn with a recklessness and a disregard for the
simplest rules of dialectics. . . . This is what is called 'science'![69]

Thus Zahm articulated a vision of the proper relationship between religion and science that he stood by in subsequent publications. Each proceeded from its own principles, operated by its own
distinctive methods, and arrived at its own conclusions. Yet these conclusions were not, *could not be*, mutually exclusive nor ultimately an-
tagonistic, for they both sought to explain and describe the wonders
of God's creation. The priest-scientist was, therefore, the perfect person to demonstrate the harmony between the conclusions of science
and of theology, for he respected each method in its integrity while
appreciating the implications of one for the other.[70]

Having settled the methodological question to his own satisfaction, Zahm entered a new phase in his career, marked by two themes.
First, he came to respect the idea of evolution, without regard to
its specific post-Darwinian formulations, as a sound explanation of
creation and of the development of plant, animal, and human life.
Second, he recognized the need for a synthetic view of the unfolding
of God's providence in human history, wedding traditional Roman
Catholic doctrines to the new insights of the evolutionists. In the period from late 1893 to 1896, he moved beyond Gmeiner's tentative
speculations about the possibility of theistic evolution to a position
that insisted adamantly that speculation be replaced by advocation.
Evolutionary theory had unavoidable implications for religious understanding, which Zahm prepared to articulate for the faithful. By late
1893 he felt himself on the verge of an important contribution to the
intellectual life of the American Catholic Church. To the founder of
Notre Dame he wrote: "I am beginning to feel that I have a great
mission before me in making known to the Protestant world the true
relation of Catholic dogma towards modern science."[71] During the
next four years he produced five books and countless articles assess-
ing evolutionary theory vis-à-vis Catholic dogma and popularizing his
belief that theistic evolution was a viable and desirable intellectual
position for American Catholics.

What occasioned this development in Zahm? Certainly a number of factors contributed to it. First, by 1894 the European scientific
community, including several Catholics, had by and large endorsed the

general theory of evolution. Darwinism was subject to constant revision, but this process made it more palatable to many observers. Zahm was in constant communication with European scientists: Mivart, for example, exercised considerable influence over him and thanked him for "carrying on" his own work in the United States.[72] Second, Zahm's own competence as a scientist grew. As his chemical and electromagnetic experiments in the laboratories at Notre Dame won greater recognition from colleagues, he became more comfortable with and adept at the scientific method of inquiry, and correspondingly less patient with fellow clerics who retained a vague fear of modern science.[73]

Perhaps equally important to Zahm's development was his perception that he could reassure lay Catholics that they need not fear modern science and encourage them to investigate its conclusions without fear of ecclesiastical reprisal. This feeling was no doubt reinforced in Zahm by the tremendous response he received as he toured the country on the lecture circuit for the Catholic Summer and Winter Schools beginning in 1893. The topic seemed of great concern to the faithful.[74]

It was this sense for publicity, exaggerated by a fancy for the sensational, that impelled Zahm to orchestrate a series of headline-grabbing events during the years of his Americanist activity. To ensure that the public would remember him, in February 1893 Zahm made an unusual request of his friend and fellow Americanist Denis O'Connell, rector of North American College in Rome:

> I need another favor, *"strictly confidential,"* until the favor is granted. For 21 years I have been trying to build the science department at ND. . . . We now have the best equipped, most complete "Catholic scientific establishment in the world." Catholics have long needed this. . . . [But] buildings are not enough. . . . I have lectured and written articles on subjects connected with science and religion. In a word, I have endeavored to show the world that the Church is now, as she ever has been, the patron of science, and that no conflict between religion and science is possible. . . . The favor I ask is not entirely personal. It could reflect on Notre Dame and on Catholic science in America as well, and will call attention to the fact that Rome—& especially the Pope—is the first to foster science and encourage those who devote themselves to its cultivation. The favor I ask is the honorary degree or Doctor of Science—*Scientiae Doctor*—given by

the proper authorities in Rome & if possible, *signed by the Holy Father himself.* . . . I will be glad to meet any little expenses incident to securing the degree. For a very special reason, I would be pleased if it could be obtained *at once.*[75]

The "very special reason" for the request no doubt had to do with the upcoming Catholic Summer School lectures at Plattsburgh that, as it turned out, touched off Zahm's rise to fame. A dramatic display of papal approval would help to silence critics of theistic evolution. When the doctorate was awarded, two years after the request and in philosophy rather than science, Zahm was delighted. He interpreted the event as a signal that his party was in ascendancy at Rome: "So far as I know, Leo XIII has given this degree to only two persons—both heretics—Mivart and Zahm!"[76]

Zahm's new-found confidence in himself as a Catholic apologist on matters scientific and, particularly, on evolutionary theory, emerged first in an 1894 article for the *American Ecclesiastical Review* entitled, "Moses and Modern Science," followed closely by a book-length collection of his summer lectures, entitled *Bible, Science and Faith.* In these works and in published lectures that he delivered that year before crowds at the Catholic Summer School in Madison and the Catholic Winter School in New Orleans, Zahm attempted to co-opt for the Catholic faith the very theories that he had previously found questionable. He found precedent for notions such as the "nebular hypothesis" in the teachings of St. Gregory of Nyssa.[77] Although he was neither a Darwinist nor a Huxleyan, he did not wish to imply that he found "nothing good" in their work; indeed, blessed saints Augustine and Aquinas had accepted theistic evolution.[78] The transmutation of species Zahm now identified with Augustine's belief in a successive creation governed by divine law; likewise, the theory of spontaneous generation could be understood as a tentative explanation of the performance of God's will for the world through a series of secondary causes.[79]

Furthermore, Zahm contended, there was nothing in Catholic dogma to preclude the possibility that man descended from an anthropoid ape or some other animal. Even Mivart's doctrine that man's body had evolved with the subsequent infusion of a rational soul by God had not been condemned; indeed, it was congenial to the words of St. Thomas on this point. And Zahm now believed the account of creation in Genesis to be in strict accord with modern science: both maintained, or allowed the possibility, that God had created primitive matter and, after an indefinite period of time, proceeding from the simpler to the more complex, supervised the development of the innumerable forms of the organic and inorganic world.[80]

For Zahm, all of this pointed to one overriding truth expressed in the greatest work of individuals who were both competent scientists and faithful Catholics: science has nothing to fear from the Catholic faith, but everything to gain.

> The faith of Catholics, consequently, far from restricting their liberty of research, gives it a vivifying principle which it could not otherwise possess. And far from circumscribing [scientists'] views of nature, or giving them false notions of the laws and phenomena of the material world, it extends their horizon and illumines the field of their investigation with a brilliance all its own.[81]

The public press response to the summer school lectures and to their publication in *Bible, Science, and Faith* was overwhelming. *Catholic World* termed it "a veritable Godsend" and recommended it for Catholics and Protestants alike "who wish accurate information concerning current controversies regarding Science and Faith."[82] *Ave Maria* judged it to be one of the most important Catholic books published in English within the last decade.[83] For the *American Catholic Quarterly Review* it was "the most valuable contribution made by an American talent and industry to the cause of Christian apologetics."[84] "To timid and troubled souls," the *Sacred Heart Review* assured, "Father Zahm's book will be a great comfort and support."[85]

Significantly, the welcome extended to Zahm's work was not restricted to the religious press. The *Baltimore Sun* praised it as a "most important and learned contribution toward the adjustment of some divergent views of the present day as to the relation of the Bible and modern investigations in the field of the natural sciences."[86] Newspapers in Boston, Buffalo, New York, and London applauded the midwesterner as "a man of the age, cognizant of all the movements of modern thought and able to give a reason for the faith that is in him."[87] The *Independent* perceived Zahm's defense of science as a crusade in which learned Catholics and Protestants might make common cause.[88] One of the most comprehensive reviews, published in *The Tablet*, deemed the volume invaluable for a number of reasons. First, although biblical scholars in France had written on the relations of the earlier chapters of Genesis to the conclusions and hypotheses of physical science, Zahm's was the first complete work on this theme to appear in English. Second, Zahm performed an important service in disseminating among the English and American public the advanced ideas of European scientist-theists such as Vigoroux and Motais. Third, Zahm contributed to this material his own conclusions and arguments in support of them. When these conclusions seemed to depart from the outlines of "true Catholic conservatism," Zahm had labored either to demonstrate that the church left open to discussion the particular point in question or to substantiate his affirmations with quotes from respected Catholic authorities of the past. For example, in the case of the Deluge, Zahm called into question its racial or "anthropological" no less than its geographical universality. In so doing he invoked modern Catholic scientists but also appealed to the authority of Cardinal Gonzalez (*La Biblia y la Ciencia*) in favor of the question being regarded as fully open to discussion.[89] *The Tablet* reported in some detail the particulars of Zahm's argument:

> Father Zahm, rightly as we think, declares for the Septuagint as against the Hebrew and Samaritan computation of the ages of the patriarches, &c., though he hardly touches on the reasons derivable—it seems to us—from a comparison of the three texts, in favour of this preference. But beyond this, he deems it more than probable that the genealogical lists of Gen. v., and xi., do not profess to be complete. Combining the indications afforded by physical science, by historical archaeology, and by Holy Scripture, he reaches the provisional conclusion that man has probably been on the earth not less than 10,000 years; and that there is no evidence to prove a higher antiquity than this. Father Zahm's chapter on "Geological Chronometers," in spite of the awkwardness of the title, strikes us as particularly good.[90]

The publication of *Bible, Science, and Faith*, and the summer school controversy, sharpened Zahm's skills for the most significant accomplishment of this period, the preparation of his most mature work, *Evolution and Dogma*, which appeared in February 1896. The fruit of thirteen years of participation in the public debate, *Evolution and Dogma* confirmed Zahm's reputation as a leading Catholic apologist and educator. He was not an original theorist, nor did he aspire to be one. He wrote not to advance a new, revised interpretation of evolution that would avoid the miscalculations of Darwin or Lamarck; that ideal theory, he promised, would come in time. Rather, his purpose was to demonstrate the comparative advantages and disadvantages of the various schools of thought and to contend that the limitations of each ought not to discredit the concept of evolution itself. Zahm described this general concept or theory of evolution, which was shared by Darwin and Lamarck alike, as "ennobling" and "uplifting."[91]

Although Zahm proposed no startling new theories, he was the first American Catholic scientist to accept fully and to apply with exacting precision Darwin's own innovative mode of scientific reasoning. Before Darwin, British philosophers of science had subscribed to a type of Baconian inductivism in which they held that the systematic collection and classification of data, done without preconceptions on the part of the classifier, would lead to inductive generalizations, a series of propositions, and ultimately "those laws and determinations of absolute actuality" that can be known to be certainly true.[92] Darwin qualified this quest for ultimate certainty in scientific inferences by formulating hypotheses that governed the choice of facts and accounted for those chosen for every investigation. He set forth natural selection, for example, not as a theory for which absolute proof had been obtained, but merely as the most probable explanation for the largest number of facts pertaining to the origin of species. "The line of argument pursued throughout my theory," he explained, "is to establish a point as a probability by induction, and to apply it as a hypothesis to other points, and see whether it will solve them." [93]

In *Evolution and Dogma* Zahm adopted this form of hypothetico-deductive reasoning as a *via media* between an "inconceivable" empiricism that guaranteed final certitude and a dogmatism, an "ultraconservatism," based exclusively on deduction from *a priori* principles, that leads to "a fanatical obstinacy in the assertion of traditional views which are demonstrably untenable."[94] Zahm did allow himself one *a priori* principle: science would not, could not, overturn truths revealed by God in scripture and tradition, for God is one and truth is one. In rejecting dualism, Catholicism allowed the scientists to proceed in their own realm of investigation, accepting the explanation of the origin of species most credible on scientific grounds, confident that the procedure would lead inexorably to a profound affirmation of theism.[95] This approach did not hide fallible human science from the light of revelation, Zahm insisted, but it did restrain metaphysics from imposing prematurely upon the course of rational inquiry. Ultimately compatible in their respective conclusions, natural science and metaphysics are nonetheless different disciplines, each with its own integrity:

> The Copernican theory was denounced as anti-Scriptural. . . Newton's discovery of universal gravitation was condemned as atheistic. . . . That the theory of evolution should be obliged to pass through the same ordeal is not surprising to those familiar with the history of science; but there are yet those among us who derive such little profit from the lessons of the past, and who still persist in their futile attempt to solve by metaphysics problems which, by their very nature, can be worked out only by methods of induction.
>
> Naturalists and philosophers are continually intruding on each other's territory. The naturalist philosophizes and the philosopher. . . naturalizes. For naturalists are very much given to making excursions into the domain of metaphysics and to substitute speculations for rigid inductions from observed facts. And metaphysicians sin in a similar manner by attempting to explain, by methods of their own, the various phenomena of the material world, and in seeking by simple *a priori* reasons to evolve from their inner consciousness a logical system of the physical universe. The result is inextricable confusion and errors without number. It is neither science nor philosophy, but a *mixtum compositum*, which not only gives false views of nature but still falser views of the Author of nature.[96]

Opponents of evolution tended to ignore the axiom that science "discloses the method of the world, not its cause; religion, its cause and not its method."[97] In a misbegotten attempt to safeguard divine providence, Zahm charged, they accepted special creation of immutable species despite overwhelming evidence of transmutation. To preserve belief in human creation in the image of God, they excluded *a priori* the possibility of human descent from lower forms of animal life.

In Zahm's estimation this attempt produced inferior theology as well as inferior science. Modern science had weakened irrevocably the foundation of the creationist's worldview. Against the spontaneous generation of life, for example, Redi and Pasteur had demonstrated that in every instance life originates from antecedent life. Geologists described in convincing detail the fluctuations of the earth and "the multifold extinct forms entombed in its crust." Thus one must reckon the age of the earth not at six thousand years but "by millions if not tens of millions of years." Again, paleontologists confirmed that "a hundred million species or more have appeared and died out." Zahm concluded from empirical demonstrations of this sort that "everything seems to point conclusively to a development from the simple to the complex, and to disclose, in Spencer's words, 'change from the homogeneous to the heterogeneous through continuous differentiations and integrations.'" The changes and developments are the result "not of so many separate creative acts, but rather of a single creation and of a subsequent uniform process of Evolution, according to certain definite and immutable laws."[98]

Consequently, Zahm argued, the older views regarding creation must be materially modified to harmonize with modern science: "Between the two theories, that of creation and that of Evolution, the lines are drawn tautly, and one or the other theory must be accepted. . . . No compromise, no *via media*, is possible. We must needs be either creationists or evolutionists. We cannot be both."[99]

For Zahm the choice between the two was a question "of natural science, not of metaphysics, and hence one of evidence which is more or less tangible." In delineating the grounds for "the almost universal acceptance of the theory by contemporary scientists," Zahm followed a procedure that he believed to be at the heart of Catholic wisdom: seek truth wherever it may be found, separate it from error, and reconcile it with other truths.[100] In evaluating the thought of the leading naturalists of the modern era, he found "elements of truth" in Darwin, Lamarck, Cuvier, Romanes, Mivart, and others. Neither "a Darwinist or a Huxleyist," he was equally comfortable quoting Agassiz against certain implications of natural selection and Darwin against the theory of abiogenesis held by the creationists. His one allegiance was to the general theory of evolution that, he was convinced, eventually would absorb and incorporate salient aspects of each modification of merit.[101]

Zahm thus refrained from endorsing *in toto* any particular system, lest its imperfections detract from the general theory. If, for example, Darwin's first description of natural selection was challenged in its assumption of the existence and development of infinitesimal forms of life from lower to higher by a lack of evidence of these forms in the fossil record, it would "not strictly follow that such difficulties can validly be urged against the general theory of organic Evolution, as distinguished from Evolution through natural selection."[102] Zahm recalled that Darwin himself had modified his theory as new data demanded. In the second edition of *The Origin of Species*, for example, he revised a previous estimate that all animal and plant life derived from four or five progenitors, acknowledging that "all organic beings which have ever lived on the earth have descended from some one primordial form, into which life was first breathed by the Creator." Zahm found this adjustment to be in keeping with scientific fact and thus in closer conformity to revealed truth.[103] At the same time, Zahm lashed out at neo-Darwinists for regarding natural selection as the sole and sufficient cause for all organic development even as Darwin was reducing its role by allowing for environmental factors.[104]

Although each theory contained an element of truth, there was as yet no theory competent "to coordinate all the facts that Evolution is supposed to embrace." Nonetheless, Zahm predicted, the development of a "true, comprehensive, irrefragable" theory demonstrating the "ordained becoming of new species by the operation of secondary causes" is inevitable. This ideal theory would admit "of a preconceived progress 'towards a foreseen goal' and disclose the unmistakable evidence and the certain impress of a Divine Intelligence and purpose." Zahm hastened to add that

> the lack of this perfected theory, however, does not imply that we have not already an adequate basis for a rational assent to the theory of Organic Evolution. By no means. The arguments adduced in behalf of Evolution . . . are of sufficient weight to give the theory a degree of probability which permits of little doubt as to its truth. Whatever, then, may be said of Lamarckism, Darwinism, and other theories of Evolution, the fact of Evolution, as the evidence now stands, is scarcely any longer a matter for controversy.[105]

In spite of Zahm's professed zeal for the independence of scientific inquiry from metaphysical deduction, dogmatic considerations did play a role in his assessments of various theories. This point is quite clear in Zahm's treatment of the origin and development of the human race, a topic especially delicate for a Catholic apologist. Forced to declare himself on this issue, Zahm sided with the neo-Lamarckians or, in the terminology of James R. Moore, the proponents of "Christian Darwinisticism." He joined them in advancing modifications of Darwin's theory in order to circumnavigate certain philosophical implications of the stark struggle for survival depicted by natural selection in unqualified form. Zahm took this position to avoid the spectre of agnosticism he saw lurking in the neo-Darwinism of the day.[106]

Lamarck had posited a theory of transmutation that in its most general form embraced two causal factors: an innate power conferred on nature by God that tends to produce a series of plants and animals of increasing complexity and perfection; and an inner, adapting disposition peculiar to living bodies that assures the performance of actions sufficient to the needs created by a changing environment, those actions becoming instinctive and inheritable.[107] Zahm joined a distinguished company who advocated theistic evolution by integrating these Lamarckian "powers" into a Christian understanding of the ordered progression of species under God. Their softening of Darwinian theory allowed these theists—Asa Gray, Richard Owen, Robert Chambers, St. George Jackson Mivart, among others—to reduce the level of intellectual tension or "cognitive dissonance" between the rival "epistemes" or ways of knowing the world presented by modern science on the one hand, and traditional theism on the other.[108] The addition of the Lamarckian "powers" helped to make credible a scientific worldview that featured design and intention in nature and purposeful, teleological variations in organisms.

Zahm drew on this tradition when he endorsed the theory of human evolution explicated in Mivart's 1871 work, *On the Genesis of Species*, which subordinated natural selection to the role played by "special powers and tendencies existing in each organism." According to this English Catholic, these special powers were the divine instrument employed in directing organisms to produce those forms that God had preconceived. The human body was derived by this evolutionary process, while the soul, source of humanity's ethical and rational nature, appeared in each case by divine fiat.[109] Zahm came to be known as "the American Mivart" for his endorsement of this theory.[110]

In adopting this position Zahm made a first attempt at "a perfect synthesis between the inductions of science on the one hand and the deductions of metaphysics on the other."[111] In a sense, Zahm compromised with himself: as a naturalist, he surrendered strict adherence to inductive method by positing a supernatural act of God in infusing the rational soul; as priest, he surrendered the traditional view of the direct creation of the body of Adam. As it turned out, he ended up satisfying neither scientific nor religious purists.

In spite of the body-soul dualism that Mivart's system seemed to foster, Zahm accepted the theory as compatible with Christian belief.

He sought to vindicate theistic evolution by demonstrating that the great patristic and medieval theologians held it to be true:

> Evolution has been condemned as anti-Patristic and anti-Scholastic, although Saints Gregory of Nyssa, Augustine, and Thomas Aquinas are most explicit in their assertion of principles that are in perfect accord with all the legitimate demands of theistic Evolution. . . . The Bishop of Hippo, in his 'De Genesi ad Litteram' proleptically announced all the fundamental principles of modern Evolution. He recognized Evolution not only in individuals, but . . . in the sum of all things. God did not create the world, as it now exists, actually, *actualiter*, but potentially and causally, *potentialiter et causaliter*.[112]

To lend additional support to Mivart, Zahm mounted a lengthy exegesis of texts of Aquinas that seemed to affirm that the rational soul is specially created and infused into the human body by God.[113]

Moreover, Zahm argued that acceptance of evolution would enhance rather than imperil authentic Catholic teaching on divine providence and human nature:

> And from the theistic point of view [evolution] exhibits the Deity creating matter and force, and putting them under the dominion of law. It tells of a God who inaugurates the era of terrestrial life by the creation of one or more simple organisms . . . and causing them, under the action of His Providence, to evolve in the course of time into all the myriad, complicated, specialized, and perfect forms which now people the earth. Surely this is a nobler conception than that which represents him as experimenting, as it were, with crude materials and succeeding, only after numerous attempts, in producing the organism which He is supposed to have had in view from the beginning. To picture the Deity thus working tentatively, is an anthropomorphic view of the Creator, which is as little warranted by Catholic dogma as it is by genuine science.[114]

Furthermore, Zahm claimed, there is nothing in evolution contrary to Scripture. "God did potentially what the ordinary Scripture interpreter believes he did by a distinct, immediate exercise of infinite power," he argued, citing Augustine's exegesis of Genesis. There the great theologian held that animals and plants were brought into existence by natural causes: "He tells us explicitly that they were created potentially, and that they were afterwards developed into the manifold forms we now behold."[115]

Certain scientific discoveries called into question traditional interpretations of the Bible on a number of points: the age of the world, the universality of the flood, and the creation of Adam and Eve. On these questions Zahm invoked Pope Leo XIII. It was not the purpose of sacred Scripture to teach science, the pope had written. Accordingly, Zahm accepted Newman's *obiter dicta* theory in claiming that certain biblical passages admit of no uniform interpretation: "It seems unworthy of the divine greatness that the Almighty should, in the revelation of Himself to us, undertake mere secular duties and assume the office of a narrator, as such, or an historian, or geographer, except in so far as the secular matters bear directly upon the revealed truth."[116]

Obviously, Zahm claimed a freedom of interpretation in matters not defined dogmatically by the church, including the question of human origins. He announced boldly that the church is not committed to a theory about the origin of the world or its inhabitants: "Hence as a Catholic I am bound to no theory of Evolution or special creation, except in so far as there may be positive evidence on behalf of such theory."[117] And as one who seemed at times to thrive on controversy, Zahm could not resist taking a swipe at his ecclesiastical opponents in Rome and America. He was unambiguous and undiplomatic in pointing the finger at the integralists who, in support of creationism and the process of deduction from metaphysical principles, refused to acknowledge the high degree of probability resting with evolutionary theory. Instead, Zahm charged, "they love to descant on the dictum of the Scholastics, *a possibili ad actum non valet consecutio*—possibility is far from implying existence."[118]

Evolution and Dogma was not the first occasion upon which Zahm criticized the neo-scholastic obstruction of scientific inquiry. Nor was this Zahm's first call for revisions in the Roman Catholic interpretation of the biblical and traditional witness on creation, providence, and human nature. But it was the first to attract international attention. It was translated into Italian (1896), French (1897), and Spanish (1904) and was promoted with an advertising campaign by publisher D. H. McBride that played up the controversial aspects of the book. It is not surprising, therefore, that *Evolution and Dogma* soon incited the antagonisms of curial officials whose worldview it seemed to subvert.

The time of Zahm's intense and highly publicized activity as an apologist for science coincided with a period of ferment in the confrontation of Roman Catholicism and the modern age. From 1894 to 1899 conservative Roman ecclesial officials mounted a fresh assault in the campaign against modernity that culminated in the papal condemnation of Americanism in 1899. Because the heresies of modernity appeared to infect culture in all of its diverse expressions, traditionalists perceived the presence of the disease everywhere: in the application of the higher criticism to sacred texts; in the separation of church and state; in the attempt to assimilate Catholicism to the local and national communities to which the churches belonged; and, invariably, in the advances of the natural sciences. While in Europe in 1894, Zahm learned that Mivart had come under suspicion for views which he had first expressed twenty-three years earlier. At the same time the rumor circulated in ecclesiastical circles that the theory of evolution itself was to be condemned by the Vatican.[119] Fueled by the debate over Leo XIII's encyclical on biblical criticism, *Providentissimus Deus*, controversy raged in the ensuing months between liberal and conservative Catholics over the meaning of the book of Genesis and the authorship of the Pentateuch.[120]

In this context Zahm's unflinching advocacy of the general theory of evolution placed him at the center of the storm, in large part because he also was identified by conservatives as a prominent member of the group of American priests and bishops attempting to "Americanize" the church. Zahm understood his crusade for evolution as a significant contribution to the self-conscious effort on the part of many progressives to assimilate Catholics into the mainstream of American political and intellectual life. One cause especially dear to "the movement" was education on every level: at the Catholic University of America, in public and parochial schools, and on the lecture circuits Zahm frequented in the 1890s. In his sustained defense of the principle of freedom of inquiry—a principle cherished by American Catholic progressives—in matters scientific, Zahm understood himself to be promoting "the movement" in a most public and persuasive way. Indeed, Zahm's concern with accumulating favorable notices, including his manipulations in acquiring the honorary doctorate from the pope, may be seen as consonant with his hope of nudging public opinion in a direction more favorable to the Americanist program. However, the integralist neo-scholatics of the Roman curia did not act in concert with American or European public opinion.

The tide began to turn against Zahm as early as 1894. That year witnessed both the publication of *Bible, Science and Faith* and, co-incidentally, a mood swing in Rome, where conservatives seemed to awaken to the threat evolutionism posed to the neo-scholastic world-view. After a triumphant year which included a celebrated address before the Scientific Congress in 1894, a private audience with the pope, and the awarding of the honorary doctorate in February of 1895, Zahm delivered the inaugural lectures at the Catholic Columbian Summer School in Madison, Wisconsin, in July 1895. He took that opportunity to introduce the major themes of the forthcoming *Evolution and Dogma* discussed above, emphasizing the "simian origin of man," the infusion of the rational soul, and the heritage of theistic evolution in the church fathers and Aquinas. From that moment forward he was embroiled in controversy.

In an open letter to Milwaukee's *Catholic Citizen* following the lectures, Rev. J. W. Vahey called Zahm an "agnostic scientist." John Gmeiner replied that he shared Zahm's views completely and referred readers to an earlier book of his own.[121] Meanwhile, Zahm sent a rough draft of *Evolution and Dogma* to Paulist priest Augustine Hewit, who advised against publication. The business about the evolution of Adam's body, he worried, would arouse opposition.[122]

Indeed, the prominent cleric from Notre Dame seemed to relish his role as provocateur. He loved to shock his audience with un-expected pronouncements, as when he first advocated publicly the doctrine of human evolution at the Madison Summer School. "He followed somewhat the juggler's methods: conceal and reveal in order to enjoy your confusion," wrote Father Patrick J. Carroll of Notre Dame's *Ave Maria* magazine. Carroll reported also that Zahm himself helped to edit the famous article in the *New York Herald* asking "Is Zahm a Heretic?"[123] That Zahm became increasingly impressed with his own role in the unfolding drama of evolution and religion is evident from his correspondence during these years with his one confidant, his brother Albert. His obvious pride in his numerous accomplishments stemmed from his conviction that he had earned a measure of respect and approval from European Catholics and from Rome itself by competently representing the best interests of the church—not, as was the case in Tyrrell's similar boasts and obfuscations, from a sense that he was deftly eluding his ecclesiastical persecutors. After receiving a round of honors, he recounted to Albert the response of the assembled fathers of Holy Cross at Notre Dame: "All are amazed and many half dazed . . . Dr. Zahm is the Hero of the hour. What next? Many ask with fluttering hearts and bated breath—Fr. Burns gravely replies, 'The Cardinal's Hat!'"[124]

The scope and depth of the public response and approbation of Zahm's work in 1895 and early 1896 aroused concern on the part of conservative clergy in America and integralist leaders in Europe.[125]

In the United States, after Zahm's second appearance at Plattsburgh in August 1895, Father Thomas J. Conaty, president of the board, disavowed responsibility for Zahm's opinions. The episcopal supervisor of the program, Sebastian Messmer of Green Bay, initiated a campaign to remove progressives from the lecture circuit. He was infuriated not only by Zahm's lectures and publications, but by the Notre Dame priest's invitation to other "liberals" to appear on the lecture circuit. A terse exchange of letters between Zahm and Messmer ensued. Messmer objected to Zahm's inclusion on the program of Catholic University professors Thomas O'Gorman and Edward Pace: "Add to the names of Dr. O'Gorman and Pace those of Rev. Lambert and Mr. Desmond and the cry of *Liberalism* would go up against the C.C.S.S. (Columbian Catholic Summer School) from all sides."[126] Messmer then informed O'Gorman that he would not be permitted to lecture on the C.C.S.S. circuit, in part because "the fact cannot be denied that the Catholic University, its professors and rector, are not looked upon with favor by many of our Catholics."[127] He might be allowed to lecture in the future, Messmer continued, only if he chose a subject "where there will be no danger of advancing theories or opinions which would or might involve the school into [sic] difficulties or controversies."[128]

Apparently, Messmer was at this time especially sensitive to criticism from a number of American Jesuits, including apologist James F. X. Hoeffer, who threatened to and in fact did resign from the summer school board over the inclusions of "liberals" on the program.[129] They felt that Zahm had almost single-handedly polluted the pure orthodoxy of the program by his advanced stand on evolution. Messmer explained to O'Gorman, "Again, having been exposed to a great deal of *incrimination* last year on account of Dr. Zahm's expression on the evolution of man, we have to be much more careful this year to have no theories or opinions put forth from our boards which would not find acceptance with all."[130]

Zahm responded to these charges with righteous indignation. As head of the board of studies for the summer school, he defended its selection of O'Gorman and Pace. The board, he insisted, "looked for men who would *attract large audiences*; men known for ability and scholarship." He refused to boycott them because "I. . . hear [that] they may, on controverted questions, entertain views different from my own." Zahm then noted that these men had never been silenced or condemned by Catholic authorities:

> Speaking for my single self I never knew, until I received your letter, that Drs. O'Gorman, Pace, Fr. Lambert and Desmond were regarded as "liberals." Surely the Holy Father would not have made the first a bishop if there had been any doubt about his orthodoxy. Neither is it conceivable that the board of regents, composed of distinguished bishops and archbishops, would retain Dr. Pace in the faculty of the university if his teaching were unsound.[131]

The Jesuits on the board tried to block Zahm from the circuit, in part because he had, they charged, misunderstood and misrepresented to his audiences the nature of the reconciliation or "concord" that the great doctors of the church, including St. Thomas, had established between science and revelation.

Zahm countered by quoting Bishop of Peoria John Lancaster Spalding's declaration that Aquinas's "point of view in all that concerns natural knowledge has long since vanished from sight." Zahm suggested that modern Catholics should not attempt to shore up Thomas's concord but should emulate his boldness by devising innovative ways to deal with new facts discovered by science. Were they living today, Zahm charged, Augustine and Aquinas would not be pathetically defending past solutions but would be "the boldest and the most comprehensive and the most liberal minds the world has ever known."[132]

Undaunted, Zahm published *Evolution and Dogma* in February 1896 and lectured on it at the Catholic Winter School in New Orleans. However, upon his return from New Orleans he learned to his dismay that he had been transferred to Rome by Gilbert Français, superior-general of Holy Cross, to take the post of procurator-general for the congregation. Critics in the Catholic press speculated that the transfer was designed to deter Zahm from further publication. "The evolution bacillus is a dangerous thing," chirped Arthur Preuss, editor of the conservative *Review*. He suggested that the pure air of Catholic orthodoxy would help Zahm recuperate.[133] "I have never been 'disciplined,' as they put it, and it is not likely that I shall be," Zahm replied bravely. "My views may be not looked upon with favor by all in Rome," he admitted, "but I know that every eminent man of science throughout Europe is in perfect sympathy with my opinions." Nonetheless, he rushed into print a slender volume, *Scientific Theory and Catholic Doctrine*, in which he repudiated Darwin and Huxley unequivocally.[134]

As Zahm arrived in Rome on 1 April 1896, the controversy over Americanism was entering a crucial phase. On 19 April Americanist bishop John Ireland spoke at O'Gorman's consecration on the respective roles of diocesan and religious order priests; his comments offended Jesuits and Redemptorists, whom he blamed for Catholic setbacks in England during penal times. Within months Americanist John J. Keane was forced to resign from the office of rector at Catholic University of America. By year's end the American press reported harsh criticisms of Keane and Ireland by Cardinal Francesco Satolli, former apostolic delegate to the United States.[135]

Once in Rome, Zahm too was caught up in ecclesiastical politics. He scored quick victories for his congregation by securing papal commendation for the college in Washington, D.C., and confirmation of the rules and constitution of the Holy Cross Sisters. O'Connell welcomed Zahm to "the Club," a group of churchmen in sympathy with the Americanist movement that included Cardinals Serafino and Vincenzo Vanutelli. Zahm became another agent in Rome for the liberal cause.[136]

This activity did not go unnoticed by the Roman opponents of Americanism, whose leader was Salvatore Brandi, S.J., editor of the influential journal *La Civiltà Cattolica*. In July 1896 he wrote to his episcopal ally in New York, Michael Corrigan, that Zahm's "recent utterances on transformism, and his relations with the liberal party, well known in the Vatican and Propaganda, will interfere with his work as Procurator of Holy Cross."[137]

The Italian translation of *Evolution and Dogma*, which appeared that fall, exacerbated Zahm's problems. He reported to his brother in December that "the Jesuits are already training their biggest guns on me. . . . The die is cast."[138] In January 1897 the first in a series of negative reviews of *Evolution and Dogma* appeared in *La Civiltà Cattolica*. Although Zahm was still confident enough to assure Cardinal Gibbons of Baltimore that "the future is ours—Leo and Rampolla still with us," he delivered his last formal paper on evolution five months later at the fourth International Catholic Scientific Congress.[139]

In December Zahm returned reluctantly to Notre Dame to serve as provincial of the congregation in America. Three months later Ireland visited him to discuss the situation in Rome. Ireland was struck by Zahm's dedication to the cause and wrote O'Connell: "You have surely fixed him in the movement. He is 'the movement' and will drive the Holy Cross, Ave Maria, and C. onward with great force."[140] Obviously the archbishop of St. Paul felt that from his position of leadership at Notre Dame, Zahm would serve ably the Americanist cause.

The news from Rome that year proved Ireland's optimism unfounded, however. In July O'Connell informed Zahm that Charles Maignen's book attacking Americanism had received the *imprimatur* and that the pope was considering the question. On 10 September 1898 Zahm received word from Français that an edict by the Roman Congregation of the Index had banned *Evolution and Dogma*. The edict read, in part:

> the most reverend Cardinals in a general meeting on September 1, 1898, having heard the exposition and the vote of the consultors, after mature deliberation have decreed: The work of the Reverend Zahm is prohibited; the decree, however, is not to be published until . . . the author will be heard out by his Father General whether he is willing to submit to the decree and reprove his work. . . . The prohibition . . . extends to all translations made in any language.[141]

For the next eight months Français, Zahm, O'Connell, and Ireland worked assiduously to prevent publication of the decree. Zahm's mood fluctuated from bitter disappointment to outrage. He wrote Français immediately, promising full submission to the decree. Yet he maneuvered to avoid any public retraction of his position and expressed frustration about the shadow cast on Holy Cross by the affair. He wrote to Ireland:

> The Index decree must be permanently suppressed & the present incumbent [Zahm] must be confirmed in the provincialship. . . . We shall win in the long war, for truth and justice are on our side; the intelligence of the world and the increasing might of America are with us . . . it is a fight for progress, for true Americanism, for the Catholic University, a fight against Jesuitical tyranny,

against obscurantism and medievalism. . . . It would, no doubt, be a great victory for the enemy to get me out of my present position, but it would cripple Notre Dame, ruin Holy Cross & give a terrible setback to our community.[142]

The decree remained unpublished, although the *New York Daily Tribune* ran a letter from Zahm asking his Italian translator to withdraw the book from distribution, on the orders of the Holy See.[143]

Who delated Zahm? The answer is unclear, but the list of candidates includes Brandi, Satolli, and the American Jesuits on the summer school board. Français did some investigative work in Zahm's behalf and enumerated the reasons for the judgment against him: curial officials were displeased that Zahm had portrayed Augustine and Aquinas as evolutionists; they felt that Zahm and Mivart had jeopardized the integrity of Scripture by threatening to reduce the story of Adam and Eve to a myth; they resented Zahm's penchant for ecclesiastical intrigue, his friendship with the imprudent O'Connell, and his support of the Americanists.[144]

It was hardly a coincidence that the decree banning *Evolution and Dogma* was followed four months later by the encyclical condemning Americanism. By the turn of the century neo-scholastic philosophers and theologians in power at Rome began to perceive Americanism and evolutionism as aspects of a larger historical movement that challenged their positions of privilege in the church, insofar as it threatened to overturn the philosophical and theological assumptions upon which the institutional system of their era was founded.[145] In the view of the editors of *La Civiltà Cattolica*, Zahm embodied the link between Americanism and evolutionism. Thus he was the object of the conservatives' resentment of the Americanist advocacy of options in areas that had been settled upon and closed to debate, in official expression if not actual practice: the nature of religious life; the ideal of Catholic education; the unity of church and state, and the preference for supernatural over natural virtues.[146]

Zahm represented a threat of a different kind as well. As an evolutionist he adopted a methodology that seemed to reflect a new and dangerous way of thinking about church and world—a new "episteme." It was this methodology that troubled Brandi most about *Evolution and Dogma*. Zahm took as a starting point not deductions from revealed truth, but "unbiased" inductions from empirical data. He promised a "synthesis" of these inductions and the "authentic" teaching of the Catholic tradition. He interpreted Scripture critically, assigning different levels of authority to different passages and scientific competence to very few. And he claimed that the defined teachings of the church on these matters were few in number, which allowed him to proceed liberally in most questions.[147]

Most egregious to Brandi was Zahm's grounding of his positions in Pope Leo's teaching on Scripture on the one hand and in the authority of the church fathers and medieval scholastics on the other. At stake in this battle was the interpretation of these figures, especially Thomas, upon whose authority the worldview of the neo-scholastic was based. Brandi wrote:

> Speaking of St. Thomas Aquinas, Zahm acknowledges that the Angelic Doctor, in perfect accord with the traditional doctrine of the Fathers, maintains that the body of the first human was formed directly and immediately by God Himself. It would therefore seem that the Angelic Doctor cannot and must not be cited in favor of evolution. . . . But this is not the case.
>
> After quoting Mivart that "God created the soul of man directly and his body indirectly, through the operation of secondary causes," Professor Zahm, with a truly American lack of restraint, writes: "This opinion favoring the derived origin of the human body is in perfect harmony with other principles set forth by the great luminaries of the Church, St. Augustine and St. Thomas." As if this were not enough, in the following pages he adds: "This opinion of the derived origin of the human body can be held in conformity with the teachings of the Angelic Doctor under another aspect." Evidently, whatever this "aspect" may be, if you believe Dr. Zahm, it is necessary to say that the Angelic Doctor is incoherent and illogical.[148]

Brandi charged that Zahm's mistakes reflected an insufficient training in neo-scholasticism: "Because he does not seem to be familiar with Thomistic philosophy, he has misinterpreted these principles and for this reason he cites and makes application of them incorrectly." Most disturbingly, Brandi concluded, Zahm assures us of the victory of the theory of evolution over other explanations of creation and recommends it "not only for Christian philosophy but also for Catholic apologetics."[149]

To propose that Thomas had condoned the theory of bodily evolution was to introduce an undesirable pluralism of interpretation into the reading of scholasticism. Zahm had attempted to do the same with the Fathers and with the Bible. This approach threatened the neo-scholastic monopoly on the interpretation of these sources. Accordingly, Brandi derided Zahm's method of interpretation, with its characteristic American foolhardiness, as much as he did the conclusions to which the method led.[150]

Neither Brandi nor Zahm followed the implications of this inductive, or hypothetico-deductive, method to its unforeseen ends. But in 1899 they jousted on the tip of an iceberg against which neo-scholasticism and the church it claimed to represent would crash in the first decade of the new century. By the time of the condemnation of modernism in 1907 Zahm had long since retired from independent research and apologetics for science and Catholic dogma. Zahm had been one of the first casualties in the war against the proposed syntheses of "the ancient faith and modern thought."[151] To the larger context in which that war was waged we now turn.

2. The Signs of the Times:
Modernism and Anti-Modernism

John Zahm ran afoul of a Roman Catholic theological orthodoxy that was assuming the shape of an impenetrable dogmatic fortress. Fortified by neo-scholastic thought, it was designed to stand with full integrity in each of its various formulations and to persevere as a unified system whose every tenet was seen as absolutely essential to the survival of the whole. In the twentieth century the defenders of this system came to be known as "integralists."

A series of definitive acts and declarations of the magisterium prepared the way for the integralists. Expressions of Catholic identity which appeared to challenge the assumptions of the neo-scholastic system were outlawed in the condemnations of conciliarism and localism (1863); liberalism, progressivism, and individualism (1864); and naturalism, immanentism, pragmatism, and Americanism (1899). In 1870 the First Vatican Council defined the doctrine of papal infallibility in matters of faith and morals, and nine years later Pope Leo XIII called for an exclusive commitment on the part of Catholic educators to the theological method of St. Thomas Aquinas. Patterns of thought deviating from his example came under suspicion, and Rome unleashed a stream of condemnations that served to narrow considerably the boundaries of orthodox Catholic belief.[1]

Rome thereby defined itself by what it was—authoritarian, hierarchical, monarchical, traditional—and by what it was not—democratic, progressive, pragmatic, open to autonomous science. This Roman fortress mentality was not a prelude to dialogue with anticlericalism in France, Darwinism in England, or pluralism in America. It was an identity bequeathed to the faithful in their resistance against the heretical impulses of the modern age. Confronted by heresy on all sides, the neo-scholastics began as early as 1849 to identify a common

malady at the root of the various ailments afflicting the Body of Christ. By 1907 they had designated this "system" opposing integral Catholicism as "the synthesis of all heresies."[2] Thus the battle between the neo-scholastics or "integralists" and those they identified as "modernists" defined the ecclesial context and the major intellectual issues to which Zahm, Sullivan, Slattery, and the contributors to the *New York Review* responded.

The question at issue was the nature of the "act of faith" and, by implication, the proper relationship between human cognitive capacities and the supernatural character of revelation. Those holding the condemned positions had misrepresented this relationship, emphasizing one aspect of it at the expense of the other. To one extreme ran the tendencies of fideism and traditionalism; at the opposite pole, the error of rationalism. An important phase of the debate over natural knowledge and revelation culminated in the 1861 condemnation of ontologism, which held that human knowledge of God's existence is the result of intuitive rather than deductive thought.[3]

In identifying ontologism, fideism, and rationalism as unacceptable interpretations of Catholic teaching on the question of human knowledge of God, the Holy Office sought to preserve the proper place of natural cognition in the act of faith, and in so doing, to fortify the neo-scholastic doctrine that human reason can, by deduction from *a priori* universal concepts, arrive at metaphysical truth. Post-Kantian epistemologies rejected this claim outright. In response the Roman school made a series of interdependent affirmations about faith and knowledge the centerpiece of Catholic epistemology. First, there are two kinds of religious cognition, natural and supernatural. Second, by natural powers of deduction, one can know, in an analogous sense, the premises of religion such as the existence of God. Third, this knowledge is also supernatural because it is God who is revealed, and such revelation is necessary if one is to perceive natural religious truths accurately. Fourth, the fact of revelation can be proved with certainty by objective miracles. Fifth, the content of revelation is unalterable.[4]

Of course, these principles did not emerge overnight. They were articulated gradually in the wake of the renascence of a time-tested ally of Romanism, the scholastic method.[5] The primary weakness of the nineteenth-century appropriation of scholastic thought was an utter lack of genuine historical sensibility. The Thomist synthesis had itself undergone significant evolution in content and conceptual form. Leading nineteenth century scholastics like Joseph Kleutgen and Louis

Billot, both Jesuits, declared forthrightly their contempt for doing theology in an historical context. To their way of thinking, the word "historical" was synonymous with "relative."[6] This ahistorical inclination
precluded any recognition by the Roman school of the limitations of
Aquinas's thought and allowed its adherents to gloss over the very
real differences in method and content present in the work of various
medieval scholastics. Kleutgen and Billot replaced the complexities of
history with a logical and metaphysical analysis of scholastic texts that
derived essential theses common to all of the doctors. This trend of
presenting scholasticism as a coherent Thomistic system encouraged
Franciscan and Augustinian scholars to present their theological and
spiritual forebears as contributing little more than subtle variations on
Thomistic themes. Thus, when dissenting Catholic historians and theologians began to uncover the historical record and to introduce the notion of pluralism into this comfortable picture, the integralists rebuked
them. Among the sources of irritation for the integralists were publications like the *New York Review*, whose first number included an article
challenging Thomistic (and Jesuit and Dominican) ascendancy in the
nineteenth century and rehabilitating the thought of Duns Scotus.[7]

Thus was a cavalier attitude toward history fostered in the manuals *ad mentem* Ste. Thomas and an image created of a profoundly rationalistic and impersonal Aristotelian science, the arguments of which
proceeded deductively to their certain conclusions, and the epistemology of which depended almost exclusively on discursive understanding. The sense of certitude accorded the divinely revealed first
principles of this science established a principle of theological control over them. It followed logically that the (nonrevealed) findings of
modern scientific and historical scholarship were subordinate to theology's first principles and must defer to its component of transrational
(supernatural) truth. Revelation would be the norm of historical and
scientific judgment. Anathema to this school were those scholars who
would reverse this relationship by subjecting theological principles to
the rigors of scientific, historical, and literary criticism.

Lost to this approach were, ironically, some of the subtleties of
Thomas's thought as well, including his unique metaphysics of existence, the role he gave to abstraction and judgment in his epistemology
and, most significant to those who would be labeled "modernists," the
connections he drew between his metaphysical system and his own
personal religious experience.[8] The Roman dominance of nineteenth-
century scholasticism resulted in a lack of appreciation for the vital

role of personal experience and nonconceptual intuition in religious knowledge of God. In contrast, a French "school" identified with the work of Maurice Blondel and Lucien Laberthonnière emphasized that faith is an act of the total personality, a religious response of the will to the indwelling spirit of God—a theme later taken up by the American Paulist William L. Sullivan.[9]

To the neo-scholastic this "doctrine of vital immanence" contradicted the traditional notion of revelation, which was described as totally extrinsic to the recipient, supernatural in origin and in mode of communication, its occurrence demonstrated, as Giovanni Perrone wrote, "by signs of indisputably supernatural provenance. . . . [the signs] by common consent were miracles and prophecies."[10] Billot, assigned to the Gregorian by Pope Leo XIII in 1888, rejected apologetic writings that relied on a role for human affections, experience, or intuition during the event of revelation. These elements, he claimed, would call into question the credibility of rationally apprehensible arguments and signs as the extrinsic condition preceding the act of faith. Other than the authority of God undergirding the arguments and signs objectively given, the believer has no immediate knowledge, and certainly no intuition, of the fact of revelation. God's truth imposes itself on the believer and demands a simple adherence to God's authority alone. For Billot the evidence for belief must be external, supernatural, and miraculous, precisely because the human subject lacks an interior, natural intuition of divine revelation. Untouched by miracle or prophecy, the human subject is unprepared for faith.

Against the ambiguity of human intuition, Billot and his colleagues affirmed the ability of speculative reason to discern the essential attributes of the divine nature by the analogy of being. Moreover, they argued that "the actual fact of revelation" can be demonstrated by historical investigation and authenticated empirically. In this system the primary role of theology is the exposition of the content of this objectively given public revelation, contained in a "deposit of faith" given by Jesus and his disciples during the apostolic age. Any "development" of this doctrine consisted in the logical, deductive elaboration of truths already contained in the original revelation, albeit implicitly and indistinctly.[11]

This network of assumptions served as the framework for the integralist understanding of apologetics, history, and biblical studies. Apologetics would convince the skeptic with scriptural proof-texts and "objective" miracles, history would substantiate these claims, and scriptural commentary would explicate the themes and teachings grounding both apologetics and history. Without regard for the context of sacred text or for the intention of the author, key words and thematic statements were culled from conciliar documents or liturgical sources or Scripture, and their meaning made to conform to apologetic purposes. If revelation consisted of a deposit of truths absolute in content and independent of the mind of the human subject, then "differences in time, historical outlook, and cultural expression were accidental."[12] A corollary flowing from this notion of truth was the refusal to consider corrective data from scientific disciplines working independently of theology.

In the decade following Zahm's silencing, certain European Catholics subjected these criteria of neo-scholasticism to rigorous scrutiny and found them wanting. Not only were the procedures disconsonant with canons of scientific inquiry, they were untrue to their own sources. Not only did the integralist approach betray many of the wisest insights of the Catholic tradition and those that would enable the church to adapt to the requirements of the modern age, they argued, but it also misunderstood the apostolic meaning of the very "categories" of faith and revelation. George Tyrrell addressed his objections to a prominent leader of the integralist group:

> Those who, like Your Eminence, believe that the object of Faith is a revealed theology, a body of divinely guaranteed terms and definitions and statements final and valid for all ages and nations, are quite consistent in holding that the Encyclical [*Pascendi*] is the friend and protector of scientific truth and liberty. . . . If God's word vouches for any one science that science must be the rule and criterion of all the rest. To be under its control is not slavery but liberty—liberty from error. . . . Such it must be if scientific propositions form, however implicitly, part of the substance of divine revelation. But if they do not; if revelation be not theology, the bondage of science to the fallible conceptions of a past age is a bondage indeed, an insuperable obstacle to progress.[13]

The modernists, in challenging the assumptions, content, and expressions of neo-scholasticism, eventually came to question the authority structure that sustained it. Loisy judged the scholastic enterprise as "routine passing itself off as tradition."[14] Tyrrell concluded that the ultimate aim of the scholastics was political, for they desired "a progressive centralization of the Roman Church by which first laity, then the priests, and finally the bishops, have been deprived of all active share in church life and government." He called for "constitutional guarantees for the liberty of the subject against the caprices of authority" and admitted that they were "inspired by the idea of democracy as well as by knowledge of the original constitution of the Church."[15]

The integralist response to these challenges was swift and sure. The integralists, or anti-modernists, understood that if these criticisms proved successful on any single point, the entire interdependent network of assumptions would be in jeopardy. They depicted their opponents as disciples of Kant, who had introduced into theological reflection the errors of immanentism, subjectivism, and agnosticism.[16] Each of the propositions condemned in the decree *Lamentabili* (1907), most of which were drawn from Alfred Loisy's books, repudiated integralism in one way or another. Among the condemned theses, for example, was an objection to the integralist view of revelation: "The dogmas the Church holds out as revealed are not truths fallen from heaven."[17]

The most incisive portrait of the "heresy," as it was labeled in 1907, came from the pen of J. B. Lemius, O.M.I., the ghostwriter of *Pascendi*. Lemius' depiction of the "movement" relied disproportionately on the writings of Loisy. His *A Catechism of Modernism* expounded on the themes of the encyclical and set out to prove that the other historians and Bible critics implicated in the condemnation were not "objective scientists" at all but post-Kantian ideologues. Were the agnosticism at the base of Loisy's criticism called for what it was, Lemius reasoned, then his movement and the critical methods at its service might be easily discredited.[18] For, in spite of their dissembling, each modernist followed the same basic pattern of approach. "Modernists employ clever artifice," Lemius wrote, "namely, to present their doctrines without order and systematic arrangement into one whole, scattered and disjointed one from the other so as to appear to be in doubt and uncertainty, while they are in reality firm and steadfast."[19]

According to Lemius, agnosticism and historical relativism comprised the negative or destructive component of modernism, whereas vital immanence, subjectivism, naturalism, pragmatism, and psychologism together formed the positive or constructive component.[20]

Lemius perceived within the negative component a series of increasingly erroneous positions, including the reduction of human knowledge to consciousness and to pale impressions of subjective images (reductionism); the restriction of ideas to the phenomenal world (positivism); and, the consequent rendering of "ideas" beyond the phenomenal world as logical abstractions void of reality (idealism). "Loisy's conception of history," Lemius wrote, "is finally atheistic precisely because it rules out *a priori* the possibility of a historical manifestation of the transcendent."

Lemius was gripped with a real fear—the loss of the transcendent altogether. If the modernist tendency to conceive of the transcendent as the object of a purely internal, psychological phenomenon without an objectively verifiable "fact" as its source were to prevail, then sacred books and institutions would be seen as but the externalizations of inner psychological phenomena and thus subject to the relativizing rules and analysis of ordinary, secular history. Modernists contend, Lemius wrote, "that God can never be the direct object of science; He must not be considered as an historical subject. . . . It is a fixed and established principle among them that both science and history must be atheistic, leaving room for nothing but phenomena." In similar fashion he reduced historical method to "Agnosticism: whatever there is in History suggestive of the Divine must be rejected; Transfiguration: everything that raises the historical Christ above historical conditions must be removed; Disfigurement: all must be excluded not in keeping with His character, circumstances, education, and the place and time in which He lived." Agnosticism having destroyed the role of natural theology in apprehending revelation, the modernists denied the intellect's ability to conform itself to external, supernatural "data," and located the manifestation of the religious impulse solely in the movement of the heart called "sentiment." Latent in the subconscious is a *need* for the divine that produces the sentiment of faith. This religious sentiment possesses within itself "both as its own object and intrinsic cause the *reality* of the divine."[21]

Herein Lemius perceived the way to dogmatic evolutionism. Modernists were those who held that faith transfigures the phenomenon (for example, Christ in the tomb on the third day) elevating it above this true (i.e., historically verifiable) condition and adapting it to faith's own sense of the divine (faith's sentiment about Christ's victory over death empties the tomb and proclaims the bodily resurrection). Thus the religious sentiment, by this vital immanence, emerges from subconsciousness into the germ of all religion. The supernatural is destroyed as religion emanates spontaneously from the natural human condition.

What role is left to the intellect in the modernist scheme—as understood by the anti-modernists? According to Enrico Rosa of *La Civiltà Cattolica*, the intellect in this scheme analyzes the religious sentiment, expressing the vital phenomenon in mental pictures and then in words. The intellect first produces simple statements about the phenomenon and then, gradually, more complex formulations that are dogmas. Dogmas, then, are no more than formulas that furnish the believer with a means of giving an account of her faith to herself, an account that in turn strengthens faith and leads to the formulation of more appropriate dogmas—that is, dogmas which more accurately articulate the progressively stronger religious sentiment. As such, dogmas are always in part inadequate, symbolic expressions of personal, or communal, faith.[22]

That this "programme of modernism" was not elaborated in its entirety by any of the accused left the accusers undaunted. For the magisterium and its neo-scholastic agents shared the sincere conviction that the enemy confronting them was united in the crucial epistemological principles—that the eternal may be known only in and through the temporal and contingent, that this knowledge may be appropriately expressed by symbol and not by analogy, that the human will plays a role in this process prior to the role played by the intellect. These principles led to methodological errors—the removal of the transcendent element from the facts of history, the evaluation of those facts according solely to the preconditions of scientific laws and previous historical patterns, the assignment of inexplicable (read: supernatural) elements to the realm of faith. These methodological errors in turn produced unsound conclusions—that the Jesus of history cannot be reconciled with the Christ of faith; that formulaic statements of faith (dogmas) have as their object not the verifiable phenomena studied by science but rather the interior religious sentiment; that this sentiment evolves and deepens as time passes with consequent development of dogma. And this complex of missteps served as prologue, in the eyes of the integralists, to a death-dealing blow to the very notion of authority. It was this threat above all that alarmed Pius X: "They claim that tradition is relative and subject to change and thereby they reduce to nothing the authority of the Holy Fathers. . . . They wish to subject church teachings to the . . . so-called scientific criticism, thus enslaving theology."[23]

All of these fears and accusations surfaced in the encyclical *Pascendi*. To each modernist the encyclical imparted stunning versatility: the modernist was at once a philosopher, a believer, a theologian, an historian and critic, an apologist, and a reformer. As a believer, for example, the modernist based his faith on his direct experience of the divine reality, an "idea of God" that engages not the mind but the will and is subject to philosophical and scientific investigation as well as to the requirements of the moral and intellectual evolution of the community of faith. As a theologian, to take another example, the modernist professed a heterodox notion of divine immanence fatal because it identified the action of the divine with that of nature, eliminating the supernatural and substituting for it a crude pantheism. The immanence is "vital," an example of organic imagery popular with evolutionists; it refines the faith gradually as human needs become clearer in time. Most alarming to the authors of the encyclical was the modernist's assertion that this refinement is given direction by a necessary antagonism between the conservative forces of religious authority and the forces of progress to be found in individual consciences.[24]

In what ways, if any, did the definition of modernism developed by Rome correspond to the actual enterprise of European and American Catholics from 1895 to 1907? Did Rome simply fabricate a heretical movement in order to discipline or expel certain individuals? Do others who happened to escape reprisal belong in this group as well? The definition attempted to trace a consensus that had not yet emerged, to expose a detailed agenda that was in fact no more than a few common methodological (and perhaps philosophical) assumptions. *Pascendi*'s authors relied on only a fraction of the writings of the modernists, overlooked the development of the thought of each individual, and quoted the modernists out of context, a context that they failed fully to comprehend. In its place they substituted neo-scholastic categories and horizons of understanding. Von Hügel complained that "the vehemently scholastic redactor's determination to piece together a strictly coherent, complete *a priori* system of 'Modernism' and his self-imposed restriction to medieval categories of thought as the vehicles for describing essentially modern discoveries and requirements of mind, make the identification of precise authors and passages very difficult."[25]

Others, sympathetic to the modernist "reality," attempted to recast the "image" of modernism presented in *Pascendi*. An anonymous

"Programme of Modernism," written as if by a group, acknowledged modernism's debt to the "criticism of pure reason which Kant and Spencer have made" but maintained that their appropriation of these thinkers had been selective and critical. "Far from falling back, like Kant, on the a prioristic witness of the practical reason," they wrote, "we maintain the existence of other powers in the human spirit, every bit as reliable as the argumentative reason, for attaining to truth."[26] Furthermore, the concept of "pure reason" held by the integralists precluded an appreciation of these "powers in the human spirit":

> It is impossible for us today to conceive a purely intellectual and speculative faculty, immune from all influence of the will and the emotions. To the latest psychology, reason seems more and more to be a sort of instrument of formulation and definition which human nature has instinctively fashioned for itself, and which it uses unconsciously in order to arrange, express and control the experiences of the more elementary and external faculties of will and feeling and external sensation.[27]

Although this type of equivocation and/or clarification could hardly have eased the fears of the Romanists, the response of a group of young Italian priests in the letter *Quello che vogliamo* vindicated the worst fears of the Vatican. Employing the Blondellian method of immanence, the letter rejected outright the neo-scholastic deductive method as irrelevant in light of the findings of positive sciences, for "man is driven to find *within himself and in the dynamic circumstances and demands of his life* the practical reason for his own action." The metaphysical system of the magisterium was outdated and dispensable:

> Religion, if it is to be accepted, cannot be imposed by means of a syllogism. . . . God, revelation, the Church cannot be imposed from without by reasoned arguments. The soul must first seek them through its own free action, must find their reasons and learn their worth under the stimulus of its own religious experience, and bring this experience into relation with the religious experience of the human spirit throughout the ages.[28]

God does not offer Himself to sensible experience, the priests continued. Thus the scholastic notion that revelation is an external communication of immutable certitude "does not respond to historico-psychological reality."[29]

The response of these priests reconfirmed the Roman hierarchy's suspicion that modernism threatened the very foundations of the church (identified, as it was, with the neo-scholastic synthesis). The language of the encyclical might well have been inflammatory and imprecise, but these radical responses were seen as vindicating the integralist fear that a groundswell of support for Kantian subjectivism, immanentism, and dogmatic relativism existed in seminaries and universities. Nonetheless, contrary to what *Pascendi* suggested, the modernists subscribed to no single policy or program; their correspondences and writings reveal a range of disparate opinions and methodologies within a broad set of shared assumptions and goals that set them apart from liberal Catholics of a previous era no less than from the neo-scholastics of their own.[30]

The diversity of modernist opinions was evident in the debate over the proper application of the findings of critical history to the teachings of the faith. In *Historie et Dogma* Blondel posed a *via media* between the extrinsicism of the integralists and what he perceived as the "historicism" of Alfred Loisy. How and why does one proceed from history to dogma? How is one to remedy the damage done by history's inability to perceive spiritual reality in historical phenomena? Blondel responded with a theory of tradition. The Catholic must believe that the religious value of certain facts is bound to their historical reality *without* historical demonstration. Nonetheless, he argued, these beliefs must not be justified in apologetics by relying solely on a purely mystical inspiration or by understanding dogmas to be merely subjective and symbolical. Tradition does not confirm historical realities by deducing them from dogmas, but by responding to Christ's past, present, and ongoing action in the church. As an expression of Blondel's "philosophy of action," this notion of tradition presumed that the collective experience of believers enabled them to see more clearly what was implied in "the direct and concrete impression of the first witnesses." "To speak accurately, the journey from facts to dogma is inescapably bound up with the return journey from dogmas to facts: separable for purposes of scientific analysis, these two moments are emphatically inseparable in concrete reality and in the living exercise of the faith."[31]

Behind Loisy's radical historicism Blondel perceived an historian who could not believe in the claims of Christian faith: one must either remove the supernatural element from history or abandon criticism in the name of faith. Blondel sought to reconcile in the historian a pursuit of critical method with a total religious commitment: his "way out" for criticism lay in his insistence that science allow for the "fact" that generations of Christians believed certain conditions and events to have been historically given, whether or not they are historically verifiable. Loisy had preserved a diminished role for faith by liberating dogma from any obligation to incorporate in its formulation positive facts; Blondel retained the positive facts but pointed as evidence for them to their immanent presence in the believing community.[32]

Blondel's position did resemble his opponent's in one particular: he too constructed a role for the critical method from *a priori* philosophical assumptions, an approach that earned the criticism of Friedrich von Hügel. Von Hügel's alternative was a modified retrieval of the tradition of historical criticism of the "scientific liberal Catholicism" of Döllinger and Acton: the results of such criticism must be applied within the context and requirements of late nineteenth-century Roman Catholicism, namely, the ultramontanism advanced by Vatican I. Consequently, von Hügel favored Fénélon, "the ideal Ultramontane," and Jean Mabillon, "the scholar-saint," over Acton and Döllinger. Von Hügel's battle was not with "Romanism" generally understood, but with the narrow, anti-historical scholasticism that had erroneously identified itself with orthodoxy and had trivialized the "method, duty, autonomy, and authority" of the "historico-philosophical Sciences and Researches."[33]

The English Jesuit George Tyrrell developed his thought on this issue over a decade in which he moved from a phase of "mediating liberalism" influenced by Wilfrid Ward and John Henry Newman to a "modernist phase" culminating in his final work, *Christianity at the Crossroads*. In this treatise Tyrrell summarized his ultimate appraisal of the role of critical methods in "true modernism":

> [Modernism is] the hope of a synthesis between the essentials of Christianity and the assured results of criticism [producing] a marked division of Modernists according as their tendency is to consider that alone to be essential to Christianity which agrees with their idea of the assured results of criticism or to consider as the only assured results of criticism those that fit in with their conception of the essentials of Christianity. Both tendencies are visions and, if unchecked, destroy the very idea of modernism which professes to consider each interest impartially without respect to the other, in the belief and hope that the results will

prove harmonious. Religion cannot be the criterion of scientific truth, nor science of religious truth. Each must be criticized by its own principles.[34]

The range of opinion indicates that modernists did not enjoy the consensus on this question that might be expected of a "movement," but they did share a commitment to the established results of historical criticism as an essential ingredient in a statement of Christian faith that might prove acceptable, and even persuasive, to the modern world.

Among four of the modernists who devoted considerable attention to the question of immanence and the personal appropriation of religious truths, however, there was in fact greater progress toward such a consensus. Blondel, Laberthonnière, von Hügel, and Tyrrell agreed on certain basic assumptions, including the notion that the believer must be prepared for, and open to, the event of revelation. For Blondel, post-Kantian philosophical thought required that the Catholic apologist shift the emphasis and focus in the expression of religious beliefs. But Blondel sought to develop a synthesis of contemporary psychological analysis and traditional statements of faith that would entail a critique of both Aquinas and Kant:

> Between Aristotelianism which devalues and subordinates practice to thought, and Kantianism which segregates them and exalts the practical order to the detriment of the other, there is something needing definition, and it is in a very concrete manner, by an analysis of action, that I should like to establish what that something is.[35]

In his philosophy of action Blondel proposed a means of reconciliation between the insights of modern psychology and philosophy on the one hand, and theology's affirmation of the transcendence of the divine, on the other. Starting from an exploration of immanence, the philosophy of action moved inexorably toward a transcendent term. Blondel spoke, in effect, a new and different language that was not immediately accessible to philosophers working within the conceptual framework of neo-scholasticism. In the language of Aristotelian teleology, *"l'action"* is the link between the efficient cause and the final cause. In post-Kantian terminology, "action" translates as "the perpetual point of junction between belief and knowledge." It is the means by which the transcendent interpenetrates the mundane and generates a dynamism, which Blondel called "the will willing." This dynamism is never exhausted by the concrete choices of the human subject ("the will willed") but continually compels the subject toward self-transcendence. The subject is coaxed "out of himself" to God. Only in this context may one speak accurately of Blondel's description of a human "need" for supernature. Far from abandoning the transcendent Other, Blondel stressed it as the very ground of being and thereby drew upon a tradition of belief articulated most consistently by the great mystics:

> Modern thought, with jealous susceptibility, takes the notion of *immanence* to be the very condition of philosophy; that is to say, if there is among its controlling ideas an issue which it sponsors as a decided advance, it is the idea, basically quite correct, that nothing can enter into a man which does not emerge from him and correspond in some way to a developmental need, and that there is nothing, whether it be historical fact, traditional teaching, or an obligation imposed from without, no compelling truth or admissable precept, which is not in some way autonomous or autochthonous. On the other hand, however, nothing is Catholic which is not *supernatural*—not only transcendent in the simple metaphysical sense of the word.[36]

Like Blondel, Laberthonniere sought a *via media* between the extrinsicism of the neo-scholastics and the historical and doctrinal positivism of Loisy. Neither of these approaches took sufficient account of the interpenetration of the natural and supernatural orders; neither understood "mere" nature as itself a gratuitous gift of God. In order to modify what he saw as an unnecessarily exclusive definition of faith as an assent of the intellect motivated by an extrinsic fact, Laberthonniere retrieved the notion of the moral and metaphysical unity between the creative and salvific work of God. In this view the human subject is not passive, but participates in his or her redemption by an integrated response of mind, emotion, and will to the event of divine revelation. However, Laberthonniere pioneered an understanding of doctrines and their meanings that in its peculiarity separated him from other writers about immanence. If those who originally formulated doctrines did so in response to the immanent presence of the divine in their lives, then the intepretation of those doctrines requires an affirmation of the subjectivity of others and thus demands a moral conversion on the part of the believer. One will not find in others what one does not find within oneself. The interpretation of a religious truth is a process of mutuality: one accepts the given fact at the same time as one projects something of oneself into that fact.[37]

Laberthonniere also retrieved an aspect of Catholic thought neglected by the neo-scholastics, namely, the emphasis on the *fait intérieur* in Augustine and Pascal. This line of thought did not deny the authority of God as the basis of faith, but located that authority within, rather than outside, the believer. The interior affirmation takes precedence over any external manifestation of divine authority; otherwise, faith is imposed heteronomously, and is foreign to the experience of the subject. Following Pascal, Laberthonniere wrote of supernature impregnating nature from within. The act of faith is at once an interior apprehension of the presence and authority of God operating within the believer and a moment of knowledge: the two must not be separated arbitrarily.[38]

Von Hügel was less concerned with the distinctions to be drawn between faith and its doctrinal expression than with the question of experience, specifically, "how can finite and contingent man solidly experience the Abiding and Infinite?" Like Blondel and Laberthonniere, von Hügel rejected deductive theology and read Pascal as a "positivist of interior reality." The epistemic link between God and the human being, von Hügel asserted, is dim experience that, if articulated at all, is not expressed as a distinct comprehension or concept, still less as a starting point and objective of strict deductive science. On the other hand, he argued, Kant was wrong to assume that our subjective conceptions of objective reality are necessarily inadequate and misleading. Von Hügel drew insights from both Kantian philosophy and neo-scholastic theology: our experience of God is a fact objectively given and dimly apprehended together with our painful contingency. God is experienced immanently *as transcendent reality.* The results of biblical and doctrinal criticism were not to attenuate this notion in any way.[39]

For von Hügel, the fundamental error of the neo-scholastics was their failure to acknowledge or even to understand fully the distinction between precisely formulated statements about the personal encounter with the transcendent God on the one hand, and the ineffable reality to which those statements point, on the other. According to von Hügel, the appropriate response to the ontological presence of God is simple adoration; analysis and conceptualization of that experience—the formulation of doctrines—is always a secondary and derivative endeavor. It is not the doctrines themselves, but the genuine religious experience, that is "fallen from heaven." Religion precedes theology; doctrine proceeds from experience divinely inspired. At the same time, the mystical element of religion must not ignore the rational element. In his theory of immanence, von Hügel sought to restore balance by emphasizing the experiential (mystical, emotional, intuitive) elements overlooked in the neo-scholastic revival of the nineteenth century. Like other modernists, the baron claimed that his efforts were not creative but conservative, reclaiming the teachings of "the true teachers of the church—not the theologians, but the saints."[40]

Tyrrell's mature approach to the question developed a distinction between the original deposit of faith, the concrete and imaginative articulation of the divine mysteries experienced by the apostles, and the later systematization of this original articulation through its application to philosophical categories and concepts. He understood primitive revelation as a concrete religion rather than a set of creedal statements, in his words, a "lex orandi" rather than a "lex credendi"; accordingly, all expressions of divine truth are symbolic and are "true" (adequate) relative to their control over religious practice and experience. If one believes that these symbols are guaranteed in every age by the Holy Spirit guiding the mind of the faithful, Tyrrell continued, then one accepts these symbols as relatively adequate and eminently determinative for the practical experience of the believing community. The neo-scholastic "system of mediated transcendence" and the consequent exaltation of ecclesiastical authority had obscured the precedent for this approach. This precedent existed in a "tradition of immanence" represented by the Augustinian, Franciscan, and Carmelite heritages.[41]

This emphasis on immanence became a controlling principle for Tyrrell, as for the other modernists, and provided a framework for his ideas on doctrinal and ecclesial development. Ultimately Tyrrell rejected not only traditional scholastic tenets but also the "Idea" of development propounded by his onetime hero, John Henry Newman. Tyrrell had come to understand that Newman's concept of revelation was also propositional; that is, it failed to reflect and preserve the experiential, mystical character of the prophetic vision recorded as normative by Scripture. Tyrrell adopted in its place an understanding of the deposit of faith as a Spirit, "an Idea" subject to growth and development according to an organic model (and not according to the architectural model employed by Newman). In the architectural model, ideas are added quantitatively to the original deposit; additions are made without changing the structure. In the organic model, addition of ideas leads to qualitative changes: the grown man is not identical to the child. Development means change, and an earlier stage of that development is not to be the sole criterion by which to evaluate later stages of growth and conformity to the Spirit of Christ. The proper criterion is the conformity of doctrines to the ongoing experience of the Spirit of Christ. Tyrrell applied the organic model to all aspects of ecclesiology, describing the church as "an extension of that human frame through which His spirit and personality makes itself felt, as it were sacramentally. The Church is not merely a society or a school, but a mystery and a sacrament like the humanity of Christ of which it is an extension." The sacramental model is uniquely Roman Catholic, Tyrrell argued, and demands a recognition of the living, developing, changing principle of identity at its heart.[42]

The range of opinions summarized above, and the developments of each modernist's thought over the course of a generation, provided a rich and diverse conceptual well from which progressive-minded Catholics in Europe drank. In Italy, for example, the philosophical-theological discussion informed the elaboration of agenda for political and social change articulated in the pages of *Il Rinnovamento*. This agenda emerged from a commitment to autonomy for the sciences, and was designed to liberate Catholic laymen and society at large from the exploitation of "clerical autocracy."[43] The condemnations of 1907 did not apprehend each of these movements in its particularities and distinctiveness but, because they shared a source of inspiration in the religious worldview articulated by the modernists, clustered them together indiscriminately. Reprisals were also indiscriminate: anyone believed to be in sympathy with this religious worldview came under suspicion.

This religious worldview took shape only gradually in the writings of the European modernists; its contents, or particular affirmations, were never systematized or presented by that generation of Catholics as a rich tapestry enfolding the historical tradition. But the modernists did evoke a strong sense of the divine presence as permeating historical events and individual lives with a subtlety of presence and hiddenness of purpose that mocked self-important legalistic and rationalistic systems and institutions. The implication seemed to be that in attempting to institutionalize and thus contain this presence, the church was misguided at best, and a petty and grasping human contrivance at worst. The anti-modernists may have perceived in modernism a completely realized (and threatening) worldview, but the modernists in fact concerned themselves, in their constructive mode, with the prior task of crafting the philosophical principles and critical-scientific methodologies by which a modern religious worldview could be substantiated and elaborated. This would be possible only through a critical and comprehensive examination of the historical tradition.

Thus the modernists' constructive work proceeded from a self-conscious rejection of scholastic methodology in philosophy, theology, and apologetics, followed by an appropriation of the procedures of critical scientific inquiry, and an assimilation of the generally accepted theories of the modern sciences. The modernist found in the history of the church the patterns of change, development, and diversity that the evolutionist found in species. Modernists rejected "the argument from authority," which protected the entire neo-scholastic enterprise from self-criticism and renewal, as a self-justifying, *a priori* controlling assumption that refused to distinguish the sources, Scripture and Tradition, from their contemporary interpretation. Instead, the modernists endorsed methods designed to uncover and account for empirical evidence, be it a new archaeological discovery or a breakthrough in textual criticism. This left room in principle for the constant readjustment and updating of present theological methods and the assumptions grounding them. They refused, for example, to exempt the Bible from the standard operating procedures and questions of historical and literary criticism.

Although they shared with liberal Protestantism and with the Tübingen school both the methodology of historical criticism and the desire to adapt the Christian religion to the intellectual, moral, and social needs of the modern age, the Catholic modernists concerned themselves with the foundational question of the proper limits of ecclesiastical and Scriptural inerrancy.[44] They raised objections to the received teaching on inerrancy, considered the question from the dual perspectives of critical exegesis and the history of the development of Catholic dogmas and institutions, and proposed reforms on these bases. The modernists saw that critical history involved more than a disavowal of certain post-Tridentine developments in Catholicism: the demands of critical history included a thoroughgoing reappraisal of the earliest institutions and dogmas of the church and, quite possibly, a complete revision of theological categories.[45] As Tyrrell put it, "Modernism does not question this or that dogma, this or that ecclesiastical institution [but] . . . the very idea of dogma, of ecclesiasticism, of revelation, of faith, of heresy, of theology, of sacramentalism."[46]

The modernists did have at their disposal a tool employed previously by a select group of liberals from Richard Simon to Ignaz von Döllinger, namely, the historico-critical method. But one factor set them apart from this company: the modernists were the first to fully recognize the nature and extent of the threat posed to Catholicism—indeed, to all of Christianity—by the possible results of the application of critical methods to the sources of revelation.[47] They perceived that this "tool" used by Simon to defend Christianity from rationalist critics like Locke and Hobbes was potentially a weapon aimed at the heart of Catholicism and its claims of scriptural and ecclesiastical inerrancy. Previous adepts at critical history, from Tübingen's Möhler to Munich's Döllinger, had begun to apply the concept of development to the history of dogma. Döllinger had criticized the 1870 definition of papal infallability for lack of historical foundation. But the modernists understood that unless the magisterium revised its expression of the concept of inerrancy so as to incorporate the acknowledged results of criticism, the modern world would reject not only the ultramontane formulation of inerrancy, but the underlying notion of religious authority as well. Catholic modernists did help to refine the application of critical methods of inquiry to Scripture and Tradition, but they were also concerned at this time to reconcile critical methods and the conclusions their application produced with the traditional religious categories and "ultimate ideas" of Roman Catholicism. As we have seen, for example, John Zahm conceived of *Evolution and Dogma* as his initial contribution to the reconciliation of modern biological sciences and the traditional understandings of divine providence.[48]

At the same time, the modernists did not see themselves as uncritical advocates of modernity. To the contrary, they believed themselves to be the defenders and proponents of an authentic Catholic tradition denied, suppressed, or overlooked by the ruling scholastic network. Modernists opposed, for example, the representation of ultramontanism as *the* Catholic tradition. For the modernists Catholicism was not a theory—a single, monolithic theological system. Nor was it primarily an institution governed by a hierarchy. Rather, the modernist believed in "the historical Catholic community as the living outgrowth of the apostolic mission."[49] The church was neither a system nor a theory, but a living, growing, developing body. In their insistence that the nuanced distinctions between visible and invisible church, institution and Body of Christ, be preserved, the modernists anticipated major themes of twentieth-century ecclesiology. And in all of this, to counteract the charge that they had abandoned Christian tradition for modernity, they deliberately invoked and reappropriated images and themes developed in medieval Catholicism and harkening back to the apostolic age. Positions inconsistent with authentic Catholicism were those claiming a direct and definitive exemption to growth and change. Upon reading *Pascendi* Tyrrell remarked that the encyclical had not demonstrated that he was no Catholic, only that he was no scholastic.[50] The debate was over the proper understanding of authentic Catholic tradition. The Romanists appealed to tradition as immutable and as grounded on a supernaturally bestowed deposit of faith, the communication of which transcended the historical order. The modernists understood tradition to be grounded in and conditioned by the human history from which it continually emerged. The integralists feared that this focus on critical history would lead to a relativizing of eternal truth; the modernists, by contrast, believed that it was consistent with faith in the *ecclesia* as a historical community shaped uniquely in each age by God.

By failing to appreciate the nuanced positions of the thinkers they cast under suspicion, and by anticipating the conclusions of the modernist synthesis-in-the-making, the authors of *Pascendi* tainted scholars in Europe and America who were undeserving of the label "modernist." Many of these scholars had pursued their researches with the presumed approval of their ecclesiastical superiors before the storm, but after 1907 they were required to abandon original research and return to the direct explication of previous knowledge and received teaching. The road to communion with Rome narrowed significantly as the magisterium reasserted pre-Leonine fortress Catholicism and rejected the proposed rapprochement with secular knowledge.[51]

To a significant degree progressive Catholic priests in the United States were influenced by the efforts and travails of modernists in Europe before 1907. But their appropriation of the themes and insights of their mentors in Europe was filtered through the context of an American Catholic intellectual community struggling to establish its own theological and apologetic tradition. This it did in a milieu formed by the American ethos and shaped, in part, by a distinctive heritage of religious thought.

MODERNISM AND THE AMERICAN RELIGIOUS MILIEU

Like the great faiths of Protestantism and Judaism, Catholicism changed when it took root in American soil. It transformed, and was transformed by, the social, cultural, political, economic, and religious structures of American society.

At the turn of the century the United States was in the midst of a transition from an agricultural to an industrial economic system. Industrialization and urbanization were accompanied by the rise of bureaucracies and the advance of the empirical sciences.[52] No one better captured the ethos of this changing society than William James. The philosopher and psychologist personified several central themes of modern American life: a distaste for elitism, an emphasis on individualism, an insistence that ideas take concrete shape, and a respect for freedom of choice in human enterprise.[53] James's writings and lectures explored the tensions between the rationalist's search for universals and the empiricist's affirmation of pluralism and disparateness. To reconcile these seemingly antithetical concerns, he promoted a philosophy of pragmatism that would "remain religious like the rationalisms but like the empiricisms preserve the richest intimacy with facts."[54] According to pragmatic method, experimentation would settle metaphysical disputes: each competing explanation of reality must withstand the test to its validity posed by its practical consequences. James defined beliefs as rules for action, guidelines for behavior. In this he rejected the systems of abstract thought that many American thinkers found wanting and promoted a method of ends-oriented reasoning:

> Against rationalism as a pretension and a method pragmatism is fully armed and militant. But at the outset at least it stands for no particular results. It has no dogma and no doctrines save for its method . . . the attitude of looking away from first things, principles, categories, supposed necessities; and of looking towards last things, fruits, consequences, facts.[55]

The implications for theological and philosophical systems based on *a priori* affirmations of faith or reason were considerable, for these systems relied very little on empirical support. The criteria set forth in modern methods of scientific investigation, James wrote, are valid as criteria for philosophical truth:

> truth in our ideas and beliefs means the same thing that it means in science . . . that ideas (which themselves are but part of our

experience) become true just in so far as they help us to get into satisfactory relations with other parts of our experience. . . . If theological ideas prove to have a value for concrete life, they will be true for pragmatism, in the sense of being good for so much. For how much more they are true, will depend entirely on their relations to the other truths that also have to be acknowledged.[56]

In this insistence on the serviceability of truth and the plurality of serviceable truths, James proved himself thoroughly modern. Furthermore, he claimed that pragmatism was no more than the perfection and consolidation of a tradition of modern philosophical insights, including those of nominalism, utilitarianism, and positivism. Although pragmatism was not the only important philosophy of the day, its eclectic character made it paradigmatic of modern American thought. In that capacity it was profoundly influential in other disciplines, especially in theology.[57] In religious thought at the turn of the century this pragmatic turn found expression in movements for social and political reform. From Protestant Social Gospel to post-Jewish Ethical Culture, progressive believers committed to the adaptation of their faith to the American environment were faced with the challenges of empirical science and the increasing societal concern for the deplorable social circumstances in which many lived.

The pragmatic turn raised questions of identity for American religionists. Does societal orientation towards progress and the future render traditional religion irrelevant and obsolete? Could the old theism survive an age that scorned idealism? How might religious institutions justify their existence before the pragmatist's demand that beliefs translate into problem-solving activities? Would American endorsement of liberty, democracy, and freedom of choice undermine once and for all the principle of authority in religion? How might institutional religion survive pluralism, denominationalism, and voluntarism without being drained of influence in the larger community?

Inseparable from these external challenges to organized religion was the internal confusion provoked by the onset of a developmentalist worldview. The quandary bedeviling scholars since the Enlightenment penetrated the general religious sensibility: How to preserve the idea of divine revelation given the new historical consciousness? What would become of the notion of revealed truths originating beyond time and space if ideas, institutions, and ethical and social movements might be comprehended as products of historical adaptation to the requirements of each age? Religion might be reduced to a socio-cultural phenomenon divested of any transcendent point of origin. As the emerging disciplines of paleontology, archaeology, and linguistics lent a greater aura of scientific expertise to the study of human history, it became evident that neither sacred texts nor religious traditions would be spared the relativizing scrutiny of the new criticism. What place would remain for the Bible, by now a sort of American icon? Should the preacher continue to defend the entire text as fully authoritative, or approach it selectively, extracting here and there grains of timeless wisdom? Once the embellishments in the Scriptural depiction of Jesus were seared away by criticism, who would remain? The ethical sage and supreme moral educator, or God in human form? American Catholics were no more immune to these questions than their European coreligionists or their Protestant and Jewish countrymen. The neo-scholastic mind, possessed of *a priori* truths given in the Deposit of Faith, looked with suspicion upon the American exaltation of mere experience as an indicator of truth.[58]

At the turn of the century religious communities divided over tactics and regrouped under different banners according to the degree of their incorporation of the new ideas. When Christians, for example, reassessed the identity of their Lord, they often found themselves allied with liberals or conservatives of other denominations rather than with members of their own flock. In this situation the intellectual centers of the churches—the seminaries and divinity schools—and of the secular culture—the colleges and universities—became the arena for the inevitable confrontation between European scholarship and American religion. From 1870 to 1920 sectarian control of many leading universities waned, the educational format changed, and science assumed a prominent place in the curriculum. Modernity made inroads into religion by way of institutions of higher learning in the United States.[59]

The modernist impulse in American Protestantism did not emerge as a fully self-conscious movement until late in the first decade of the new century, and then in the writings of Shailer Mathews, D. C. McIntosh, and others. By this time the inchoate modernism in American Catholic thought had been crushed by the Vatican. The American Catholic priests of this study resembled more closely in their efforts Protestant precursors to Mathews's modernism, men like William Adams Brown and George Gordon. These thinkers stressed the need for a scientific definition of Christianity in which critical history might guard the "essence" of Christian truth. This would, they recognized, require a method by which central themes of a religion are selected as determinative of its essence. For Brown this principle of selectivity was necessarily subjective, "found in the interest and need of the man who defines. . . those particular qualities for which at the time we happen to have use, and ignores the rest."[60] Although George Gordon agreed with Brown's basic program, he complained that critical history might too readily arrogate to itself final judgments on the essence of Christianity. He found Brown's preference for the modern altogether too uncritical and ultimately ahistorical. Too often, he argued, the method took over the critical study of an issue; for example:

> If it can be shown that Greek philosophy, Stoic preaching, and Roman law, institution and ritual went to the formation of early Christianity, it is assumed that these contributions are alien elements, discolorations of the stream of the primitive faith, which, now that it is flowing through the fine white sand of historical analysis, is regaining its original purity, it is this assumption which must be resisted, for it amounts to the denial of the worth of history.[61]

Gordon did not reject historical criticism; he simply insisted that it be employed constructively to rediscover pristine Christian religious experience. In so doing it could lead modern believers to a renewed experience of Christ.

The first question posed by American Protestant modernists in the last decade of the nineteenth century, then, was this: How might scientific methods best be applied to the study of religion? In the minds of many of these early modernists this question led to a hope, namely, that the use of scientific method might become a decisive factor in the movement toward Christian reunion. All the old rivalries were suspended, Brown proclaimed, for modernity introduced concepts so radically new as to place the twentieth-century Christian in a context wholly discontinuous from anything that had gone before. His new scientific definition of Christianity would no doubt undermine any denominational claims of absoluteness. Brown described Roman Catholicism as an example of an absolutist faith that was doomed, at least in its neo-scholastic expression. He rejected its "ontological conception" of absoluteness, by which the Absolute is a reality independent of all finite experience. This assumption led Rome to an anti-modern, unscientific prejudice. "How, then, can reason sit as judge upon that before which it is its duty to bow?" Brown asked. Any religion dependent upon prophecy and miracles as "proof" of the validity of its teaching stood the risk of suffering dismissal at the hands of modern science.[62]

Gordon suggested that Christians form conceptions of Christ in keeping with the vast and infinite character of the universe revealed by modern science. The boundaries of traditional Christology must be reconstructed in the light of the new understandings of geology, archeology, and biology, which have together served to expand the very idea of human history. Gordon echoed the call of Catholic modernists in Europe for a reformulation of basic concepts and categories:

> The ideal of a Christ for humanity, ultimate as a form of thought though it is, is capable of infinite expansion in answer to the developments of time and the facts of the case. It could not have meant what it must mean for the believer today. The consciousness of history as of unmeasured extent...is one of the great forces calling for a new conception of salvation.[63]

Like Brown, Gordon was confident that this step would facilitate the offering of Christ to all people and thus serve as a basis for Christian unity. In this regard he was exceedingly pragmatic: Which conception of Christ would best take advantage of the practical opportunity for religious unity in an age of communication? "A Kingdom of the Spirit" was emerging in the modern world, he believed, "appropriating the wealth of all faiths, isolating itself from particular times and places...getting ready for a new conception of Christ."[64]

Some of the Protestant modernists believed that both Protestantism and neo-scholastic Catholicism would soon be displaced by a "mediating Catholicism" introduced by European Catholic modernists. Newman Smyth hoped for the success of the Roman Catholic modernists, whom he believed to be harbingers of the next stage of the evolution of Christianity. These rebels against Vatican-sponsored neo-scholasticism, Smyth felt, offered to waning Protestant churches lessons about the historical development of doctrine. Their researches might indeed hold the key freeing Christianity from its squabbles over creeds and dogmas. In integrating this historical approach with Catholicism's organic views of the church, the Catholic modernists offered a model for ecumenical relations unparalled in modern times:

> Protestantism may find itself more indebted than we know to those Roman Catholic thinkers and historians for the answer which they have been compelled to discover in order to save

the loyalties of their own faith. It is given in their principle of the historical development of the dogmas of the Church. . . . Apply (as they do) without hesitation the first principles of organic evolution to the development of the Church and its dogmas, and you will have secured both the integrity and historical continuity of its life, and at the same time the progress and ever renewed adaptations of it to the knowledge and life of the world.[65]

Smyth did not expect or desire the death of creedal religions. Various creeds would survive and occasion celebrations of the universal Christian truths inherent in each of them. In similar fashion Charles Briggs defended doctrines such as the virgin birth without flinching on the principle of doctrinal development. As a member of the Episcopalian Church, he campaigned vigorously for Christian unity on the modernist pattern and intentionally used the language of the European Catholic modernists. Echoing Tyrrell, he complained that the major obstacle to Christian unity was not creedalism but "medievalism," against which progressive Protestants and Catholic modernists alike struggled.[66]

Thus the openness of the New Theology to certain themes in Catholic thought was extended and reinforced by this conscious appropriation of ideas congenial to Roman Catholic modernism. In this effort Protestants like Smyth and Briggs encouraged and, as we shall see, actively cooperated with, the incipient modernism evident in the work of the American priests attempting their own synthesis of faith and modern thought. And these priests read and corresponded with many of the leading proponents of the New Theology.[67]

It is more appropriate to speak, as William Hutchison does, of a "modernist impulse" within liberal Protestant theology before 1900, rather than to conceive of American modernism as a self-directed and wholly distinct movement unto itself. In the later writings of Shailer Mathews there is a self-awareness and independence that bespeaks a more mature modernism; but such precision of methodology and clarity of conclusions were largely absent from the writings of early European Catholic or American Protestant modernists.

Indeed, if the Protestants are to be taken as an example, one would not expect that a modernist impulse within American Catholicism would have emerged in this era as a distinct school of thought, much less as a coordinated movement. Between 1870 and 1910, however, certain themes did emerge in the writing of liberal Christian and Jewish theologians that would form the basis of an identifiably new approach to the challenges of doing theology in an age of scientific criticism. Figures such as Charles Briggs, Felix Adler, and John Zahm may with some justification be characterized as modernists in that they furthered the development of the modernist impulse in liberal thought; at the same time, each represented a different stage along a liberal-modernist trajectory. Any generality suffixed by an "ism," be it conservatism, liberalism, or empiricism, includes under its wide umbrella a variety of subtler distinctions. And so with modernism: to say that Felix Adler was a modernist is not to say that modernist Charles Briggs shared his concept of theism. It is rather to suggest that Briggs and Adler did share certain convictions that set them apart from other progressive thinkers: a belief that the modern age offered a grand opportunity for a total reconstruction of the very *ideas* of theology, dogma, and religion; a demand for an unprejudiced synthesis of modern thought and ancient faith; and a conviction that an evolutionary model of religion promised both real continuity with past truths and irresistible progress toward greater realization and expression of them.[68]

If the modernists affirmed a type of theism expressed through the conceptual forms of an increasingly sophisticated scientific worldview, they claimed they did so because the figure of the scientist-as-theist would be most persuasive to the modern mind. If modernists strove with varying degrees of success to rehabilitate the image of Jesus Christ in their preaching and writing, they insisted that they did so out of respect for the results of literary and historical criticism which was carrying the day. If liberals leaning toward modernism openly embraced the values of modern age, they also argued that their focus on ethical activity and social salvation reflected the vital concerns of their congregants. Lest they be seen as employing the new criticism to destroy faith, these nascent modernists wished rather to reawaken the faith of people who had tired of hearing hackneyed platitudes and ahistorical simplicities from the pulpit.[69]

The experiences of these early modernists suggest that their instincts were not misleading. The most hostile reactions to their preaching and writings came from denominational leaders who defended the old order. The modernists who did attract a following within denominations related the findings of modern sciences and biblical criticism to the practical, emotional, and moral concerns of the congregants. In so doing they tended to alienate those churchmen who had not studied enough to engage them in meaningful debate, but who were wary of what seemed to be radical ideas. Modernists offered an easy target to conservatives and traditionalists, and provided justification for separatist movements and the resulting splintering and divisiveness that came to characterize organized religious activity at the turn of the century.

Modernism did not spring up overnight in the Protestant denominations. It developed in the context of a liberal movement that sought adaptation to American democratic society and capitalist enterprise. Liberal Protestants thereby paved the way for the more intentional and coherent modernism that appeared in the writing of Gordon and Brown and, later, Mathews. A similar pattern can be seen in American Catholicism.

AMERICANISM IN THE CATHOLIC CHURCH

At the turn of the century American Catholic liberals were beset with a "great crisis" brought about by the condemnation of "Americanism" by Pope Leo in *Testem Benevolentiae* (1899). It seemed to Pope Leo's advisers that the United States provided a religious and intellectual environment in which liberal theology flourished. Although certain observers of the controversy, as well as the priests and bishops implicated but not named in the encyclical, denied that the tendencies denounced by the pope actually existed in the United States, Americanism was in fact a precursor to the appearance of theological modernism in the American Catholic community. Those priests and bishops to whom the label "Americanist" applies endorsed the principle of freedom of religion enshrined in the Consitition of the United States, and celebrated those American citizens of prominence who had successfully wed their religious faith to a scientifically informed worldview. The Americanists conveyed an important message to their brother priests, namely, that vigorous activity designed to bring Catholics into the mainstream of American intellectual life and culture would receive the blessing of their ecclesiastical superiors. Liberal American Catholic bishops such as James Cardinal Gibbons, John Ireland, John Keane, and John Lancaster Spalding promoted the development of reform-minded scholars within the ranks of the American priesthood. These bishops enjoyed a close and supportive friendship with clerics like Zahm, Driscoll, and Sullivan, who in turn felt, for a time at least, that their intellectual endeavors were not only approved but appreciated by the church.[70]

Americanism did not express itself primarily through theological or philosophical systems of thought. Instead, it took the form of a working strategy, initially articulated by Isaac Hecker, for the accommodation of Catholic life to the situation of American pluralism and freedom of religious expression. This pragmatic, ends-oriented approach to religious and cultural adaptation reflected a distinctively American treatment of ideological questions, that Alexis de Tocqueville had contrasted to the patterns of European thought.

The Americanist solution to the problems of an immigrant church did of course demand a level of theoretical reflection upon which later apologists built.[71] But experiment and action often preceded the elaboration of a theoretical framework for action. In surveying the implicit ecclesiologies and the often explicit strategies of adaptation pursued within the American Catholic community in the late nineteenth and early twentieth centuries, one can perceive a trajectory of thought moving from a point of origin in liberal or progressive Catholicism to a terminus in modernism. Hecker's plan for converting Americans to Catholicism implied, for example, the type of institutional commitment to the intellectual life that was subsequently promoted by Gibbons, Keane, Ireland, and Spalding. In the same way, the explicitly theoretical and theological writings of Zahm, Driscoll, Sullivan and others working with "modernist" methodologies can be seen as a type of apologetics for the liberal cause.

In Isaac Hecker's apologetical writing, themes and emphases appeared that were later condemned in papal encyclicals on Americanism and modernism: a minimalist appreciation of ecclesiastical authority, a marked preference for mystical and immanentist theologies over against scholasticism, a rejection of the vows regulating religious life (especially those inhibiting mobility from place to place), and a selective adherence to teachings of the magisterium on democracy and religious liberty. Hecker, the founder of the missionary congregation of St. Paul, envisioned the advent of an American spirituality in which "there could be a synthesis between true piety and all that was good in modern civilization." In anticipation of a modernist theme, he argued that this synthesis could serve as a legitimate Catholic alternative to the extrinsicist theology in favor at the Vatican.[72]

A key to Hecker's thought lay in his profound conviction that the Holy Spirit of God, "the Sanctifier," at work in individual human souls was the same spirit at work in the history of the church and in a new and dramatic way in nineteenth-century America. The goal of this life-giving Spirit was to impart a measure of spiritual perfection to each individual. In Hecker's view, all external means—vows, pious devotions, even the reception of the sacraments—were subservient to this end.[73]

Hecker organized the Paulists according to this principle. He deemphasized priestly mediation of the Divine Spirit; no confessor should stand between the individual and the Holy Spirit, the true "Superior and Director" in the life of the regenerate man. No communal standard would stand in the way of the unique spiritual pilgrimage of each individual; no rule would "repress, suppress, [or] annihilate the instincts, aspirations, and capacities God-given to human nature."[74] The Rule and Constitution that Hecker composed for the Paulists promoted the personal sanctity of each member and of all the souls they could evangelize. The rule wedded the life of constant missionary work to contemplative prayer, for Hecker believed that spiritual perfection "depends on the Holy Ghost . . . being the instigator of our enterprises." The traditional vows of religious orders were unnecessary for the Paulist living the apostolic life. "What a member of another religious community might do from that divine guidance which is external," Hecker wrote, "the Paulist does from the promptings of the indwelling Holy Spirit." He viewed his religious community as the very embodiment of the dynamic Divine Spirit and confided to his diary that, because "the Eternal Absolute is ever creating new forms of expressing itself," he would not presume to restrict those forms by regulating the community. "One of the natural signs of the true Paulist," he wrote "is that he would prefer to suffer from the excesses of liberty than from the arbitrary actions of tyranny."[75]

Hecker deplored the tactic of making obedience to external ecclesiastical authority the test of religious orthodoxy. The inspiration of the Holy Spirit was not, according to Hecker, resticted to the magisterium. Despite holding views that were not shared by the curia,[76] Hecker made considerable strides during his lifetime in charting a new direction and strategy for Catholic missionary efforts in a pluralistic society. Setting the tone for a generation of Americanists, he taught that the Holy Spirit was at work preparing the United States for Catholicism by means of American democracy, pluralism, voluntarism, and church-state separation. By acknowledging the immanent presence of the Spirit in the human soul, this new, uniquely American expression of Catholicism would relegate Protestantism and its doctrine of total depravity to the pages of history. Convinced that his own personal experience of the leading of the Holy Spirit was at once consonant with the ideal of Catholicism represented by a litany of saints and mystics of the past (among them, Julian of Norwich, Francis de Sales, and Louis Lallemant) and, more significantly, paradigmatic of the religious experience of modern Americans, Hecker promoted ideas and values that he considered both American and Catholic. These ideas and values included the freedom of the will, individual liberty, moral growth, "the perfection of activity," and the acceptance of all that is good in secular society. Hecker challenged the lay Catholic to become more responsible for his or her own spiritual development and to make prudent use of the liberty of conscience and of political action available in the United States.

Hecker was not a modernist. In calling for a "synthesis between true piety and modernity" he seemed not to acknowledge a need for a deliberate reconstruction of dogmatic formulas and theological categories. Nor did he fully comprehend the implications of the new scientific methods of inquiry for religious thought. And although his name was linked with several of the erroneous tenets cited in *Testem Benevolentiae*, only one of these, the reputed preference of certain liberals for active rather than passive virtues, received explicit mention in *Pascendi*.

Yet Hecker played a central role in the emergence of a tradition of liberal Catholicism in America. He celebrated progress, encouraged advances in biblical criticism and scientific investigation of human origins and development, and praised the separation of church and state in America. He presented popular lectures exploring themes of Protestant theology congenial to Catholicism and reached out to "humanitarians, nationalists, indifferentists, and skeptics."[77]

Hecker's influence on later American Catholic modernists, some of whom published encomiums to him and analyses of his life and thought in the *New York Review*,[78] was considerable. He personified a Catholicism renewed in and by the modern world rather than cowed by it. Like many modernists, he anchored his vision of renewed Catholicism to the bedrock of traditions overlooked by nineteenth-century scholasticism.[79] "The interest shown by my audience was remarkable," he once wrote, "and my experience convinces me that, if this work were continued, it would prepare the way for a great change of religion in this country."[80]

Even after the ignominy visited upon Hecker's name after a French translation of his biography launched the Americanist crisis, influential liberal American prelates continued to invoke it. James Cardinal Gibbons, leader of the American hierarchy for a generation, called Hecker a "true child of the Church" and applauded his apostolic zeal that attracted Protestants to the Catholic faith "without sacrifice of orthodoxy." Like Hecker, Gibbons favored the integration of modern methods of critical inquiry with traditional methods of Catholic education. He is most remembered in this regard for championing the fledgling Catholic University of America as a potential national center for disciplined reflection on faith and secular knowledge. Yet he also supported critical scholarship in more controversial ways. In 1889, for example, Italian canon Salvatore di Bartolo published a book translated into English as *Criterions of Catholic Truth*. At his request Gibbons reviewed it, writing that it would surely "strengthen faith and remove prejudices" of those who considered Catholicism to be inimical to modern thought.[81]

Gibbons's endorsement, no less than the book itself, sparked a debate in the pages of Catholic periodicals. Joseph Schroeder spoke for the ultramontane party: di Bartolo was guilty of "theological minimizing" and would be punished accordingly.[82] His words proved prophetic, for the book landed on the *Index of Forbidden Books* even before Gibbons could muster a reply. Chagrined, the cardinal lapsed into an embarrassed silence.

Gibbons's closest episcopal allies, John Ireland and John Lancaster Spalding, shared the conviction that Roman Catholicism was at a crucial point in its history, and that America would lead the way in transforming the relationship between the church and the age. Although Ireland and Spalding differed in levels of understanding of the new sciences and apologetics, and had a falling out, they were the two most prominent articulators of the progressive vision of American Catholicism that modernists would later adopt as their own.[83] Neither foresaw the calamitous results of their stirring call for intellectual excellence. For, as their opponents hastened to point out, Ireland and Spalding offered a kind of official endorsement for bold experimentation in Catholic apologetics and theology. Ireland's enthusiasm for American civil liberties moved him to urge his church to adapt to the American ethos. At the anniversary of Gibbons's elevation to the episcopacy he said:

The Church, too, has her accidentals and her essentials; we should be ready, while jealously guarding the essentials, to abandon the accidentals, as circumstances of time and place demand. What the Church at any time was, certain people hold she must ever remain. They do her much harm, making her rigid and unbending, incapable of adapting herself to new and changing surroundings. The Church, created by Christ for all time, lives in every age and is of every age.[84]

Much like early Protestant liberals who endorsed evolutionary theory without fully understanding the implications for the faith of Darwinian natural selection, Ireland held forth with a cheery naivete on the topic of reconciliation between democracy and magisterium, religious faith and scientific method. He did in fact promote the building of a synthesis between the ancient faith and modern thought, but did not seem to grasp the ambiguities and complexities involved in this task:

Between reason and revelation there can never be a contradiction; the so-called war between faith and science is a war between the misrepresentations of faith, or, rather, between ignorance of some scientists and the ignorance of some theologians. . . . The discoveries of the age, whether in minute animalcules or in vast fiery orbs, demonstrate God. Through all the laws of the universe they show forth an absolute cause, all-wise, all-powerful, eternal. The fruits of all historical research, of all social and moral inquiry, give us Christ rising from the dead and raising the world from the dead. They give us Christ's Church as the enduring embodiment of Christ's mission. The knowledge of the age! The age has not a sufficiency of knowledge; and the need of the hour, the duty of the Church, is to stimulate the age to deeper researches, to more extensive surveyings, until it has left untouched no particle of matter that may conceal a secret, no incident of history, no act in the life of humanity, that may solve a problem. The knowledge of the age, the Church blesses it; the Church promotes its onward growth with all her might.[85]

The volatile combination of forceful progressivism and incomplete scientific understanding blinded Ireland to the implications of his rhetoric and undermined his prestige at Rome. He gave unwitting encouragement, time and again, to men and ideas that the Vatican condemned. On the eve of the promulgation of *Testem Benevolentiae* he praised Hecker as "providential" in his demand for a new form of Catholic spirituality suited to modern America.[86] In 1892 he publicly praised Loisy and supported his new review of biblical criticism, *L'Enseignement biblique,* identifying it with the highest aspirations of Catholic theology:

> Must we say to the whole world that we prefer more our refuge in silence and darkness than an exposition of the faith to serious and impartial examination? Must we justify the accusation often made against us, that we neither have the science nor the courage to treat biblical questions? Yours is the only publication in the arena in the name of faith. . . . The biblical question has great importance among the Protestants in America, and without the help which I receive from your writing, I would not know where to turn. After all, a Catholic today is obliged to take cognizance of the biblical controversies. As far as I am concerned, I say quite openly, that with our old ideas of Scripture we could not sustain the authority of the Sacred Book.[87]

Ireland soon wished he had not spoken so openly. After Loisy left the pretension to orthodoxy behind in *Autour d'un petit livre,* Ireland realized with horror that he had helped spur a heretical movement. The archbishop of St. Paul promptly reversed course and began to denounce the new methods, often with a vehemence he had reserved for the modernists' opponents in the decade before *Pascendi.* Although scandalized at the temerity of the modernists as the encyclical portrayed them, Ireland had nonetheless helped to build momentum in his own national church community for a similar "movement."[88]

John Lancaster Spalding, bishop of Peoria, was a man of considerable erudition who felt more comfortable than did Ireland amid the nuances of modern philosophy and theology. He was more deliberate in his encouragement of the new theology and more determined to resist the encroachments of Roman neo-scholastics in the intellectual affairs of American Catholicism. From an early date Spalding established a reputation as a maverick. During seminary training at Louvain he absorbed the philosophical insights of ontologism and traditionalism.[89] This led him to challenge the assertions made by neo-scholastics about the plausibility of rational proofs for God's existence. As a young priest he defended ontologism in a debate with James McMaster, editor of *Freeman's Journal.* "Ontologism, the fundamental doctrine of which affirms the intuition of the infinite—of God—has not been condemned, and I as a Catholic priest am free to hold this doctrine."[90] He was soon forced to reverse himself on this position as it became clear that Rome did, indeed, hold ontologism as a heretical doctrine. Spalding was also notably in disagreement with ultramontane opinion. As the bishops deliberated at the First Vatican Council, Spalding wrote to his erstwhile rector at Louvain that "nothing but a definition of the Church will ever elicit an act of faith from me in the infallibility of the Pope or that of any man. . . . I have little confidence . . . in those cliques that sacrilegiously arrogate to themselves the mission of guiding aright in the Church of Jesus Christ." When that definition was promulgated, he did submit.[91]

In spite of his reputation as a liberal, and after delays caused by his ecclesial opponents, Spalding was appointed bishop of Peoria, where he continued to provide leadership to the Americanists. He led the protests against the appointment of a permanent Apostolic Delegate to the United States. American Catholics, he wrote, "are devoted to the Church; they recognize in the Pope Christ's Vicar, and gladly receive from him the doctrines of faith and morals; but for the rest, they ask him to interfere as little as may be." He gave thanks for church-state separation in America and, with Ireland, urged that the church "adapt herself to all forms of government . . . with their differences of laws, customs, education and sentiment."[92] In a private audience with Leo XIII the year after the condemnation of Americanism, Spalding defended Hecker against the pope's claim that the founder of the Paulists "taught the guidance of the Holy Spirit without the Sacraments." "Holy Father," Spalding responded, "I knew Father Hecker well and intimately, and he was a holy, disinterested, zealous and enlightened priest. I am certain that he never believed or taught what they accuse him of."[93]

With greater clarity and self-awareness than did other liberals, Spalding articulated the clear choice that American Catholic thinkers faced between an anachronistic scholasticism and an eclectic, modern approach to scholarship. He assailed as illusory the prevalent notion that medieval Catholicism had achieved the ideal relationship between church and state, or faith and reason. The "indefectible power" of the church, he argued, was its ability to "survive the destruction of social forms which seemed to be part of her life, and develop new strength in surroundings which had been held to be very fatal to her very existence." Certainly Spalding's most obvious attack on nineteenth-century scholasticism came during the inaugural address he presented at the laying of the cornerstone for Catholic University on 24 May 1888.

> Aristotle is a great mind, but his learning is crude and his ideas of nature are frequently grotesque. Saint Thomas is a powerful intellect but his point of view in all that concerns natural knowledge has long since vanished from sight. What a poverty of learning does the early medieval scheme of education reveal . . . and so when we read the great names of the past, the mists of illusions fill the skies, and our eyes are dimmed by the glory of clouds tinged with the splendors of a sun that has set.[94]

Spalding continued the assault on the integralist mentality during an address at the dedication of Holy Cross College, which John Zahm had invited him to deliver. The modern enthusiasm for scientific method originated in the United States, which, Spalding announced, was the perfect setting for the passing of the torch of knowledge and truth to a new generation. He identified Europe with the ancient and inappropriate: "What sacredness is there in Europe more than in America? Is not the history of Europe largely a history of wars, tyrannies, oppressions? . . . Why should Europe be the object of awe and admiration for Catholics . . . what vital manifestation of religious life and power can we behold [there]?"[95]

Although Spalding was not considered a modernist, he began to publicize ideas and issues that modernists later took up. In 1900 Spalding repeatedly called for a positive and supportive attitude from church officials concerning scientific research, an attitude that had been notably absent in their dealings with John Zahm. If the ancient faith of Christians were to thrive in modern America, it must seek protection from the researches of science. This would be possible, Spalding insisted, only if Catholic scientists and theologians were willing, if necessary, "to abandon positions which are no longer defensible, to assume new attitudes in the face of new conditions." He did not speak of specific doctrines or scientific theories in need of revision, but left the details of this program to others. But he did call for a "re-vivification of faith" expressed in large part by reform of priestly training. The educated priest, Spalding affirmed, could no longer settle within the walls of monastery or cloister, but must go forth into the world armed with sophisticated opinions, a scientific worldview, and a flexible approach to religious pluralism.[96] Within two years, James

Driscoll, the Sulpician president of St. Joseph's Seminary, Dunwoodie, New York, would begin to implement curricular reforms in line with this mandate.

Like the careers of other liberal American Catholic prelates, Spalding's was shadowed by the implication of heresy after 1899. But Spalding especially drew the fire of integralists, who implied that he nurtured an inclination for modernist thought. Denis O'Connell politely understated the case when he suggested that "Bp. Spalding is not considered strongly attached to Rome nor to Roman training." Cardinal Simeoni, the prefect of the Congregation of the Propaganda, warned Corrigan of New York that Spalding's cornerstone speech "contained many unusual and not very sound ideas." And Spalding's 1900 response to *Testem Benevolentiae*, given in the Church of the Gesu in Rome, incited the opposition of the Jesuits, as did his friendship with scholars suspected of modernism, including Lucien Laberthonnière, Friedrich von Hügel, Loisy and Tyrrell. Tyrrell found Spalding's lectures "in sympathy with all that is best and most Catholic in modern thought."[97]

It would be inaccurate to label any of these progressive priests and bishops "modernists." Although each encouraged the church to adapt itself to the intellectual, social, and political demands of the age, none of them anticipated a thoroughgoing attempt to reconceptualize the essential teachings of the church. Yet each of these men helped make possible the brief appearance in American Catholic liberal theology of a modernist impulse. Indeed, "the fresh wave of intellectualism that surged through the 'elite' of the American clergy in the early 1900s was, at least partially, due to the encouragement given progressive thought by the Americanists in the previous decade."[98]

Yet this encouragement and support were not enough to shield Notre Dame priest-scientist John Zahm from the judgment of the Roman censors. Like the other American Catholic modernists of his era, Zahm was influenced by the work of Catholic modernists in Europe, American Protestant liberals in science and theology, and his own liberal coreligionists in the United States. And, like them, his attempts to meld these diverse influences into a coherent apology for Roman Catholicism in modern America were doomed to failure. This failure did not, however, prevent a group of priests in New York, similarly influenced, from attempting to develop an American Catholic "program of modernism" at St. Joseph's Seminary, just five years after Zahm was silenced.

3. The Program of Modernism at Dunwoodie

The termination of John Zahm's career as reconciler of modern science and Roman Catholic faith coincided with Pope Leo XIII's warning to the American hierarchy of "things to be avoided and corrected" amid the "contentions which have arisen lately among you." With this papal rebuke of "Americanism" coming on the heels of the censure of Zahm, it appeared that progressive thinkers might sound the retreat before the forces of traditionalism. Yet the controversies provoked greater polarization in the American Catholic community. For the first seven years of the new century a groups of priests persevered in the study of the new thought, even as their conservative coreligionists took heart from the efforts of the new pontiff, Pope Pius X (1903–1914), to end the challenge to neo-scholasticism as the dominant conceptual paradigm in the church.

Why, then, was there, in Michael Gannon's words, "a modest flowering of American Catholic clerical culture" in the wake of the 1899 condemnation of Americanism and the reassertion of Romanism under Pius X? A number of historical developments contributed to the survival of a measure of intellectual creativity in the American Catholic community. First, at the Third Plenary Council of Baltimore in 1884, the American hierarchy had provided official endorsement to critical scholarship by urging that "the priest should have a wide acquaintance with every department of learning that has a bearing on religious truth." The American priests who, after 1899, continued to explore the implications for "religious truth" suggested by the nascent disciplines of paleontology, post-Darwinian biology, cultural anthropology, semitics, and the higher criticism of the Bible could, and did, cite this general mandate.[1] Second, the founding of Catholic University in Washington, D.C., as the first school of graduate studies in the United States fostered a sense of critical inquiry in line with Pope Leo's admonition (*Aeterni Patris*, 1879), to priest and layperson alike, to become familiar with the discoveries of modern science. Under the initial leadership of John J. Keane, bishop of Richmond, the university attempted to attract to its faculty the leading Catholic scholars of Europe. After his dismissal in 1896 for ecclesio-political reasons, the mantle passed to others, notably former Americanist Denis J. O'Connell, who assumed the rectorship in 1903 and continued, with only limited success, to build the school into a respectable university. In spite of financial difficulties, however, the institution did provide a national center for American Catholic scholarship.[2] It thereby also became a focal point at the turn of the century for ecclesial tensions and for controversies over the method and content of Catholic education. Third, the Catholic press diversified, with the Paulist *Catholic World*, Notre Dame's *Ave Maria*, and the *Catholic University Bulletin*, among other periodicals, providing a moderate-to-liberal counterpoint for conservative publications such as Herman Preuss's *Fortnightly Review*. While many of the issues included conventional devotional, pastoral, or historical essays, others reported on the latest researches of European and American exegetes, philosophers, and historians, some of whom even contributed articles to their pages.[3] Finally, the questions and issues raised earlier by Gmeiner, Zahm, and the Americanist bishops did not subside but continued to be relevant in the new century and were taken up with renewed vigor by other apologists.

Although the modernist impulse in American Catholic liberalism did not wane after the silencing of Zahm, it faced stronger challenges from traditionalists wary of any type of thought deviating from the methodological norms of the received scholasticism. Nowhere was this polarization more evident than in the company of priests dedicated to the education and formation of the American clergy, the Society of St. Sulpice.

THE SULPICIAN PRESENCE AT ST. JOSEPH'S SEMINARY, NEW YORK

Along with other Roman Catholic religious communities of this era, the Sulpicians faced the potentially divisive challenge of modernization and Americanization. With practical considerations in mind, some urged the adaptation of traditional Sulpician piety to the relatively informal character of the American ethos, and applauded the inevitable modification of the strict regulations governing seminary life. If we are to attract young Americans to the priesthood, the reasoning went, we must put a contemporary face on long-standing practices. They also encouraged their seminarians to forego the ethnic particularities of the immigrant churches in which they had been nurtured and to embrace American principles and institutions. Some progressive Sulpicians endeavored to modernize seminary programs and to Americanize seminarians. Both steps were calculated to maximize the effectiveness of the Society's service to the American Catholic community.

However, these new ideas angered as many Sulpicians as they stirred to activity. Resentment arose from their impression that the Americanizers were compromising the bedrock principles of the society. As the new century dawned these traditionalists, ensconced in key administrative positions within the society, worked to curtail the success of their liberal confrères in the United States. Both sides in this disagreement over tactics understood that the proper response to the challenge of modernity could go a long way toward vindicating the society before its many critics.

Founded by Jean Jacques Olier in 1641, the Society of St. Sulpice met a need in the French church for the religious formation of seminarians. As part of a broader renewal of the diocesan clergy, the Sulpicians were imbued with the spirit of moderate Gallicanism. Although ultimately loyal to Rome, Olier and his disciples were nonetheless influenced by an ecclesiology inspired by French nationalism and by a theology with Jansenistic overtones. The spirituality that they developed reflected the ascetical tendencies of the Augustinian tradition and its emphasis on the unmerited character of divine grace. The Sulpician ideal stressed a rigorous discipline in devoted service to the church. The Sulpicians supervised closely the development of seminarians in their charge, participating with them in a structured prayer life, academic investigation, spiritual training, and even recreation. Each Sulpician served the dual function of educator and spiritual director—a practice that made them exceedingly influential in the formation of the clergy and worried curial officials accustomed to the Roman system.[4]

When the first Sulpicians arrived in the United States in the summer of 1791 and opened the first American seminary, St. Mary's of Baltimore, they brought with them the distinctively French ethos of the society. John England, bishop of Charleston after 1820, complained

to Rome that "the progress of faith [is] being hindered by the administrative methods of the Baltimore group . . . [they] should be replaced
by secular priests either born and educated in America or belonging
to a race more easily adaptable to American ways than the French."[5]
A generation later, Baltimore archbishop Martin John Spalding took
up the refrain by urging the superior at St. Mary's and the superior
general in Paris to "Americanize" the seminary by installing a director whose native tongue was English and who could teach pastoral
theology and preaching skills for an American audience.

In 1878 the new superior in Baltimore, Alphonse Magnien, initiated a program of Americanization in the seminary. He attempted
to achieve a measure of autonomy from the society headquarters in
Paris, and recruited American men to the society and the seminary and
Americanized priests to the seminary faculty. Similar emphases characterized the early years of seminaries that opened in Boston (1884),
New York (1896), and San Francisco (1898).

Over the course of the next two decades, Magnien became increasingly involved in the Americanist controversy as a supporter and
confidant of Ireland, John J. Keane (first rector of Catholic University, later bishop of Richmond), Denis O' Connell (as rector of the
North American College in Rome, the primary "Americanist agent"
there) and, to a lesser extent, Cardinal Gibbons. Magnien had been
an advocate of moderate Gallicanism in France, a liberal movement
that exalted the role of the national church but remained loyal to the
papacy. In the Americanist movement Magnien found a renewed expression of this ecclesiology, which had been suppressed in the wake
of the neo-scholastic victory at the First Vatican Council. He read Ireland's speeches in the 1890s and found the archbishop of St. Paul's
endorsement of a "free church in a free state" reminiscent of Mon-
talembart and Dupanloup in the 1860s. With enthusiasm he quoted to
his seminarians O'Connell's 1898 address to the Fourth International
Catholic Scientific Congress in praise of Isaac Hecker's "new idea"
(ecclesiastical and political Americanism). Magnien also supervised
the establishment of a Sulpician house of studies adjacent to Catholic
University in Washington, D.C. He encouraged young priests to famil-
iarize themselves with the findings of modern science and historical
scholarship and supported their travels to Europe to study with leading
exegetes and theologians, among them Alfred Loisy.[6]

John Hogan shared this commitment to Americanism and perceived more clearly than did Magnien its theological and philosophical

underpinnings in modernism. Born in Ireland in 1829, Hogan joined the Sulpicians in 1851 and was assigned the chair of fundamental theology at St. Sulpice in Paris upon his ordination to the priesthood the following year. There he absorbed the insights of Sulpician philosopher and immanentist Louis Branchereau (who also influenced Ireland), became a disciple of Cardinal Newman, and developed a profound distaste for neo-scholasticism. He imparted developmentalist views to a generation of seminarians in France, including many who would later become involved in the controversies over Americanism and modernism, such as Felix Klein, E. I. Mignot, and Maurice d'Hulst, the eventual rector of Institut Catholique in Paris. In 1884 Hogan was appointed superior of St. John's Seminary in Brighton, Massachusetts. "Primarily a pedagogue rather than a scholar,"[7] Hogan's teaching, correspondences, and published treatises reflected the influence of European modernists. He was one of the first Sulpicians to acknowledge the higher criticism of the Bible and to advance arguments in favor of a revised theory of inspiration. He termed Loisy's article on the inerrancy question "the clearest and strongest I have seen yet," and lauded his use of literary and historical methodology. His correspondences reveal that he encouraged both Loisy and d'Hulst in their (competing) efforts to reconceptualize the doctrine of biblical inerrancy. He also agreed with Loisy's general analysis of "dogmatic formulation," including the notion that the post-apostolic doctrine of the church could not be found in Scripture. But, because "the world is not ready for these facts," he told Loisy, "it is necessary to form a synthesis of the facts to make them acceptable."[8]

Yet Hogan preferred to leave the building of such a synthesis to bolder men and more accomplished scholars. He was content with the preparatory work of alerting his students to the deficiencies in neo-scholastic method, especially its ahistorical approach to the Bible, which necessitated such a synthesis. As part of this effort he introduced at St. John's a series of Scripture courses for the entire six years, and recruited Francis Gigot, a French Sulpician Scripture scholar, for the faculty. In describing the rationale for these moves in 1886, Hogan also noted how American Catholic studies lagged behind the institutions of Protestant theological education with their strong emphasis on advanced Scripture studies.[9]

Although Hogan did not consider himself a pioneer of the modernist synthesis, his own book on biblical criticism, *Clerical Studies*, did, however, discuss the reconciliation of the traditional theories of inspiration and inerrancy with the factual evidence uncovered by modern archaeological and historical research. Originating in 1891 as a series of articles for the *American Ecclesiastical Review*, the book criticized the tendency of scholastic theologians to inhibit the development of a biblically based theology by depending on *a priori* principles to settle the difficult questions posed by the scientific method. The predominance of the methods of (an ahistorical) theology over those of biblical scholarship had impoverished Catholic seminary education since the Middle Ages, and had put Catholics far behind Protestants in the modern attempt to interpret newly discovered manuscripts and to apply scientific and literary criticism to the Bible. Nonetheless, Hogan predicted that the day would come when all Catholic scholars would employ critical methods and renounce outdated notions such as the Mosaic authorship of the Pentateuch. Pope Leo's encyclical on biblical studies, *Providentissimus Deus*, was not, after all, to be considered binding, and left substantive points open to careful consideration and further discussion. Gerald Fogarty has described Hogan's own approach to the interpretation of scripture as "daring," for *Clerical Studies* held that "inspiration does not change the established literary habits of a people or of a writer," which include "loose and inexact statements side by side with what is strictly accurate; figurative language of all kinds . . . [and] all the ordinary modes of human speech . . . and all the literary peculiarities of eastern peoples."[10]

Hogan proposed a general program of seminary studies that "did not accord with the accepted norms." The scientific and historical study of the Bible in its original languages was to be the center of the curriculum, with advanced students consulting the most recent European journals, such as the *Revue Biblique* and Alfred Loisy's *Revue d'Historie et de Littérature Religieuse*.[11] In some of its particulars, Hogan's proposal would be followed by the Sulpicians staffing St. Joseph's Seminary in New York.

The Americanizing and modernizing efforts of Magnien and Hogan did not go unnoticed in neo-scholastic circles. On the contrary, they were interpreted within the framework of a sustained examination of suspected liberalizing tendencies within the Society of St. Sulpice, tendencies in which the neo-scholastics discerned the now-familiar trajectory of error extending from Gallicanism, ontologism, and immanentism, through French republicanism and Americanism, to its culmination in modernism and atheism. Although the founder, Olier, had been under a cloud of suspicion, the nineteenth-century scholastics focused on the more immediate target of Branchereau, whose theory of religious knowledge appeared in manuals read by seminarians. They charged that Branchereau confused the idea of God with the Divine Reality itself and thus led his followers to the heretical conclusions of ontologism, subjectivism, and pantheism. These philosophical errors were compounded by the questionable ecclesiological doctrines that had been associated with the Sulpicians since certain American bishops, including former Sulpician Augustin Verot, had adopted Dupanloup's minimalist interpretation of the *Syllabus of Errors* issued by Pope Pius IX in 1864. Cardinal Johann Franzelin, S.J., went so far as to blame the "inopportunist" position of American bishops debating the definition of papal infallibility at Vatican I on the influence of "Gallican Sulpicians" at Baltimore.[12]

In other words, even a generation before *Pascendi* portrayed modernism as a synthesis of heresies, the integralist neo-scholastics perceived within the Catholic clergy an organized opposition with its own equally well-integrated intellectual system—a system with radically different ecclesiological and political implications. "Gallican Sulpicians" and "Americanist Sulpicians" were, by this reasoning, barely to be distinguished one from the other. The Jesuits who published *La Civiltà Cattolica* and other prominent proponents of neo-scholasticism in the Roman colleges perceived in both tendencies the same spirit of opposition to the ultramontane ecclesiology and to the extrinsicist philosophy certified by the First Vatican Council. Ontologism, with its stress on the immediate personal intuition of the divine presence, was seen as the philosophical basis for the Americanist emphasis upon the agency of the Holy Spirit in individual and corporate spiritual life. As Americanists, Magnien and Hogan believed that the religious and civil liberties of the United States provided the most desirable environment for the modern growth of Catholicism, and both men therefore supported the idea of a strong national church. As Christopher Kauffman put it, "French liberalism was without an ecclesiastical base until Americanism supplied one."[13]

Given this prolonged period of scrutiny of Sulpician orthodoxy, it is not surprising that the leaders of the society in Paris inaugurated a campaign, as the new century dawned, to restore the image of the Society in Rome. The new superior-general of the Sulpicians, Jules Lebas, presided over the tightening of censorship policies and gave particular attention to books and articles by Sulpicians in the United

States. Lebas called Hogan to Paris in 1901 and delayed the granting of an *imprimatur* for *Clerical Studies*. Hogan died that year.

This renewed vigilance polarized the Sulpician communities in Paris and in the United States. By regulation, Sulpicians in America were to submit their scholarship to French censors at St. Sulpice. Knowing full well that the verdict likely depended on the identity of the censor, the more progressive scholars attempted to direct the manuscripts into sympathetic hands. The censorship policies of the society under Lebas were particularly aggravating to five American Sulpicians at St. Joseph's Seminary in Yonkers, New York, who were dedicated to the pursuit of scholarship and critical reflection on the truths of the faith. In 1902 under the leadership of the new seminary president, James Francis Driscoll, S.S. (1859–1922), they attempted to establish a vital center for American Catholic scholarship at Dunwoodie (as the seminary was known, in reference to its location in Yonkers).

Born in Vermont, Driscoll decided at an early age that he had a vocation to the priesthood. After attending seminary in Montreal he was ordained and joined the Sulpicians in 1887. He pursued advanced studies in Paris, at St. Sulpice and Institut Catholique, where his mature intellectual outlook was forged in the crucible of early European modernism. While abroad, he came under the influence of leading liberal Catholic exegetes, historians, and theologians, including Albert Houtin, Alfred Loisy, and Felix Klein. His specialty was the study of semitic languages and biblical literature, subjects he taught at Montreal (1889–1896), during his first assignment to Dunwoodie (1896-1901), and at St. Augustine's, the Sulpician house of studies adjacent to Catholic University (1901–1902). At Catholic University he renewed the acquaintance of Orientalist Henry Hyvernat, who influenced Driscoll's appreciation of linguistics and archaeology. In 1900, as a member of the New York Oriental Club, Driscoll formed a friendship with Scripture scholar Charles A. Briggs of Union Seminary that would prove to be significant.[14]

As president of Dunwoodie, Driscoll was committed to the task of communicating to the American clergy the insights of his European mentors. This commitment took a number of forms. Among other roles Driscoll played the publicist, advertising not only the work of the European modernists but also the inchoate efforts of American priests to approximate their methods. He translated Loisy's *L'Evangile et l'église* and *Autour d'un petit livre* into English and helped facilitate its circulation in the United States. He also published the writings of European modernists in the scholarly journal he founded, the *New York Review*. He developed a network of correspondences through which new ideas and opinions were exchanged. As seminary president Driscoll eliminated certain outmoded courses in the curriculum and supervised the development of replacements designed to instruct seminarians in the nuances of the higher criticism and the new theologies. Moreover, he dismantled the traditional structure and routines of seminary life, including the ban on outside reading and interaction. In order to broaden the scope of the faculty's acquaintance with contemporary topics and theological ideas, Driscoll continued the faculty exchange program with Columbia University (arranged by his predecessor Edward Dyer) and encouraged students to take courses there, and at Union Theological Seminary. By the end of Driscoll's tenure as president in 1909 the seminary had become the primary center for the dissemination of modernist ideas and methodologies in the American Catholic church. In appreciation of these efforts George Tyrrell judged Driscoll to be the best theological thinker in the United States at the turn of the century. Von Hügel described him as "the much-beloved pupil of Loisy," one who "is in a position to give and get a hearing and a public for Catholic work of the most modern sort."[15]

As this new intellectual openness gathered momentum during the first four years of Driscoll's leadership, the conflicts with the Sulpicians in Paris sharpened, forcing the priests to decide between their membership in the society and their loyalty to "the cause." Driscoll's correspondences during this period reflected his growing awareness that the society had become dominated by "the enemy camp." To his close friend Edward Dyer, now the vicar-general of the Sulpicians in the United States, he first expressed his concern over Lebas's treatment of Hogan and interpreted the episode as symptomatic of the malaise gripping the Sulpicians in Paris. Hogan was "a fine great figure, a grand old man, a credit to the society," regardless of the suspicions of "the party in ascendancy at present." The conservatives, Driscoll believed, "attribute a portion of the evils that have overtaken Sulpitianism within recent years in the shape of intellectual temerity and laxity of discipline etc. etc. to his influence."[16]

At first Driscoll played ecclesiastical politics, seeking to influence the Sulpician policy as a member of the loyal opposition. He attempted to build among his American Sulpician correspondents the unanimity necessary "if we are to do anything effective in warding off the incubus of a legislation intended for conditions of time and surroundings totally different from ours."[17] Driscoll hoped to see progressive Sulpicians represent the society in matters of importance to the universal church. When Pope Leo XIII decided in 1902 to name a commission to oversee biblical studies, Driscoll wrote to Dyer:

> The idea is certainly excellent *provided the right men are on the board*, otherwise things will be much worse than before. I shudder at the idea of such a commission being made up of men like Satolli, Mazella, etc. (I know of course that the latter is dead (*deo gratias—I mean requiescat in pace*) but there are plenty like him left).[18]

In their stead Driscoll recommended Francis Ernest Charles Gigot (1859–1920), the most accomplished Scripture scholar in the American church. Ordained at the Institut Catholique in 1883, Gigot took his first teaching assignment as professor of dogma and sacred Scripture under John Hogan at St. John's Seminary in 1885. In 1899 he was transferred to St. Mary's Seminary in Baltimore, and in 1904 he joined Driscoll's faculty at Dunwoodie.

In the texts on Scripture study for which he was known, Gigot surveyed the contemporary debates among Catholic scholars on controversial issues in biblical studies. He did not restrict the scope of his coverage to the various opinions of the scholastic commentators. Alongside excerpts from the *Summa Theologica* and *Providentissimus Deus*, he quoted from texts produced by critical exegetes of the progressive French and German schools, such as Loisy's *La Question biblique et l'inspiration des Ecritures*. On the question of biblical inspiration, he cited with approval the theories of Newman, di Bartolo, and d'Hulst; and he presented a minimalist interpretation of the strictures on critical inquiry established in 1893 by Leo XIII's *Providentissimus Deus*.

In textbooks of this sort one would not expect the author to present original and constructive arguments for contribution to the ongoing debate—and, by and large, Gigot avoided this direct approach. Gigot maintained that the "new" or "modern" theories of inspiration and inerrancy were in truth no more than updated versions of long-standing opinions dating back to the earliest centuries of the Christian experience. As did modernists in Europe, Gigot argued that a departure from scholasticism did not necessarily signal a departure from traditional Roman Catholic opinions.[19]

For example, even in his least controversial work, *A General Introduction to the Study of the Holy Scriptures* (1900), Gigot was careful to include a section on the contemporary revision of the verbal inspiration theory. "While many [Catholic scholars] would restrict such relativeness of truth to a comparatively few biblical passages which refer to purely scientific matters, others think it should be extended to all scientific matters," Gigot informed his readers, "and to many historical statements besides." Without fully sanctioning this view Gigot went on to elaborate the persuasive arguments supporting it: the discrepancies in the historical books, the numerous inaccuracies in chronology and geography and, most important, the words of St. Jerome to this effect.[20] Indeed Gigot did not privilege the received or "orthodox" position on controversial questions. When he published two articles on the Book of Isaiah in the *New York Review*, for example, he presented the modern critical theories of the question of the authorship of the books alongside the traditional teaching. "Both opinions are beset with numerous and great difficulties," he wrote, "and, on that account, the readers of the *New York Review* cannot expect us to define what is the true position."[21]

It was, however, Gigot's more specialized work, the two-volume *Special Introduction to the Study of the Old Testament and the New Testament*, that provoked a confrontation with Sulpician censors in Paris. In 1901 Gigot published the first of two parts of this series, *Special Introduction to the Study of the Old Testament, Part 1: The Historical Books*, in which he defended the theory that the Pentateuch was not written by Moses as being in accord with "the Fathers of Trent," who had settled "only the question of the sacred and canonical character of the books enumerated."[22] Perhaps due to the fact that conservatives in the American Catholic press criticized the book for citing censured thinkers such as Mivart and Loisy, Gigot attracted the attention of the Sulpician censors in France as he was preparing the second part of the *Special Introduction*.

The ensuing conflict, which dragged on from 1902 to the eventual publication of the volume in 1906, revealed the extent to which both Driscoll and Gigot were at odds with the received scholastic theological tradition. In 1902 Driscoll alerted Dyer that "someone has denounced Father Gigot at headquarters and they are after him."[23] All would depend on which censors handled the case. Gigot, Driscoll reported, was already considering resignation from the society in the event that the "reactionnaires" Vigoroux and Fillion in Paris denounced his ideas and methods. Driscoll would not blame Gigot for such an action; in fact, he confided to Dyer, he might join him in retreat. In a revealing passage of this letter, Driscoll indicated clearly that he understood himself and Gigot to be harbingers of a new and timely approach to theology and biblical studies in the American Catholic church. The old ideas and methods of nineteenth-century scholasticism could not satisfy the intellectual demands of twentieth-century Americans; they should be replaced by critical methods, whatever the cost:

> I do not know how far the war will be carried on, but it is coming round in my direction, and I begin to foresee ugly possibilities for myself. Already last summer I was denounced in France as holding unsound, heretical doctrines concerning scripture and, according to the standard that is now in the ascendancy over there, I must plead guilty. My "nihil obstat" is on the most compromising of Fr. Gigot's books. I am using the same for my class in Baltimore so any campaign that should culminate in the withdrawal of Fr. Gigot would probably involve me as well and I cannot help giving a thought to what I would do in such an emergency. I am not very aggressive or revolutionary in my presentation or defense of the new views but my convictions in the matter are very definite and it would be impossible for me to teach the old rubbish—the word may be strong but it is the only one that fits my appreciation as it would be for Dr. Herrick to teach the physics of Aristotle or the alchemy of the schoolmen.[24]

In a letter to Dyer after the Parisian censor's first rejection of Gigot's *Special Introduction*, Driscoll wrote of the "reactionary principles" of the society and of Gigot's conviction that his work would be suppressed. "Fr. Gigot has arrived at the conclusion," Driscoll reported, "that the best thing for him to do—the best thing for us, and for the work—is to leave now of his own accord before he is asked to do so." By leaving the Sulpicians, the priests hoped to guard their work from immediate censorship and avoid any embarrassment for the American church. Secession from the Sulpicians would, Driscoll explained to a disbelieving Dyer, hold several immediate advantages for Gigot:

> 1) He will be free to go on with his work whereas if he remains, there can certainly be no question of his publishing any more on the lines he has been following. . . . 2) His own interest requires

that he provide a terminus ad quem if he leaves us. Now if he be sent away, or has to leave because of adverse rulings concerning his books, it will be very hard for him to find a place, and moreover in that case anything he might write would be discredited ipso facto. On the other hand, if he leaves now . . . no fuss having been made, he can go on teaching as well as writing. It cannot be said that he was excluded from S.S. on account of his teaching. 3) This move, i.e., his spontaneous withdrawal, would preclude any opposition on our part, and thus, he thinks would be an advantage for us and for the American work, because a protest will . . . [cause] us Americans to go on record as opposing the traditional methods and upholding tendencies that are represented in the [Sulpician] circular as being so baneful. If we protest, we will merely compromise our own reputation and confirm the anti-American prejudices, whereas if there be nothing said the storm will blow over in due time. There is no use irritating the present administration [in Rome], rather hope and wait for a change. He is sure that he will be required to withdraw his book and to change his entire tenor of teaching—a thing which he will not do.[25]

This passage revealed Driscoll and Gigot's concern for the reputation of the American Catholic church no less than their awareness that their work might compromise it at least in the eyes of "the present administration." Their only hope was to avoid controversy and "hope for a change" in the prevailing attitudes. But, unlike Zahm before them, they recognized that such a change was necessary if their work was to gain acceptance. In the interim the most prudent course of action was to remove their studies and publications from the watchful eyes of the Sulpician censors. "Lebas will rejoice at [the resignation]," Driscoll believed, "and there will be no exhibition of dangerous American tendencies."[26]

The controversy over Gigot's writings continued for four years, during which he joined Driscoll on the faculty at Dunwoodie. The censors in Paris prevented the publication of his second volume of the *Special Introduction* and he was reduced to asking Dyer's permission to use these pages in his own class lectures. "Of course," he wrote Dyer, "If the matter must be submitted again to Paris, I had better give it up at once. Paris, as you know, has already—at least practically— denied me the desired freedom."[27]

Gigot grew increasingly impatient and submitted his work to American censors to offset the opinions of those in Europe. In his appeals to Dyer one senses his urgency. The strength of his text was in its contemporaneity; he felt that the delay caused by the Sulpicians might render it obsolete in the rapidly developing field of scriptural studies. "As regards to my 2nd volume of Special Introduction to Old Testament," he complained to the Vicar-General, "I am tired of waiting for an opportunity to have it appear." Gigot claimed that American bishops and priests liked volume one and awaited volume two; only the "stubborn Paris Sulpicians" stood in the way. Furthermore, he argued, the delay would render the book useless: "Besides, it is a book intended to secure prudently a transition from old to new positions among Catholics and it is desirable that its publication should not be delayed any longer." Paradoxically, in order to facilitate acceptance of the volume, Gigot offered to revise it by removing "every expression of mine that betrays a personal leaning towards new theories and opinions."[28]

As Gigot's ire increased, his arguments for acceptance of his work assumed a political character, one that could only alarm his superiors. The Sulpicians in Paris were wrong to silence him, Gigot warned, and proof of their error lay in his own popularity in the United States:

> Fr. Vigoroux's statement that, in my first volume, I do not teach the Catholic doctrine or something to that effect—can hardly be correct, seeing that the volume was allowed to pass by our American censors. . . . I do present [the question of the authorship of the Pentateuch] with its proper theological value. Vigoroux would not dare speak vs. Vol. II if it is re-examined here in America and given practical endorsement by Sulpicians in this country and by leading American reviews, priests and bishops. . . . [The Special Introduction's] appearance will be, so to speak, a proof of my orthodoxy, if any such be required, in the eyes of certain men in this country and elsewhere. The transition begun by the first volume, between old and new theories, should be continued without delay.

Gigot concluded that if this final appeal were denied, his "impression" would be confirmed that "no further scientific advance is to be expected on the part of our Sulpician professors in this country."[29]

Many of Gigot's American colleagues rushed to his defense, including Father Daniel Maher, Hogan's successor as rector of St.

John's Seminary in Brighton, Massachusetts. He regretted the pain caused Gigot by the rejection of his work but believed that "open opposition" would be useless. Maher, too, believed that in time Gigot's ideas would gain ascendancy in Roman Catholic thought. "We are in a period of transition," he wrote, "and the ideas that the examiners of Fr. Gigot's book take exception to, are gaining ground among Catholic scholars and before many years will be taught without opposition." Driscoll and Gigot did, Maher believed, represent a growing constituency of American Catholic teachers and scholars.[30]

The prolonged controversy over the orthodoxy of Gigot's scholarship was not, however, the only factor in the secession of the priests at Dunwoodie from the Society of St. Sulpice, but it did indicate to them that other aspects of their program of modernism would inevitably meet the same stifling criticism. Thus, before they formally seceded from the society, they brought these projects to a figure of authority whom they perceived as less vigilant, the archbishop of New York. There were at least three persuasive arguments for the transference of Driscoll's and Gigot's allegiance from Sulpician Vicar-General Dyer to John M. Farley, archbishop of New York after Michael Corrigan's death in 1902. First, it was no secret that Farley desired to wrest control of seminary training in his archdiocese from the French society. When the disgruntled Sulpicians from Dunwoodie consulted him for approval of curriculum changes and for permission to establish a periodical of advanced studies, Farley welcomed the requests as the most diplomatic means of transferring the seminary to his supervision. He later reminded St. Sulpice that the priests had, after all, initially approached him — not the other way around.[31] Second, Farley's enthusiasm for the move was not accompanied by careful scrutiny of the revised programs of study and publication at his new seminary. Driscoll and Gigot manipulated the archbishop with ease and were at times duplicitous in their relationship with him.[32] Third, Farley seemed sincerely committed to turning out priests well-versed in the most recent theological and biblical scholarship. Although Driscoll no doubt embellished the account of the archbishop's response to the idea of the founding of the journal, his explanation to Dyer was probably accurate:

> He (Farley) expressed his deep, long-standing regrets at the backwardness of Catholic writers in matters of modern scientific interest, and gave as his opinion that it was due in great measure to the exaggerated restrictive policy of the ecclesiastical authorities

who, through their unreasonably stringent methods of censorship, only succeed in stifling all initiative on the part of the ablest and best disposed Catholic scholars.[33]

Whereas the successor to Lebas as superior general of the Sulpicians, Père Garriguet, had demanded that each of the issues of the proposed review be submitted to censors, under Farley's supervision only the very last issue of the *New York Review* bore the imprimatur.

When Driscoll sought Farley's approval of his programs over the head of his immediate superior in the Sulpicians, Dyer rightly interpreted the action as a prelude to his erstwhile friend's secession from the society. Dyer was obviously hurt personally by what he considered to be the betrayal of the society and of his close friendship with Driscoll. The correspondence between the two men up to the actual date of the secession (9 January 1906) of Driscoll, Gigot, and three colleagues on the faculty at Dunwoodie, reveals poignantly the erosion of a once-strong friendship.[34] In defense of the Society of St. Sulpice and of his own leadership, Dyer circulated his written interpretation of the crisis, the most sensational aspects of which were leaked to the press. Dyer's primary contention was that the secession was motivated not only by Gigot's difficulties with the Sulpician censors in Paris but by the Dunwoodians' desire to pursue projects and studies, including the publication of the *New York Review*, which would not stand up to the test of orthodoxy required of such projects by the Sulpicians.[35]

In the letter informing Dyer of the secession, Driscoll had anticipated such charges and sought to dismiss them by depicting the withdrawal as part of the natural course of events in archdiocesan politics:

> We the undersigned sincerely regret to make to you the following announcement which we feel must be a painful surprise: It is that we have decided to sever our connection with the Company of St. Sulpice, and have accepted the offer of the Most Rev. Archbishop . . . to continue the seminary work as priests incorporated into the archdiocese of New York. Nothing is to be changed in the existing order of things or in the spirit of the seminary administration, with which His Grace is well satisfied. Only henceforth the seminary will be exclusively under diocesan control and the future members of the faculty will be recruited from the clergy of the diocese.

Without entering into a lengthy discussion of the motives that have prompted this action, or of the occasion that has precipitated it, it may be briefly stated . . . [that] by remaining in the conditions on which we are accepted we obtain a very practical endorsement of the work that has been done, notwithstanding the Archbishop's well known objection to having his seminary under control other than his own.[36]

With these words Driscoll merely alluded to the considerable disagreements between the two parties, implied that Farley approved of his bold initiatives at the seminary, and placed the secession in the context of the archbishop's "well-known" desires to control seminary education. Significantly, Driscoll pointed to the practical endorsement of their work that the secession obtained for the former Sulpicians. It was, indeed, a practical benefit, for without it they could not have continued their work. Dyer responded with outrage. "I do not understand," he wrote, "by what right you have undertaken to hand over to the Most Rev. Archbishop of New York a Seminary that was entrusted by his predecessor in office to the Society of St. Sulpice." He judged the action to be "treason" and claimed that it would play right into the hands of the enemies of the society in Europe.[37]

Dyer next took his case to Farley. The news of the secession was so "extraordinary" that he wished the archbishop to verify it. He reminded Farley of a contract between the archdiocese and the Sulpicians, "for whom of course the above-named gentlemen are in no way authorized to act," and objected to the "summary dismissal" of the Sulpicians, a move without precedent that would "inflict a most grievous injury upon the Society both in this country and in France." Dyer could not comprehend, he confessed, how the archbishop could do such a thing in light of the honorable service of the Sulpicians to the archdiocese of New York.[38] In his response Farley contradicted Driscoll's previous story: the former Sulpicians had come to him, he had not invited them. Had he not accepted them, he would have had no recourse but to close the seminary. "Thus, by force of circumstances that were brought about without my interference, and without my knowledge, until almost the time of their occurrence, the Sulpician Fathers ceased, by the very fact, to be connected with the Seminary, without either the Sulpicians or myself having an opportunity of giving the year's notice of withdrawal as per contract," Farley responded.[39]

Dyer's retort was swift and to the point: "I do not see that the only alternative open to your Grace was to accept the Sulpicians, . . . or to close the seminary . . . [for they] would certainly not have left St. Sulpice at all, had they not found an opening into your Archdiocese."[40]

Dyer's fulminations were to no avail. Frustrated and discredited, he composed his own account of the incident and circulated it privately among Sulpicians in the United States. In this account he repudiated Driscoll's public statement that the withdrawal of the priests from the society "was not the outcome of any controversy concerning their orthodoxy or that of the 'Review.' " Dyer recounted the series of events surrounding the founding of the *Review*:

> [The Sulpician superior general] Father Garriguet thought that Father Driscoll should write him a letter expressing regret that the circumstances in which the *Review* started did not allow of his being consulted beforehand about it. He directed that the Sulpicians should not appear too conspicuously in it, that their articles be submitted to the S.S. censorship and that they should take no financial engagement in regard to it; and he recalled the regulation of the Index that each number should bear the episcopal imprimatur. I do not know that any of these points was observed; I know that most of them were not.[41]

Dyer concluded his account by portraying the company at Dunwoodie as betrayers of the Sulpician spirit of seminary training, who preferred modern scholarship to piety. He offered it as an empty hope that in Dunwoodie's future "men may ever be admitted to her Faculty who, not in theory only but in fact, place the spiritual above the intellectual, who consider it their first duty, not to give a brilliant course or to train up a band of scholars—great aims whose importance we do not minimize—but to train holy and zealous Priests."[42]

The conservative Sulpicians rallied to Dyer's cause. From Paris the "discreet" Father de Foville urged Dyer to report the "Dunwoodie Five" to the Propaganda as heretics.[43] From St. Patrick's Seminary in Menlo Park, California, Edward Arbez, S.S., sent condolences to Dyer and termed Driscoll, Gigot, and Holland's action as "odious" and "abominable."[44] Daniel Maher of St. John's Seminary, formerly an admirer of Gigot, agreed that the telling question in the controversy was the orthodoxy of the *Review*: "Again, some of the Europeans mentioned as contributors have been and are still, I believe, engaged in the controversy concerning the new apologetics, and some of their ideas on points of doctrine have stirred up sharp criticism and determined opposition."[45] Even three years later, after the condemnation, one Sulpician wrote Dyer of "the great blessings accorded to St. Sulpice . . . the schism of Dunwoodie," for it had rid the society of heretical influence.[46] The *Boston Evening Transcript* editorialized that the affair was but one episode in the emergence of "the new liberal Catholicism," that sought as part of its agenda of reform to change the doctrines of the church. The editors surmised that the former Sulpicians had abandoned the society in anticipation of the censure of their new journal.

In a letter of response Driscoll described the purpose of the *Review* in terms similar to those used by European modernists:

> The purpose . . . is not to abandon the old in favor of the new, but rather to interpret with becoming care and reverence the old truths in the light of the new science. The task, as it appears to us, is not one involving doctrinal change, but restatement and readjustment, in other words, the preservation and not the rupture of continuity. To this end, viz: the gradual assimilation by theology of what is sound in the results of modern scholarship, we hope to contribute our mite.[47]

The foregoing rehearsal of the sequence of events leading up to the secession of Driscoll, Gigot, and three of their colleagues from the Society of St. Sulpice serves to illustrate a self-awareness about the "cause," however loosely defined, that they shared with progressives such as Zahm and Gmeiner who had earlier attempted a modernist-style synthesis between traditional faith and modern thought. The efforts of Driscoll and Gigot signaled a new stage in the emergence of modernist thought patterns in American Catholicism. They often rejected the radical conclusions of their colleagues and mentors in Europe, such as Loisy and Tyrrell, but they shared with these thinkers an aversion to scholastic methodology, a preference for critical methods of historical and literary inquiry, and a dedication to the task of constructing a synthesis of modern science and revealed truth. They stood in continuity with the efforts of Zahm, but approached the task with a boldness of vision (or with a measure of imprudence) that the apologist-scientist did not share. It remains to describe the substance and scope of their efforts.

THE MODERNIZATION OF SEMINARY EDUCATION

Michael Gannon described Dunwoodie during Driscoll's reign as the heart of a reform movement invigorating the American Catholic church at the turn of the century:

> More than any diocese, religious order, or seminary elsewhere in the country, New York was opening its eyes and ears to the proclamation of truth in the natural, historical, and social sciences. More than any other it was promoting the study of theology and Scripture in depth, in consort with the best minds in Europe, and in conjunction with the full range of human wisdom. More than any other it was preparing American Catholicism for what a later epoch would call aggiornamento.[48]

Nowhere was this more apparent than in the restructuring of the seminary curriculum that Driscoll supervised upon his appointment to the presidency of Dunwoodie. On the matter of seminary education Driscoll was of one mind with John J. Keane and John Lancaster Spalding: if the Roman Catholic priest serving in the United States is to effectively lead his people, he must be liberally educated; that is, he must possess intellectual sophistication in cultural, social, historical, and scientific matters, as well as in religious studies and theology. Traditional piety could not replace intellectual competency in every area touching upon the ordinary concerns of the lay person. The priest must understand the American character, American politics, and American religion in order to preach and pastor responsibly in American society.

For these purposes Driscoll found the curricular structure that Dyer had inherited under Archbishop Corrigan woefully inadequate. Based on the scholastic pedagogical approach, the program of studies was centered on subject matter that Driscoll found inappropriate to the needs of the modern priest: hagiography, medieval church history, and classical rhetoric, to cite a few. Latin and Greek had their rightful place in the curriculum, Driscoll judged, but courses were taught exclusively in French or Latin, languages that the future parishioners of the seminarians found inscrutable. Philosophical studies were confined to "Aristotle and the Summa"; theology to the restrictions of scholasticism. "The program does not appear to meet fully the issues of the day," Driscoll complained to Dyer. "A priest educated on these lines would not be equal to the cultured laity on those questions on which society is divided."[49]

Among the pressing needs the traditional curriculum failed to meet, Driscoll perceived, was the theological preparation for training lay people in religious thought. The priest produced by the old system possessed an understanding of theology that, by its technical language and syllogistic reasoning, precluded translation into lay vernacular. "The layman requires theological learning, not to define magisterially, but to give an account of the faith that is in him," Driscoll wrote, "[and] the nearer we bring the cultured Catholic layman to the high plane occupied in the early ages, the better it will be for religion."[50] Furthermore, Driscoll believed that, as part of the preparation of the seminarian to minister in the pluralistic milieu of America, studies in comparative religions must be mandated, with a special emphasis on the objective analysis of the dominant Christian faith in the United States, Protestantism, and of non-Catholic philosophies.

One of his colleagues on the faculty, Francis Patrick Duffy (1871–1932), shared these convictions and helped Driscoll translate them into curricular reforms. Duffy's approach to seminary training and religious formation was genuinely catholic in scope. He was a man of diverse interests, a student of biology and history no less than philosophy and theology. With appreciation he observed the early growth of the Christian ecumenical movement and predicted that Catholicism would participate in the noble endeavor only to the extent that Catholic educators pioneered the way. Pedagogically, he was not a disciple of St. Sulpice, and he never joined that company of priests. Thus he brought to Dunwoodie a fresh perspective on the purpose of seminary education and a commitment to multidisciplinary approaches to academic inquiry.

Duffy deliberately chose to serve the archdiocese rather than the Sulpicians, in part because Archbishop Michael Corrigan supported his advanced studies at Catholic University of America. Corrigan ordained Duffy in 1896 and, in a move of some significance for later events, placed him at the disposal of his auxiliary bishop, John Farley. After brief service as Farley's assistant curate, Duffy opted for the academic life and returned to Dunwoodie in 1898, this time as a faculty member.[51]

To the seminary he contributed a keenness of intellect. In preparing his classes, Duffy consulted not only the Catholic standards, but the classics of the moderns. He enthusiastically passed this knowledge on to his students. He informed Dyer that "outside of the standards—Aristotle and the Summa—I confine my reading to the moderns—Ladd, Flint, Balfour, Lilly, Mivart, Huxley, Spencer, Darwin. I am now reading 'The Origin of Species' for the first time. So you see how much there is I don't know."[52] In 1903 Dyer recommended him for an honorary doctorate, reinforcing Duffy's plans to devote himself to scholarship. "It will be a stimulus to me to live up to your expectations and exhortations," he had written to Dyer, "by devoting myself more to the work of writing." It was in fact Duffy, together with Father John F. Brady, who first proposed to Driscoll the idea of founding a journal of modern thought and served as its associate editor.[53]

Duffy and Driscoll replaced the standard fare of offerings in medieval piety and scholastic philosophy with courses modeled after those Driscoll and Gigot had taken at Institut Catholique in Paris under Loisy and Louis Duchesne in modern scriptural exegesis and church history, respectively. Felix Klein, a classmate of Driscoll's at the Institut, visited Dunwoodie in 1904 to review the new programs. He found them congenial to the highest standards of European Catholic scholarship:

> as to the curriculum, to judge from the programmes and the authors, there was no great difference between it and those of France . . . the topics are very well adapted to present needs. In the second year in the course in philosophy, for example, I was well pleased to see the studies indicated in these terms: "Origin of the Universe"; "Spontaneous Generation"; "The Materialistic View of Life"; "Periodic Evolution"; "Descent of Man"; "Is Evolution Admissible?"; "Distinction Between Man and Brute."[54]

Perhaps equally important was Driscoll's introduction of guest lectures by prominent scholars, Protestants as well as Catholics, into the routine of the seminarians' academic life. Lectures on "The Medieval Guild" and "The Literature of the Holy Grail," gave way to "The Catholic Church and Twentieth-Century Thought," "Theological Needs," and "Modern Biblical Theories." Driscoll brought in lecturers most conversant with liberal and modernist themes in both European Catholic and American Protestant theology, apologetics, and biblical criticism. Because of their publicized confrontations with ecclesiastical authority, at least two of these guest lecturers gave Dunwoodie a reputation for innovation in religion studies.[55]

The first of these visiting scholars was the Italian priest Giovanni Gennochi, once a consultant to Leo's Pontifical Biblical Commission, who quickly fell under suspicion of modernism. At the insistence of his advisers, Leo XIII had in 1898 suppressed Gennochi's chair of Holy Scripture at the Pontifical University of Apollinare. This ignominy did not prevent Driscoll from inviting Gennochi to Dunwoodie, on the eve of *Pascendi*, to share with seminarians his method of scriptural study. Gennochi had attempted to modify the historico-critical method, which, in the hands of Alfred Loisy with whom he maintained a frequent correspondence, had become an instrument of radicalism.[56]

Gennochi and Loisy agreed upon general principles of method—the necessity, for example, of integrating the discoveries of archaeological digs in the Middle East with historical and biblical scholarship; or of comparing biblical texts to recently discovered Semitic texts that placed the Holy Writ in its proper, if less extraordinary, context; or of rejecting traditional Roman assumptions, based on scriptural passages, about the age of the world in light of new geological discoveries. However, Gennochi felt strongly that, as a Catholic exegete, one must pose constantly a central methodological question: how and to what extent is exegesis to be independent from the impact of scientific discovery? In other words, what elements, if any, in the sacred texts are to be exempt from the probe of scientific criticism? Are there elements in Scripture that overwhelm mere history, that cannot be wholly apprehended by mere science?

To Gennochi, Loisy had answered these questions with the aid of an a prioristic personal philosophy; but historical method was not to be confused with philosophical method. Loisy countered that his "philosophy" proceeded from *a posteriori* considerations derived from established historical conclusions, and thus was more valid or legitimate than philosophical principles held in the service of theology.[57] In the estimation of Gennochi the scholar must respect the distinction between the role of criticism on one hand and the claims of philosophy and theology on the other. Like many other modernist scholars,[58] Gennochi sought support for this dichotomy in a revised theory of biblical inspiration that limited divine inspiration to matters of faith and morals alone; and like them he too was discredited in Rome for this endeavor.

There is, again, no way of knowing how much of the particulars of this debate Gennochi shared with the seminarians at Dunwoodie or with Driscoll himself. But two things point to Gennochi's influence on the program of modernism at Dunwoodie. First, on the controverted questions outlined above, the editorial stance of the journalistic organ of the seminary program, the *New York Review*, adopted Gennochi's more moderate positions and rejected those of Loisy.[59] Second, Gennochi did attract at least a modest following among the Dunwoodie seminarians, four of whom—John J. Mitty (the future Archbishop of San Francisco), Edwin Ryan, Daniel W. Sheerin, and Francis X. E. Albert—traveled to Rome after their ordination to study with him. In 1907 Farley received reports that these young priests were "consorting" with "a known modernist." [60]

The second prominent figure to enjoy close ties with Driscoll and to appear before the seminary faculty and student body at Dunwoodie was Charles A. Briggs of Union Theological Seminary in New York. Known for his protracted battles with Presbyterian conservatives over biblical inerrancy and inspiration,[61] Briggs had, by the time of his lectures at Dunwoodie, fled to the Episcopal church and embraced a new, if related, cause—ecumenism.

The main components of Briggs's approach to these topics were in position as early as 1883 with the publication of *Biblical Study: Its Principles, Methods and History* in which the author described theology itself as a modern science. According to Briggs exegetical theology was the fundamental discipline in the field of theology and proceeded from clear premises and by acknowledged empirical methods. The new science took as its object of investigation "the sacred Scriptures, their origin, history, character, exposition, doctrine, and rules of life" and is, Briggs maintained,

> true to the spirit and character of its fundamental discipline, is open-eyed for all truth, courts investigation and criticism of its own materials and methods, and does not assume a false position of dogmatism and traditional prejudice, or attempt to tyrannize over the other sciences in their earnest researches after the truth.[62]

This was the only method of theology that would assure for theology and the religious life it sought to articulate, an ongoing and independent role in American culture. Its primary scientific task was to determine the essence of biblical teaching above and beyond its cultural entrapments. The cultural and historical environment in which the text was composed would be identified and thus relegated to its proper, minor role in theology. Only in this way could the Bible escape the particular worldview under which it was written and appear "ever new" to each age. Briggs urged his colleagues at Union to employ the new historico-critical methods as tools in building a comprehensive biblical theology. Otherwise, he warned, the traditionalists would lead organized religion into oblivion. The conservatives failed to appreciate the irony of their situation: they threatened to become what they feared most, namely, prisoners of cultural religion. They had avoided the perils of modern culture by embracing and elevating to normative status the particularities of the culture of the Yahwist tradition or of first-century Hellenism. By refusing to recognize and allow for the culture-bound form of all expressions of religious sentiment, even those of the Bible, they trapped the liberating message of Scripture inside the worldview of a bygone era. The inevitable result of this undue subservience to culture would be creedal dogmatism, the absolutizing of the text itself, and eventually the trivializing of every aspect of scriptural religion.[63]

Briggs for some time tried to keep one foot in the door of Presbyterian orthodoxy by stressing that the Bible remained the sole infallible norm of religion. He did this by privileging the Bible over the various historic creeds derived from particular readings of it. "Every catechism and confession of faith will in time become obsolete and powerless," for each age has its unique needs that no one creed can entirely satisfy without losing its timeless appeal. "It is sufficient that the Bible gives us the material for all ages and leaves to man the noble task of shaping the material so as to suit the wants of his own time."[64]

Few in American Protestantism before or after Briggs put forth the case for a modernist synthesis more bluntly or unguardedly. Unlike other thinkers along the liberal-modernist trajectory, he made no concerted effort to convince his opponents that he was reclaiming a lost or neglected tradition of theology from Christian history. What he proposed was radically unprecedented but necessary. He did argue, however, that the traditionalists were ill-named: their literalism enjoyed no long-standing source in Christianity. It too was a spontaneous response to the highly charged atmosphere of modernity.[65]

After joining the Episcopalian priesthood in 1899, Briggs turned his attention to the young ecumenical movement. Thus he entered the halls of St. Joseph's Seminary with a keen interest in promoting modern methods of biblical study as an avenue of creedal reformulation and of increased cooperation among Christian denominations. Clearly, Briggs's espousal of modernism had moved him, perhaps ironically, to a position of greater sympathy with the ideas of European Catholic modernists regarding doctrinal development. Accordingly, he was more tolerant than many of his coreligionists regarding certain traditional Roman Catholic teachings—on purgatory, free will, and sanctification, to name a few—and hoped to promote modern biblical criticism as a primary means of increasing understanding between liberal Protestant and Catholic scholars. His contributions to Driscoll's program of modernism at Dunwoodie must be seen in this light.[66]

The list of guest lecturers at Dunwoodie during these years extended beyond these two controversial scholars, including figures who were more than sympathetic to Driscoll's endeavors to reform seminary training. Walter Elliott, for example, whose biography of Hecker launched the United States church into the Americanist controversy, extolled the virtues of his mentor and uncovered the implications of his thought for Catholic mission work and catechesis. And the professor of dogmatics at St. Bernard's Seminary, Rochester, Edward J. Hanna, first contributed to Driscoll's program of studies by lecturing on the relationship between dogma and piety.[67]

Driscoll's program required not only that visiting scholars enliven the staid academic environment of the seminary, but also that the seminarian occasionally flee that environment and experience learning in a secular, urban setting in which, after all, most of the seminarians would be working. They attended classes at New York University and, by special arrangement between Driscoll and Columbia President Nicholas Murray Butler, they enrolled in Columbia as graduate students, attending classes in a variety of disciplines. Driscoll would not allow the educational process to be confined to the grounds of the seminary or to the texts of Aristotle and Aquinas. He did, indeed, seem to be "leading the American priesthood into a new day."[68]

Driscoll and his colleagues were not content to limit their program of modernism to the seminarians in their charge; they sought a broader and more influential audience. They wanted no less than to reeducate the American clergy in the most recent religious ideas and methodologies, to introduce them to the work of European priests and scientists transforming the agenda of theology. To accomplish this goal, the priests at Dunwoodie founded a journal of "ancient faith and modern thought."

4. *The* New York Review: *A Journal of Modernist Thought*

The journal that the priests at Dunwoodie founded, the *New York Review*, was dedicated to educating the American Catholic clergy in the ideas and methodologies that, in just three years, would come to be known as "modernism."[1] During the brief span of its life (1905–1908), the editors published dozens of articles by men and women whose careers and reputations were to be tarnished as a result of *Pascendi*, including George Tyrrell, Maude Petre, American Paulist William L. Sullivan, Henri Bremond, Joseph Turmel, and Ernesto Buonaiuti.[2] The editors continued to praise and solicit contributions from George Tyrrell even after he was excommunicated. Other articles in the *Review* were authored by leading Protestant modernists such as Paul Sabatier. American Catholics from Dunwoodie and from Catholic University also contributed to the journal, and Driscoll and Gigot authored articles on the new methods of textual and historical criticism of the Bible and on the debate over the theory of inspiration and inerrancy.[3]

Through these articles, editorials, and book reviews, the editors of the *Review* presented to their readers a renewed vision of the Catholic past, a reinterpretation of traditional teachings and, most significantly, a definite alternative to the scholastic program of theology, biblical studies, and church history. The journal was, in that sense, a primer of the modernist worldview. It presented the nuances of the historico-critical method, adopted a developmentalist framework for understanding the work of the Holy Spirit in the church, opened its pages to immanentist thought, and addressed with critical rigor the questions of authority and reform in the church. In so doing, the *New York Review* was unprecedented in the history of American Catholic publications. The editors recognized from the beginning that they

117

were the heralds of, and would-be contributors to, a twentieth-century synthesis of traditional Catholic belief and modern thought.

This awareness was evident in the planning process for the *Review*. In correspondence explaining the purposes of the new journal, the editors, Driscoll and Duffy, emphasized that they would solicit contributions from "the foremost Catholic scholars of the United States, England and France—men who are really in touch with modern thought and its problem, and who are both able and willing to discuss them from the modern point of view."[4] Two months before the appearance of the first issue the editors distributed to Catholic and non-Catholic periodical offices and educational centers some 25,000 flyers announcing the purpose of their imminent publication. The *Review* would treat in a scholarly manner topics of interest in philosophy, theology, and biblical studies, presented in such a way that the educated American might grasp their implications. The articles, the flyer claimed, were designed to "draw attention to the needs of the intellectual situation in matters of religious belief"; the various authors could be expected to provide "discussion and solution of the problems and difficulties connected with Religion."[5] Driscoll promised that the review would aid the "gradual assimilation by theology of what is sound in modern scholarship" by "interpret[ing] . . . the old truths in the light of the new science."[6]

The professors at Dunwoodie were uniquely suited to the task of coordinating the various streams and emphases of liberal and modernist thought during the first decade of the twentieth century. Three of the five major staff members had studied with the leading scholars in Europe. In addition to Driscoll and Gigot, Rev. Joseph Bruneau, S.S., the acquisitions editor for the *Review*, had formed lasting friendships with Loisy, Marie Joseph Lagrange, and Henri Bremond. Through his publications in biblical studies Bruneau had established a reputation as a critical thinker.[7] He was probably the staff member responsible for soliciting articles from European modernists. Thus it was with great regret that Bruneau left the seminary and his work on the journal in 1906. He was the only one of the six Sulpicians there who refused to secede with the others from the society. Nonetheless, his later works on theology and philosophy placed him under suspicion in Rome.[8]

These priests sought to describe the progressive development of Catholic truth. The scriptural citation that opened each issue of the *Review* proclaimed that "Every scribe who is instructed in the kingdom of heaven is like a man that is a householder, who bringeth forth out of his treasures, things new and old (Mt. 13:52)." Editors of other Catholic periodicals seemed to recognize the innovative character of the *Review* and the ambition of its editors. The editors of the *Catholic World* acknowledged the importance of the proposed enterprise:

> It has become almost a truism among us that the Church's greatest need, today, is a genius who would do for our age what St. Thomas did for his, which was to bring our theological system into harmony with the advancing gains in secular knowledge. But no commanding intellect like that of the great Dominican has been vouchsafed to the Church in these later days. Indeed, the vast growth of the sciences forbids the possibility that, ever again, one single mind within the compass of a lifetime should be equal to the forming of a synthesis of science and theology. The task must be achieved by many men working under one co-ordinating principle, along many distinct lines. The *New York Review* promises to be one such co-ordinating principle.[9]

The *New York Review* did, indeed, intend to play a coordinating role for the American church in the task of constructing a synthesis of science and theology. The editors of the journal had a coherent plan. The synthesis would be framed within a religious worldview in which the will of God was seen as unfolding over time rather than given in completeness all at once. The divine will was seen further as seeking expression in a variety of human religious experiences rather than through an elite class forming a predominant school of interpretation. The two foundational principles of this worldview were consistently invoked in the pages of the *Review*. The first was the concept of immanence—the immediate, indwelling presence of the divine life in the individual subject—and the implications of this concept for Catholic understanding of the nature of the relationship between the human community and the divine, the nature of genuine religious experience, and the nature of divine self-revelation. In elaborating these implications the writers for the *Review* took care to demonstrate that the concept of immanence enjoyed an authentically Catholic and, in fact, an authentically scholastic history. Second, the sources of divine revelation were to be reconsidered in light of this retrieved emphasis on divine immanence. As inspired human expressions of the intimate, ongoing relationship with God codified in the term "immanence," the sources of revelation—scripture and tradition—could be reexamined and reinterpreted in light of, and with the assistance of, the modern philosophical turn to the personal, the experiential, and the historical. These themes overlapped in the pages of the *New York Review* but can also be seen as distinct issues.

"THE NEW APOLOGETICS": RETRIEVING A NOTION OF VITAL IMMANENCE IN RELIGIOUS EXPERIENCE

The first issue provided an accurate reflection of the themes of the seventeen numbers that were to follow. The opening article, by Wilfrid Ward, was a statement of commitment to modern apologetics. As did the modernists in Europe, Driscoll and Gigot sought in Cardinal Newman an orthodox mentor. Therefore the opening article of the *Review* celebrated "The Spirit of Newman's Apologetics." Ward characterized Newman as the champion of the loyal opposition to neo-scholasticism: "He saw truly that the questions raised, the modes of thought determining men's deepest convictions, are now largely different from those which obtained in the thirteenth century." Ward compared the rise of historical and scientific consciousness in modernity to the equally determinative passion for syllogism and logic that dominated twelfth- and thirteenth-century thought:

> If St. Thomas was the first doctor of the Church under the new intellectual regime of the thirteenth century—the regime which combined the wisdom of the fathers with the Aristotelian culture—Newman may prove to be the first of the new series which is to show us how the essential teachings of the Catholic tradition may be combined with due recognition of the claims of the positive sciences in the nineteenth and twentieth centuries.

Newman had called for freedom for those specialists working in the sphere of physical and historical sciences—a freedom, Ward wrote, "untrammeled by the premature, often ignorant, interference of theological critics." The new *Review*, dedicated as it was to reporting the conclusions of scientists and historians in matters affecting religious belief, must enjoy that same freedom in order to succeed. Quoting Newman's axiom, "Heretical questionings have been transmuted by the living power of the Church into salutary truths," Ward called for the Holy Office to tolerate deviations from the received faith, for false starts are part of the process of creating a new synthesis.[10] Ward explained that the immanentist strain in Newman's thought was no less than an element of the Catholic faith that had been suppressed by the "supernatural rationalism" of the scholastic method. In the *Grammar of Assent*, Newman had retrieved the mystical emphases in the Catholic theological tradition. The process whereby the human mind can justify belief in religion is not, Newman maintained, a matter of mere dialectic or rational investigation; indeed, human reasons and premises of belief must include that sense of the presence of God in the human conscience.[11]

Ward's tone-setting lead article was followed in the first issue by George Fonsegrive's commentary on the differences between modern Catholicism and free thought. Fonsegrive defined religion as a style of life, a "concrete" fact, informed but not determined by scientific knowledge. Science would place its conclusions at the foot of religion for assimilation. Free critical research, Fonsegrive wrote, "is a method indispensable for the begetting of science, but . . . when results are really attained, this method no longer serves a purpose."[12] Science could not threaten faith, for science dealt in theory and abstract speculations, whereas religion was eminently practical. Historical science, for example, could not undermine the historical "facts" on which Christianity is based, because these "facts" are to be tested only by the practical rules that hold in matters of actual conduct. Here, the scientific method did not reach. "For religion is a life, a series of actual concrete deeds, of separate acts of intellect, will and heart," he concluded, "[and] there is not a single religious action which is purely intellectual."[13]

The centerpiece of the first issue was "Scotus Redivivus," an article by James J. Fox of Catholic University of America that attempted to demonstrate that the new thought was grounded primarily in venerable Catholic intellectual traditions rather than in modern ideology or philosophy. Unfortunately these intellectual traditions had been overshadowed by a sterile and monolithic neo-scholasticism. The jubilee year of the dogma of the Immaculate Conception had resulted in "bringing forward honorably from comparative oblivion" the fame of John Duns Scotus, the medieval rival to Aquinas. "The present movement for his canonization," Fox stated, "is welcomed by everybody as the vindication of a name that, owing to the long reign of a rival influence, has borne much unmerited obloquy."[14]

The rehabilitation of Scotus was, Fox maintained, providential in light of the particular needs of the faithful in the modern era. In contrast to the Thomist school, Scotus had emphasized the supremacy of the will over the intellect and had limited the role of reason in apprehending metaphysical reality and religious truth. Scotus had applied this formulation to a number of fundamental theological questions: the nature of God, free will, predestination, and the act of faith. Fox judged this philosophical turn "potent enough, if not to lay in ruins the fair edifice of Thomistic intellectualism, at least to weaken it with a mighty rent," and announced that the "New Apologetics," to be demonstrated and advocated by the *New York Review*, was predicated upon it—in spite of the fact that it was identified by some with Kantian agnosticism. These modern religious apologists recognized that the mind of the great Franciscan possessed, "in a higher degree than any other scholastic mind, the characteristics which constitute what is called, to-day, the scientific spirit. This spirit will accept nothing as true and established until it is supported by reasons that compel conviction." On that basis Scotus rejected the preponderance of theological and philosophical propositions accepted by other scholastics as based on rational proof. He taught that propositions of faith are to be reached only through revelation, grasped by an act of faith in which the will dominates the intellect. "The limitations which Scot attributes to reason in search of religious truth are, at first sight, little short of shocking," Fox admitted, especially "to one who has been nurtured in the text-books of scholastic philosophy." There are many truths, Duns Scotus taught, that are outside the boundaries of rational proof—the existence of a personal Supreme Being, the immortality of the soul, the existence of future reward and punishment, to name a few—but of which Christians possess the certainty of faith.[15]

Fox recognized that this teaching was not yet accepted by Roman Catholic theology in official quarters. He cited the proclamation of Vatican I that from created things reason, unaided by revelation, may reach with certitude a knowledge of God, the Creator. But, Fox declared, that old way of understanding religious faith and life must give way to another venerable viewpoint, one that spoke to modern sensibilities:

> We have touched the point where present day thought finds itself in harmony with Scot. There prevails a widely spread impression that the dialectic objective proofs offered by our old apologetics, formed on the line of intellectualism, cannot be depended upon exclusively for the defense of the fundamental truths of religion. The mind of the age subjects them to the same pitiless, unrelenting criticism that they underwent in the mind of the Scot, with the same result. And, with the advance of knowledge, criticism

has come into possession of an apparatus of tests far beyond those that were at his disposal. . . . Those Catholic thinkers who have withdrawn their confidence from the old method do not, generally, impugn the objective value of the traditional system, but consider that, however perfect, judged by the standards of abstract reasoning, it may be, it does not attain its purpose, which is to convince.[16]

Like Ward, Fox judged Cardinal Newman to be the father of the new apologetics and theology, and credited him with initiating the revival of Scotist thought. Fox pointed out that Newman had never denied that right reason can attain to real truth; however, Newman directed his thought not to the theoretical possibility but to the concrete fact, namely, how reason operated "in fallen man." Considering the use of human reason "actually and historically," Newman judged that it tended towards agnosticism. "The fact of revelation is in itself demonstrably true," Fox paraphrased Newman, "but it is not therefore true irresistibly. . . . I cannot convert men when I ask for assumptions which they refuse to grant me; and, without assumptions, no one can prove anything."[17]

Newman had inspired the new apologetics by endorsing a "method of immanence." The neo-scholastic method confused faith with rational science and thus reduced the believer to his intellect. The dialectical, metaphysical, and historical proofs of the traditional methods of apologetics, addressed to a logical faculty conceived of as serene, impartial, and undisturbed by the volitional element of personality, failed to convince the modern mind. In its place, Fox explained, the new school held that "the apprehension of truth—at least of religious and moral truth—is an act of the entire moral personality rather than a function of the speculative intellect alone." Between science and faith there is a mysterious abyss that cannot be bridged by any process of intellect. "Christianity is not only a representation, it is a life; it appertains not only to logic, but also to conduct: it belongs in the first place to the category of being and only secondarily to that of thought. Hence the appropriation of religious truth demands something more than a passive attitude of intellect, the rigid energy of logical deduction, or the analytic ways of positive science."[18]

In this way the new apologetics set the epistemological foundations for a radically renewed vision of Christian faith and life. Prefigured are the modernist emphases on moral activity and social action, dynamic faith and the progressive journey to understanding. Science cannot threaten this vital faith if dogma is not equated with abstract, speculative reason. Fox prescribed that the scholastic definition of faith—*adequatio rei et intellectus*—be replaced by an immanentist version—*adequatio rei et spiritus*. "Truth—religious and moral—is the harmony between the objective thing and the entire personality, will as well as intellect," he wrote, "[and] the readiest argument for God and the moral law [is in] the proved harmony between these realities and the moral element within us. . . . "[19]

For his part Fox could not appreciate the controversy caused by the adoption of this "new" method by certain Catholic scholars. The critics, he argued, did not fully understand its meaning or the claims made for it. "That it has been accused of the two opposite tendencies, rationalism and fideism, affords fair presumption that it contains neither one or the other." The critics tend to exaggerate and thus distort its positions, Fox claimed. A case in point was their erroneous charge of fideism: "Certainly the evidence for religious truth drawn from its correspondence with the soul and its effects upon personality and life must, in the last analysis, be apprehended and applied by reason—[but] by reason judging from the inner experience of the entire soul."[20]

Perhaps most radical of the ideas proposed in the pages of the *New York Review* were those with ecclesiological implications. Fox applied this fluid, developmentalist, Spirit-inspired model of faith to the church itself, with results that could only trouble traditionalists. He wrote that aspects of the church, including doctrinal and juridical authority, "are living realities of the divine order; as such, they correspond to a need of the religious consciousness." This perspective, he insisted, prevented the church from appearing to be "a heterogeneous system imposed on the spirit from without." The faith would be seen as a living, and lived, reality. Furthermore, under the new perspective, the church would be immune from the advances of science. The scholastic method had mistakenly tried to beat science at its own game; but the new theology insisted that "the evidence for moral and religious truth need not be, cannot be, of the same exclusively intellectual character as that required in speculative science." The new theology rejected the assumptions of modern science—that "truth" could be obtained, for example, only by the logical methods of science—lending balance to the traditional approach and preserving the integrity of Christianity:

Immanence does not aim to destroy, but to supplement intellectualism, which has hitherto had a free hand to shape the campaign against modern unbelief. Its success has not been so complete as to justify it in rejecting any help that may be offered to it. Criticism—biblical, historical, philosophical—is making plain that many breaches are to be repaired, many weak points strengthened; that historical fact and historically demonstrable fact are not convertible terms. Modern knowledge and the scientific spirit have demolished so many ancient prepossessions, have reduced to natural proportions so many things that were once supposed to belong to the transcendental, that the age is extremely suspicious of the miraculous. The a priori is distrusted.[21]

The faith must, then, reconcile itself to the disposition of the modern age: its concern, for example, for moral values, the ethical injunctions of the Gospel, and the building of character. "It is to this spirit that the new apologetics addresses itself," Fox concluded.[22]

These were insights particularly appealing to priests influenced by Isaac Hecker's early immanentist thought. The Holy Spirit was the dynamic force stirring belief and religious fervor in the United States—not the dry logic of the scholastic manuals. American Catholics, in reexamining their cherished notions about the religious life, would do well, the editors of the *New York Review* implied, to recall this long-standing tradition of thought exemplified by Scotus, Newman, and Hecker. To demonstrate the continuity between the European and American cases, Driscoll and Duffy paired Fox's article with one on the thought of Isaac Hecker, "The Church and the Soul," by Paulist Joseph McSorley.

Hecker's portrayal of the religious life as active, even dynamic, mined a rich vein of pragmatism in the American character. It would respond dramatically, McSorley suggested, to a renewed understanding of the church that reflected the worth of the energetic efforts of the individual believer. "Let the Church be revealed, in doctrine and in deed, as the indispensable aid of the aspiring soul," he demanded. He contended that nothing would serve the church better than to set as its main object the promotion of personal holiness and the diffusion of knowledge concerning its work of spiritual development. This is what modern Americans yearned for. This could be accomplished, McSorley insisted, without harm to the traditional self-understanding of the church. The new theologian sought balance, not revolution.

"The action of the Holy Spirit embodied visibly in the authority of the Church," Hecker himself had written, "and the action of the Holy Spirit dwelling invisibly in the soul, form one inseparable synthesis."[23]

As anticipated in these themes of the first issue, a substantial portion of the journal was devoted, over a three year period, to a subtle critique of nineteenth-century scholasticism, accompanied by an ongoing demand that modern methods of critical investigation of religion be incorporated into Roman Catholic theology and philosophy. These articles and editorial "Notes" proposed to balance Thomistic principles and concepts with those of other influential Catholic thinkers of the past, the most prominent of which was Cardinal Newman. Two contributors, David Barry and Thomas J. Gerrard, submitted for publication a series of articles in this vein.[24]

Gerrard's "Newman and Conceptualism," which appeared on the eve of the condemnation of modernism, sought to defend the English divine from charges that he was a conceptualist and, by implication, very nearly an atheist. These slanders, Gerrard wrote, were fomented by "a school of ultra-scholastics whose minds are so fixed in the scholastic groove that they cannot possibly see the truth except from their own standpoint." The scholastic standpoint "is not the only true one." At this stage of the "trajectory of modernism" in American Catholic thought, it was enough to argue that scholasticism, inadequate in itself to the task of constructing a modern apologetic, be supplemented by various methods and insights that were also genuinely Catholic. Thus Gerrard judged it an asset, rather than a liability, that Newman was not indebted to scholastic philosophy. "If therefore he has built an independent structure complete in itself yet not out of harmony with scholastic thought," Gerrard wrote, "we have all the more reason to admire his genius."[25]

Gerrard demonstrated that Newman and the scholastics drew upon the same basic sources for their respective theologies and philosophies, namely, the church fathers. But the integralists refused to admit that Newman's thought was in harmony with their own; instead, they charged that Newman ignored the scholastic doctrine of universals and challenged the "moderate realism" of scholastic doctrine. In Gerrard's evaluation, the nineteenth-century "ultra scholastics" had thus repeated an error they made with countless other thinkers. Rather than see Newman's work in its full integrity and consider its stated purpose—"the sole object of the work was to show how, without having recourse to the scholastic method or any other theory of thought, the mind could arrive at practical certitude"—the integralists insisted on reading Newman "through scholastic spectacles" and expressing "Newman forms in scholastic forms."[26] By interpreting all thought according to their own presuppositions and evaluating ideas by their own categories, the neo-scholastics imposed inflexible and, for Gerrard, unbearable requirements on Catholic philosophy and theology.

The neo-scholastics disapproved of Newman because he made the "turn to experience" the starting point of his reflections; his intention was not, however, Gerrard wrote, to formulate a theory to counter scholasticism, but to present an analysis of phenomena suitable to an age that "had acquired a distaste for a priori reasoning." "His method was not a breaking away, either conscious or unconscious, from the method of the schools," Gerrard insisted, "it was a transcending of or prescinding from it." Gerrard concluded his article with a mild denunciation of those who ignored completely the "implicit and purely subjective evidence" of experience because they "are so absorbed in abstractions that these things become to them the 'realities' of life"; they would "rather be converted by the smart syllogism" than by the "less strictly logical basis" of conviction inspired by lived experience.[27]

A return to a true catholicity of theology, philosophy and apologetics within the Church of Rome, Gerrard maintained, would restore to its proper place in the understanding of revelation and the act of faith the idea that "there must be in each individual soul a detailed exigency for the detailed truths of faith." As we have seen, the neo-scholastics disavowed this "need" in fear that the objective givenness of revelation might otherwise be lost. Nonetheless Gerrard insisted upon

> the right of those who favor the subjective method of apologetic to pursue their work without incurring the suspicion of heterodoxy. It is the right of those who seek the Catholic truth by the more personal way—and they constitute by far the majority of our converts—to do so without afterwards being considered only half-converted.[28]

Gerrard emphasized that this pluralism in approach was not new or distinctively modern, but one with the "ancient faith." The subjective method of apologetics would not displace the scholastic method but, in fact, strengthen it:

> There is a head-logic and there is a heart-logic. They are not contradictory; they are complementary. The syllogism has its

place in the great scheme of truth, but it is only the skeleton of truth . . . it is the honest humble endeavor of the school of subjective apologists to make a scientific presentment of that exigency (of the human soul for divine truth). After all, the masterpiece of St. Thomas is but a summa, a synopsis. It needs a Newman to show us how to breathe into it a spirit of Life. It is possible to be a thoroughgoing disciple of St. Thomas and of Cardinal Newman at the same time. The name of Newman stands unquestionably for a sign of the truthfulness of the Catholic priesthood. Similarly, it may be held up for a sign of the right to approach the Living Truth as Christ said it must be approached, not first by reason and syllogism, but first by the whole heart and the whole soul and the whole strength and lastly, "with all thy mind."[29]

The condemnation of modernism did not deter Gerrard, nor the editors of the *New York Review*, from developing these themes in 1908. In a follow-up to "Newman and Conceptualism," Gerrard continued his explication of the compatibility of Newman's thought, properly interpreted, with Thomism. He set forth his vision of a new theological and philosophical synthesis for which "St. Thomas provides a skeleton and Cardinal Newman clothes it with flesh and skin and makes it live."[30]

Newman pursued philosophical reflection in a modern context, "assuming nothing," acting as a whole, integrated person rather than as intellect detached from will and emotion, testing each theory or concept by concrete experience. For Gerrard and for many other contributors to Driscoll's journal,[31] this approach was appealing and in keeping with Aquinas's own doctrine of the whole man. Based upon a series of such parallels between Newman and Aquinas, Gerrard felt himself to be "in a position to draw the parallels together and to make a synthesis." Whether the projected third article in the series would have made good on this claim is a matter of speculation, for the *New York Review* ceased publication three months later, in part as a result of suspicions that its contributors fancied themselves builders of a modernist "synthesis."[32]

This occurred in spite of efforts by contributors such as David Barry to portray the positions of the editors of the journal as moderate, mediating between the extremes of neo-scholasticism and modernism. This author presumed, five months after *Pascendi*, to sketch "the true function of experience in belief." This was necessary, he felt, not only because the modernists had distorted the question by "repudiating miracles and prophecy," but also due to the equally exaggerated response of their opponents. In short, Barry did not want submission to the encyclical and resort to the traditional method of apologetics to cause the church to lose sight of the significant truths in the modernist position. "And there is a danger for those who do not realize that as a rule error is merely an exaggeration of the truth," he cautioned, "that they would disclaim the aid of our individual experience, not only as an exclusive basis of faith, but even as a valuable auxiliary in confirming us in its profession when we have obtained it through external revelation." To anticipate this reaction and counter it, Barry thought it well to consider "cases where it is specially manifest that the firmness and vividness of our belief... are due to our experience of the pleasure and benefit of the living of the supernatural life." Barry would not go so far as to teach, as certain modernists allegedly did, that one's own personal experience of the immanent God led to the "actual inception" of belief, that personal experience "caused" faith. But, he averred, it did promote faith. In order to thrive, the external truths of faith must find "corroboration" in one's lived experience of the Holy Spirit:

> once we accept the faith, we find that these truths are corroborated, and our loyalty and cooperation with them are rewarded by the working of the Holy Spirit in our souls, who disposes all things sweetly for those who love Him. His yoke is sweet and His burden light, and our individual experience and consciousness of this truth is of the first importance in the economy of our spiritual life.[33]

Barry's article was an encomium to the vitality of Catholic religious experience, a reinterpretation of the tradition as distinctively founded on the workings of the Divine Spirit in the lives of ordinary Christians. By the "loyalty and devotion that even the ordinary uneducated faithful have to their religion," there exists a set of distinctive religious experiences, many of them mediated by the church, that bind each individual to the body in a unique way. Barry judged that "the Protestant hostility to some of our most cherished beliefs arises largely from the fact that they cannot be adequately appreciated except through experience."

Barry did not explore, nor fully acknowledge, the potential conflict between this emphasis on personal experience and the received Roman Catholic position on the role of authority. Instead, he introduced a subtle equation that many modernists would have endorsed: "our experience of the workings of God's grace in our souls, and our experience of the value of certain doctrines to our spiritual life have a share with authority in convincing the intellect of religious truth and in moulding the heart to virtue."[34] He did not elaborate on the extent or limits of this "share" with authority, but recommended the testing of "the value of certain doctrines" by their suitability as expressions of "our experience of the workings of God's grace in our souls." Indeed, Barry turned the received teaching to his advantage. If the Catholic can affirm even one doctrine on the basis of his personal experience, he suggested, then that affirmation carries with it "strong presumptive evidence of the truth of the other doctrines of the same Church as well." The appropriate contemporary principle of integration of the faith was the common spiritual experience of the faithful rather than an *a priori* network of doctrines imposed from above by a neo-scholastic hierarchy. Barry borrowed this idea from English modernist George Tyrrell in his treatise "Lex Orandi, Lex Credendi": genuine apostolic Christianity had established a prominent role for individual and communal religious experience.[35]

In another issue William Turner reported the influence of a contemporary French school of pragmatism on Blondel and Laberthonnière. Turner pointed out the similarities and differences between French and American pragmatism. Both, for example, were interested in the application of their method to the study of religion. The French identified religion with a supernatural body of truth and the dogmatic teaching and sacramental system of the Catholic Church. Blondel, Laberthonnière, and others associated with the body of doctrine commonly described as *l'apologetique d'immanence*, Turner judged, shared many points of contact with the methods and principles of philosophical pragmatism. In spite of the "destructive" aspects of their method, these men were, in Turner's judgment, "first, and above all else, Apologists for the truth and transcendancy of Catholic dogma and Catholic institutions."[36]

In the last issue of the *New York Review*, editor Duffy provided the clearest example of the journal's dedication to the retrieval of a pluralism of method in theological and philosophical studies. As an expert in the history of scholasticism, Duffy was aware of the pluralism of interpretations and application of the scholastic method since the thirteenth century, and thus objected to the tendency of certain Romanists of his era to "define" scholastic philosophy. Even *Pascendi* did not confine the term "scholasticism" to one particular school of interpretation, Duffy argued, even if the pope instructed priests "that the scholastic philosophy we prescribe is that which the Angelic Doctor has bequeathed to us." In Duffy's interpretation, "this, however, is evidently offered by the Holy Father not as a definition but as a limitation of the term."[37] Scholasticism itself was more fluid and adaptable to the modern era than its most prominent ecclesiastical proponents would allow. Duffy insisted that scholars agreed only that scholastic philosophy included a certain set of methods developed over a long period of time, a distinctive approach to dogmatics, and a unique theory about universals.[38]

Most revealing were Duffy's criticisms of Louvain Professor DeWulf's *Scholasticism Old and New: An Introduction to Scholastic Philosophy, Medieval and Modern*, especially the author's "unsubstantiated" assumption that scholastic philosophy was applicable to modern day problems. "The author sketches briefly, at times too briefly," Duffy complained, "the present-day questions on which the neo-scholastic philosophy has, or should have, a word to say." Most grievous to Duffy was DeWulf's facile acceptance of the neo-scholastic refusal to engage "a problem which overshadows all the rest—and which our neo-scholastics handle very gingerly—the question of evolution."

Duffy made it clear that he found turn-of-the-century neo-scholasticism inadequate to the challenges of the modern American milieu and in need of revision:

> Dr. DeWulf, though an ardent and successful defender of ancient principles, is an equally ardent, and, we hope, an equally successful advocate of modern methods. He would not do away with the methods of stating and solving philosophical questions which are traditional in the schools, but he would supplement them by modern historical methods of approach, study of the natural sciences, laboratory and seminar work, etc.[39]

"THE NEW APOLOGETICS": INCORPORATING THE HIGHER CRITICISM OF THE BIBLE AND THE IDEA OF DEVELOPMENT

In the same issue in which Ward, Fonsegrive, Fox, and McSorley developed the immanentist implications of developmentalist thought and proclaimed that faith, by their definition, had nothing to fear from critical researches, Driscoll, Duffy, Gigot, and Cornelius Clifford reported on the results of those critical researches. They addressed the question of the reconciliation of faith and science from the perspective of science.

Clifford reported on "Holtzmann's Life of Jesus." The German Bible critic analyzed the gospel accounts of Jesus' life with all the tools of literary and historical method—commenting, for example, on the theological presuppositions of the individual evangelists and their redaction of the narrative. Clifford found this approach to be convincing and free of prejudice. He was more hopeful than Fox that science and faith could ultimately complement one another as sources of religious knowledge, as "two separate but not necessarily opposed planes of thought."[40] Driscoll echoed this opinion in the first of a series of articles on "Recent Views on Biblical Inspiration." Admitting that his studies led him to a greater deference for the "substantial claims of scientific criticism," Driscoll argued that science could not be dismissed as troublesome; its conclusions must be applied to religious understanding, forging a renewed understanding. He was heartened that "the most eminent Catholic apologists and scripturists of the present day" were addressing the problem:

> Ever deferential to authority and maintaining firmly the just claims of the faith once delivered to the saints, they, at the same time, accept without misgiving or *arriere pensee,* albeit in a spirit of scholarly discrimination, the facts and inferences of modern criticism on their scientific face value. Thoroughly alive to the need of an adjustment between these facts and a certain traditional value, they are earnestly seeking to establish the basis of a more uniform solution of biblical difficulties on principles in harmony alike with the data of revealed truth in the scientific progress of the age.[41]

Driscoll remained confident that such harmony was ultimately possible. The opposition was not between faith and science, he repeated, but between inferences of the scientists and the theologians. He predicted a "peaceful issue of the present conflict."[42]

Vincent McNabb echoed this call for a pluralism in methodology in an article on "The Petrine Texts in the Fourth Gospel." After denying Johannine authorship of the Gospel, McNabb justified his departure from the received method of exegesis of the texts on Petrine supremacy. Without denying the value of scholastic presuppositions, he argued that the critical method was superior for modern biblicists:

A mere *a priori* way of dealing with biblical texts is sometimes valid and even valuable. Yet, at its best, it can never equal in validity or strength the *a posteriori* method which throughout the chronological order of ideas sees the continuity, growth, survival and validity of Christian dogmas and principles.[43]

It was precisely this *a posteriori* method that Pius X had condemned, yet McNabb applied this procedure to his study of the fourth gospel and concluded that its author "need not be looked upon as a sacred writer inspired by the Holy Ghost," but as a human historian informed or "inspired" by the things he heard and saw around him.

This treatment of Scripture was exactly the kind of reasoning that troubled the Roman neo-scholastics, who feared that the rejection of the received a priori methods of exegesis in favor of "scientific" procedures would lead the Catholic scholar to unsound, if not heretical, conclusions, and to a dangerous rearticulation of traditional Christian assumptions and concepts. McNabb combined the insights of the historian with the textual analysis of the exegete, unwittingly fulfilling *Pascendi's* description of the modernist as one who integrated an agnostic philosophy with the tools of the exegete and historian by writing a history of the evolution of the church. "To aid them in this they call to their assistance that branch of criticism that they call textual," the pope had written, ". . . it is quite clear that the criticism we are concerned with is an agnostic, immanentist and evolutionist criticism."

Furthermore, McNabb described the apostolic church as American and democratic in spirit and structure rather than Roman and hierarchical. In the ancient church, he wrote, practical needs outran the intellectual difficulties they suggested. The question of the hierarchy commanded more attention at times than even the question of the creed. Critical history demonstrated that Christian answers to both questions had evolved gradually through time. McNabb followed this criticism of nineteenth-century scholasticism with his own attenuated exercise in application of critical methods to Scripture and traditional development.[44] Thus his article exemplified the *New York Review*'s coverage of the new approaches to biblical scholarship. Other didactic articles surveyed new methods of interpreting church history, and the theological and philosophical bases of apologetics. These articles surveyed the incipient efforts of scholars who were employing the canons and criteria of scientific inquiry and producing provocative results.

Gigot's series of six articles on the higher criticism of the Bible was the outstanding example of this category of articles. It was a cautious defense of the new discipline delivered via a sober and technical discussion of the relationship of the higher criticism to the doctrine of inspiration, the authority of the teaching church, and the traditional interpretations of key scriptural passages. Gigot began with a recognition that the very name "higher criticism" posed a problem, in that it promoted the image of a self-laudatory, rationalistic tribunal bespeaking judgment over the Bible. To many it seemed "simply a euphemistic term to denote the aim and principles of unbelief. . . synonymous with Rationalism." And, Gigot acknowledged, many people judged higher criticism to be an insidious effort to undermine faith in the Bible, and demanded that the inspired books be withdrawn from the province of critical investigation altogether. However, he wrote, "most men" discerned a human element in scripture because, though divine and inspired, the books of the Bible "bear the unmistakable impress of the time, place, style, and methods of composition of their respective authors." The Catholic bibilical scholar might reverently, yet scientifically, apply critical methods "to ascertain and determine the true origin and character of ancient writings."[45]

Here Gigot followed a method of presentation that he used in his textbooks on scripture and in all of his didactic pieces in the *New York Review*. Having thus stated the opposing positions on the question before him, he would proceed to question both the conservative position and the progressive interpretation. On this particular question his sympathies were evident. Without mentioning Loisy by name, Gigot recounted his story as an example of the necessity for the church to enter the discipline. Sincere believers in the Bible, Gigot contended, felt obliged to master higher criticism to counter those negative critics who employed it to attack religion. Of the pioneers in Catholic biblical criticism Gigot wrote:

> They knew that they could only meet these negative critics on their own grounds and that they had nothing to fear for the faith that was in them from a strictly scientific investigation of the contents of Holy Scripture. And in point of fact their earnest efforts have often been crowned with the most brilliant results: for time and again it was given to these believing scholars to show either that the facts appealed to by their opponents were no facts at all, or that the irreligious theories, framed by the deniers of revelation, were not really borne out by a careful study of

the actual facts. Whence it appears that the "Higher Criticism" of the Bible should not necessarily be identified with the views and purposes of incredulity . . . like any other branch of human knowledge, if rightly cultivated, [it] must finally make for the cause of truth.[46]

Like Loisy in his debate with Harnack, the Scripture professor at Dunwoodie saw higher criticism as a weapon by which the Catholic faith might be defended from the critiques of rationalism, positivism, and empiricism. After distinguishing "Higher Criticism" (the historical and literary analysis of the Bible) from "Lower Criticism" (the analysis of the various texts and translations), Gigot concluded with an affirmation of the possibility of pursuing both types of criticism without threatening orthodoxy. Yet he gave a broad interpretation to the "province" within which the critic might work: any "questions referring to the literary form, the authenticity, the reliability, and integrity of the ancient books, whether secular or sacred, are the special object of the Higher Criticism and their study may, and should be, pursued without anti-scientific and anti-religious bias."[47]

In the second article of the series Gigot explored in detail the problems attendant upon the critic's attempt to discern the authorship, date, literary form, integrity, reliability, and theological presuppositions of the canonical writings. He mentioned, almost in passing, the demise of the mechanical theory of inspiration as well as the inadequacy of nineteenth-century attempts to avoid testing the accuracy of scientific and historical statements made by the authors. Gigot's immediate predecessors in the field of biblical studies asked little of the texts themselves, for "as long as they knew by the infallible teaching of the Church that all the books of the Bible were inspired," it did not occur to them to question the history, or literary form, or even the "purity of prophecy" of those books. These questions were viewed from the standpoint of authority; they were matters for the theologians to handle, not the critics.

But to Gigot this approach was no longer adequate or advisable. It would not do to rely upon "the data of Holy Writ" including "the words of our Blessed Savior" for accurate testimony on the authorship and historical character of certain books. In modern scholarship scientific investigation replaced authority in the task of revising church teaching on "non-revealed" questions. Without naming the integralists, Gigot seemed to refute their fundamental principle of exegesis and theology. The Bible, and theology springing from it, contained many different levels of teaching; only a portion of these doctrines were revealed to the church by God. He suggested that the integralist tendency "to present them all indiscriminately as directly and necessarily connected with the dogmas of the Catholic faith, would be a fatal mistake from the point of view of modern apologetics." The only sure means of meeting higher critics on their own ground would be to adopt the principles of the new exegesis, namely, that these questions of authorship, redaction, origin and history of the sacred texts are first secular questions, not to be placed under theological presuppositions and restrictions. Presumably, theology would take up where the task of critical exegesis left off.[48]

In supporting his position Gigot invoked an argument employed by his European colleagues who were, the next year, labelled "modernists." The idea of "a thoroughly scientific investigation" of scripture was hardly radical or even "modern," he insisted; in fact, one could point to a long line of "such great Christian scholars as Origen, St. Jerome, Eusebius" to prove that "the scientific study of the problems now dealt with by the Higher Criticism of the Bible is no novelty in the Catholic Church." Modern Catholic apologists and exegetes were simply treading, "however humbly, in the footsteps of the careful and able critics of past centuries." Indeed, even Pope Pius X seemed, to Gigot (as late as 1906), to be in support of "the true progress of the art of criticism." Gigot concluded with an unequivocal endorsement of the same method that Pius X would condemn unequivocally one year later:

> Thus, then, for the defense of the sacred writings of both Testaments, it is right not to consider the questions of criticism as decided once for all by the authority which may appear to be attached to "the usual exegesis of Scripture." It seems to be right likewise to examine these same questions with the same openmindedness which befits scientific investigation, and which alone causes one to be fully ready to gather up whatever particles of truth Higher Criticism may have discovered. In point of fact, it would be difficult to imagine a frame of mind more becoming an apologist of revealed truth, since he has nothing to fear for the solidity of defined belief.[49]

It was, of course, precisely on this statement—whether the new exegesis and apologetics posed a threat to "the solidity of defined belief"— that the Roman neo-scholastics differed with the modernists.

Gigot's third article in the series examined the general principles of the higher criticism of the Bible. The first of the principles was to examine the books of Scripture in their historical context with "all the distinctive features of individual human authorship," for, "as a rule, God acts through His creatures (in this case, the inspired writers) as if He had apparently no share in their work." Quoting Newman, Gigot contended that the Bible might be looked upon as uninspired.[50] This led to a second principle, which Gigot's detractors in the clergy deemed to be the introduction into Holy Writ of the notion of relativism, namely, that "the author of the work was a child of his day, and he meant his work to be used first by his contemporaries." Thus the critic was to gather as much data as possible on the social, moral, political, economic and religious conditions of the author's time and people, from which he might "with more or less moral certainty" infer the specific philosophical, apologetical and theological presuppositions of the author and the work itself—presuppositions that may or may not be shared by modern readers. The third principle of higher criticism followed directly from the second: no bit of "external evidence" was to be excluded *a priori* from the critical interpretation of the text. Gigot demanded that "every piece of information, whatever its origin, should be welcome." This might well include data supplied by the comparative study of Semitic languages, archaeological researches made in the Holy Land, other works of history and literature, etc. The student of higher criticism should hold bias neither for ancient principles nor modern opinions but seek "particles of truth wherever found." "Whatever is proved solid and good in time-honored positions, [the critic] will hold as precious gold," Gigot wrote, "and so will he do also with whatever amount of truth he perceives in modern views . . . nothing short of anti-scientific prejudice would prompt him to act otherwise."[51]

The final principle of higher criticism required that all theories regarding the composition, context, author, and presuppositions of the sacred writings be framed and tested in an *a posteriori* fashion. Following the scientific method Gigot insisted that ancient or modern interpretations of the biblical texts be conformable to "facts sufficiently ascertained" and in harmony with all available data. These theories and interpretations ought to be discarded "when they cannot be stretched any longer to offer a sufficient explanation for all ascertained data." The received method of biblical study should be relegated to the past:

As no number of *a priori* conceptions, however acute or often repeated, no amount of vague conjecture and strong feeling in favor of an opinion, can secure for that opinion a real scientific standing, so, in like manner . . . no number of preconceived notions, no amount of attachment to long-cherished solutions of Biblical problems, should betray us into a hasty . . . rejection of a theory which may have been slowly elaborated by generations of experts in critical matters. Pure and simple appeals to the dictum of authority, to the position of a school ancient or modern . . . will not weigh much against scientific theories. As theories must rest on facts, so must they be disposed of by appeals to facts.[52]

In thus applying the empirical standard of the modern sciences to the study and interpretation of the Bible, Gigot rejected the claim of his opponents that this process introduced empiricism into the very study of revelation.

Instead, Gigot described the constructive aspect of higher criticism in an attempt to overcome the impression that modern scholarship has only put forth negative positions, has "reopened, and left opened, questions which our ancestors regarded as settled." This seeming proclivity toward the destructive is understandable, suggested Gigot, given the extent and number of erroneous positions and "modifies the ancient opinions to the extent actually required by newly ascertained data." In order to accomplish this constructive task, modern critics "do not recoil from the use of methods which may appear rash and venturesome in the eyes of many," including an amount of speculation.[53]

As if anticipating criticism of this opinion, Gigot devoted his next article to the relationship between tradition and modern methods of biblical study. Repeating a dictum introduced previously, he taught that one must discriminate between the human and divine aspects of Scripture. The questions mooted by higher criticism did not belong to "the sacred sphere of Revealed doctrine." Questions of authorship, method of composition, and historical context of the book fell within the province of literary and historical criticism. If the critics are regarded by some as holding a bias against tradition, it is because they refuse to "ascribe the same infallibility to the pronouncements of tradition concerning mere literary and historical questions, as to the sacred teaching of tradition regarding doctrinal and moral matters." Here Gigot referred to traditional teaching as "human tradition" and applauded modern critics for not following it blindly. Instead, the

Catholic scholar "complies with his duty as a man of science, when, before endorsing tradition fully, he wishes to make sure that it fulfills all the conditions required for its validity."[54] Gigot believed that such men need not fear charges of heterodoxy; to the contrary, these faithful scholars were in the strongest position to guide the necessary work of reinterpreting and rearticulating traditions for belief by modern Roman Catholics:

> In the future, as in the past, [the higher critic] will therefore start his study . . . by consulting ancient traditions, and also by probing them, fully determined to abide by their verdict if he finds them solid, and only to the extent that they really are so . . . if he finds upon testing them, that they are only partly correct, he will preciously treasure up their actual amount of truth, diligently add to it whatever particle of truth he may detect in his other sources of information, and thus secure a re-statement of traditions that will make them acceptable to his fellow-workers; if on the contrary, the examination forces him to regard those traditions as groundless and unreliable, he will courageously discard them.[55]

Nineteenth-century scholastics would find the methodology of the modern critic objectionable. Also objectionable was the fact that Gigot, and his colleagues in New York and Europe, would prefer to submit critically-inspired revisions in the traditional statements about the Scriptures not to the ecclesiastical censors of the Vatican, but to an independent community of scholars. To the integralists, this was nothing short of an outright rebuke to the magisterium. Gigot refused to have higher criticism "bow its head before tradition, and to abide by all its dicta, right or wrong." Had not the learned Benedictines of the seventeenth and eighteenth centuries followed this same principle in producing for the world their "masterly critical edition of the Fathers and Writers of the Church"?[56]

In his final installment before the promulgation of *Pascendi*, Gigot carried these principles to their logical extreme. He characterized traditional views of the integrity, date, context, and authorship of the inspired writings as "human opinions susceptible of alteration." Hence, the proper attitude toward those "traditions" was not the more or less unthinking credulity of the ultraconservative who, absolutely wedded to the past, denies the lawfulness of any departure from them." Gigot set the highest premium on the objectivity of the higher critic, one who refuses to play the advocate of any particular position before the facts are in—only such objectivity in method would entertain the possibility of impressing the modern audience. As an impartial judge, free from bias, the critic examines and weighs evidence before formulating conclusions. Furthermore, this method dates back to Christian antiquity; the higher critic enjoys, then, "a powerful and constant means of success." Finally, his own conclusions are not perceived as infallible; in the cause of ever greater objectivity, the critic submits his work to the scrutiny of other scholars, ever able to refine and revise imperfect formulation or concepts. Gigot concluded this paean to higher criticism with a lengthy quotation from a Protestant exegete reviewing the progress of the discipline within the previous century.[57]

For the student of modernist influence upon American Catholic thought, Gigot's series of articles on the higher criticism raises basic questions. Was Gigot in any sense a modernist? Were some of his writings, even these primarily didactic articles, heretical? On the one hand, Gigot argued consistently and emphatically that critical methods be employed in the modern historical, literary, and textual studies of the Bible and promoted these methods to seminarians in the classroom and to his colleagues in the American priesthood who read the *New York Review*. Furthermore, many of Gigot's recommendations for biblical studies were similar to those of Loisy. For example, in separate articles treating of the historicity of certain characters in the Old Testament, he introduced the distinction between the actual historical existence of certain figures in the books of Job and Genesis and the virtues attributed by the text. They appear as spiritual allegories rather than historical figures, Gigot emphasized, but this is not to impugn their spiritual worth. Religion is not a matter of facts or "extrinsic" evidence, but a far more profound concept. Even the seemingly destructive elements of the higher criticism would, he asserted, contribute to the progress of vital religion.[58] He prescribed the procedure to be followed in the rearticulation of ancient traditions:

> State impartially the ancient traditions bearing on the point at issue, together with the chief grounds in their favor. Should they, upon the examination of these grounds, think that the traditions are but partially true, they carefully refrain from treating the traditional position as if altogether worthless. Much rather do they endeavor to determine the amount of truth contained therein and to modify the ancient opinions to the extent actually required by newly ascertained data.

In such passages Gigot did seem to advocate a "modernist" approach to Scripture study: he approved of the application of the higher criticism to the sources of revelation and endorsed the revision of traditional doctrines according to the results of this procedure. On the other hand, however, he did not question the very idea of dogma or the validity of the church's teaching authority in guiding the interpretation of Scripture. Nor did he address the question of the organic unity of the substantial belief and the traditional form by which it was conveyed.[59]

Nonetheless the procedures Gigot advocated in the passages quoted above were condemned by Pius X:

> The critic takes in hand the documents dealing with the history of faith and distributes them, period by period, so that they correspond with the list of needs always guided by the principle that the narration must follow the facts, as facts follow the needs . . . the rule holds that the age of any document can be determined only by the age in which each need has manifested itself in the Church. Further, a distinction must be made between the beginning of a fact and its development, for what is born one day requires time for growth. Hence the critic must once more go over his documents. . . .
>
> The result of this dismembering of the sacred books and the partition of them throughout the centuries is naturally that the Scriptures can no longer be attributed to those authors whose names they bear. The modernists have no hesitation in affirming commonly that these books, and especially the Pentateuch and the first three Gospels, have been gradually formed by additions to a primitive brief narrative—by interpolations of theological or allegorical interpretation, by transition, by joining different passages together. This means, briefly, that in the sacred books we must admit a vital evolution. . . . The traces of this evolution are so visible that (they actually write) a history of them. To aid them in this they call to their assistance that branch of criticism which they call textual. . . .
>
> . . . it is quite clear that the criticism we are concerned with is an agnostic, immanentist, and evolutionist criticism. Hence anybody who embraces it and employs it makes profession thereby of the errors contained in it and places himself in opposition to Catholic faith.[60]

Pascendi equated the very use of textual and higher criticism with agnosticism, immanentism, evolutionism—in short, modernism. And although it might with justice be said that Gigot—and other American Catholics—promoted this type of criticism before 1908 but were not agnostics, it is important to recognize that the institution that nurtured and employed them did not allow of such a distinction. The Dunwoodie professors did not, of course, accept this official identification of the higher critic with the agnostic and were chagrined, to say the least, to see that the specific examples that *Pascendi* provided of certain unacceptable conclusions flowing from the application of critical methods—for example, the revised teaching on the authorship of the Pentateuch—could have been as easily lifted from the pages of the *New York Review.*

While Gigot's series on higher criticism of the Bible did not directly confront the crucial issue of dispute—namely, the character of revelation and the relationship of its content to its form—the companion series on inspiration, penned by Driscoll, attempted to provide the theoretical foundation and presuppositions for the instructional tone of other *Review* articles. As did Gigot, Driscoll presented opposing positions on the question of inspiration and often supported the progressive view.

Driscoll narrowed the controversy down to one question: Were the conclusions of the modern biblical critics compatible with inspiration, with the divine authorship of the Bible? He advanced the distinction between "the revealed fact of inspiration" and "certain traditional inferences . . . not pertaining to the substance of the doctrine, nor all of equal theological or scientific value." The modern Christian apologist must, Driscoll believed, "ascertain if the doctrine of divine authorship really does imply all that has been deduced from it by traditional theology."[61]

Reporting with approval on the views of Lagrange, Driscoll followed that Catholic Bible critic's distinction between the concept of inspiration subjectively considered (the manner in which it affected the personality of the sacred writers) and objectively considered (the object of inspiration and its influence as manifested in its results). In the case of the former, the deductive method of neo-scholastic theology would be "beyond the realm of scientific observation, like the gift of prophecy or any other transient supernatural prerogative." Furthermore, Driscoll reasoned, because they bequeathed us no information on this subject, there is no sufficient reason to assume "that they were even conscious of the special divine influence under which they are believed to have written." Thus one could proceed only by way of logical inference from the data of revelation and, Driscoll added, from the "more or less certain" principles of modern psychology. Deductive reasoning could establish certain conclusions—for example, that inspiration involved a special illumination of the intelligence. And one could accept such conclusions "without fear of their being seriously disturbed by any subsequent facts of observation." Quoting Lagrange, Driscoll warned that any careful theologian applied this method with great reserve. In fact, the deductive method was clearly subordinate to the scientific method. Driscoll made this point by employing neo-scholastic terminology:

> In other words, the action of divine inspiration like that of revelation is a great historical fact made manifest to our faith in permanent tangible results, and since the best means of finding out the nature of an efficient cause is through a knowledge of its effects, it is precarious to reason confidently *a priori* on the nature and extent of revelation without having gathered all the light we can from the examination of what inspiration has produced. Manifestly our knowledge of God and of His works is too imperfect to warrant its being made an exclusive basis to decide upon what He must or must not have done, and instead of speculating on what, according to our theological ideas, was befitting the divine efficiency in a given case, it is rather our duty to study with reverence and humility the visible results of its action.[62]

Data ascertained by the application of critical methods of analysis of the words of Scripture should outweigh "our preconceived ideas regarding the supposed fitness of things."

The president of St. Joseph's Seminary realized that his position, stated so clearly, would incite controversy. In the same article he called for open exchange of ideas and dialogue on this crucial issue for "truth is not the exclusive possession of any individual or school." He also indicated a number of the conclusions that would follow the acceptance of his (and Lagrange's) methodology, among them the recognition that an inspired book may be anonymous, pseudonymous, or the joint work of several authors; and, that, contrary to the traditional opinion, the authors of scripture were not necessarily, in every case, apostles, prophets, or wonderworkers—or even men recognized for their holiness. Driscoll also refuted the notion that the Old Testament canon had been formed in a solemn, official manner at given moments when a recognized servant of God stepped forth to submit his inspired manuscript to a competent tribunal. Scholars recognized in Driscoll's time that the process of the formation of the canon of both Old and New Testaments was a gradual, at times informal, process.

Yet, like Gigot, Driscoll refused to admit that these conclusions of modern critical scholarship jeopardized the concept of biblical inspiration in its authentic integrity. Were the understanding of that concept revised accordingly, Driscoll suggested, the fact of multiple authorship or progressive composition of a particular book would not threaten the belief that its contents were divinely inspired. Even if the inspired prophet did not actually compose the text but simply passed down teachings orally, Driscoll pointed out, "the work in its present [written] form is inspired, and there is no valid reason why this characteristic should be limited to any particular mode of literary composition." Writing one year before *Pascendi* condemned this opinion, Driscoll judged it "beside the mark and illogical to reject *a priori*—as is sometimes done—the composite structure of the Pentateuch."[63]

Finally, as had Gigot and certain European critics, Driscoll refuted the claim that his opinions were distinctively modern or anti-traditional. In point of fact, "ancient commentators allowed that documents in themselves not inspired might be incorporated into the Bible." Ironically, Driscoll insisted, those who rejected the conclusions of contemporary scholarship were the moderns, for they imposed modern standards of literary composition upon the ancients, refusing to respect their quite different ideas of the writing of history, the use of pseudonyms, and the very process of book-making. The "ultraconservative school" neglected history at their peril. "It may, indeed, at first blush seem irreverent to ascribe to the sacred writers modes of procedure which to us appear indelicate," Driscoll wrote, "but it is well to recall that they did not appear so to them." In these matters, he counselled, there is much that is "merely relative and indifferent"; one can readily admit, without prejudice to orthodoxy, that "God adapted the grace of inspiration to the literary customs of the period."

In concluding his essay on the subjective aspect of inspiration, Driscoll approximated views of Loisy, later condemned in *Lamentabili*, suggesting that revelation is a kind of divine education, doled out by God in proportion to the receptivity and (limited) understanding of its hearers:

It is a commonplace in apologetics to affirm that God in the working out of His plans in the world, proportions his light and grace to the limited capacity and manifold imperfections of those whom He wishes to draw nearer to Himself. Thus, the moral code of the Old Testament, though recognized as having explicit divine sanctions, is confessedly imperfect, in many respects, viewed from the Christian standpoint. Yet God, who in Himself is just as perfect in the Old dispensation as in the New, made use of it for His own good purpose, and as the most conservative theologians must consistently admit, made Himself directly responsible for its provisions. May we not, therefore, without incurring censure of irreverence, allow that He likewise adapted His responsibility and supernatural action in connection with the sacred writings, to the somewhat crude literary methods of the age? . . . it is likely that the subtle grace of inspiration was as imperceptible in its mode of action as it is now in its results, and we may confidently assume in the light of the Biblical facts, that with regard to the mode of composition, the inspired writings were produced, in a manner quite similar at least to those of other books written at all external and observable conditions.[64]

Taken together as a piece, Driscoll's and Gigot's series of articles on biblical inspiration and inerrancy, on textual and higher criticism, provided the subscribers to the *New York Review* with a fairly comprehensive introduction to the methods and preliminary conclusions of "modernist" exegesis and apologetics. The Dunwoodians advocated these methods and adopted many of the conclusions; in so doing, they relegated the contrary positions and methods of nineteenth-century scholasticism to a secondary and subordinate role in the emerging synthesis of modern science and religious faith.

Driscoll and Gigot also solicited articles from critical thinkers on the cutting edge of their respective disciplines. These articles did not repeat, but presupposed, the arguments and principles set forth by the editors of the *Review*; accordingly, their authors were less concerned with justifying a non-scholastic approach to apologetics and devoted themselves almost exclusively to the task of bringing Catholics up to date with recent researches and revisions in the received understanding of traditional teachings.

F. Hugh Pope, O.P., contributed a series of articles covering topics such as "The Historical Geography of the Greek Bible," which the author found riddled with errors. After reporting on recent break-throughs in the study of the Greek Bible, Pope focused on the dis-covery of papyri scrolls of 4 B.C. and the revolution it incited in the study of biblical Greek. From the insights garnered from the scrutiny of the papyri, Pope concluded that the Septuagint was not the work of seventy-two Jews imported to Egypt for the purpose—as previously believed—but a product of diaspora Jews, most of whom were unfa-miliar with the geographical details of the Holy Land. Consequently, they erred frequently in the translation of geographical details. Any test of either the historical or geographical veracity of the Greek trans-lation would point up these mistakes, Pope reported, "for the simple reason that . . . the translators did not know the geography of Pales-tine and were only slightly acquainted with its history." Furthermore, Pope continued, a second class of errors in the Septuagint derived, incredibly, from the translators' deficiencies in Hebrew. Pope did not ignore the larger implications of these errors for the Roman Catholic understanding of the Bible; indeed, he reminded his audience that, in producing the Latin Vulgate, St. Jerome had quoted these mistakes "faithfully, and, when possible, read into them a spiritual and alle-gorical significance." Pope wished his essay to be a contribution to a clearer understanding of biblical Greek; it was not, he claimed, simply destructive.[65] Also in this genre of pointedly didactic articles were the contributions of Gabriel Oussani, an orientalist who taught at the sem-inary, and wrote of the manner in which secular history, linguistics, and archaeological findings were being incorporated in the higher crit-icism of the Bible. He promoted such an interdisciplinary approach to exegesis and admonished American Catholic apologists not to ignore the wisdom of the archaeologist and the historian of religion.[66]

Traditions of the Roman Catholic faith were equally subject to rigorous investigation in the pages of the *Review*, yet the tone of the majority of these articles can fairly be described as moderate, the im-pact noncontroversial. Ironically, the author who best exemplified this approach, Edward J. Hanna of Rochester Seminary, was one of the few contributors to the *Review* later singled out as sympathetic to modernism. Hanna sought a middle ground between the essentialist views of the neo-scholastics and the historico-critical methods pre-ferred by European theologians. For example, in "The Power of the Keys," Hanna rejected the extreme postion of Dr. Henry Charles Lea, who had argued that the growth of the penitential system in the Cath-olic Church enjoys no warrant in the teachings of Christ. Although he did not challenge Lea's central contention, that "it required the ingenuity of theologians . . . to build up from this simplicity the complex structure of dogma and observances on which were based sacramental absolution," Hanna refused to sacrifice the apostolic integrity of the sacrament to the concept of development. "That there has been a gradual development in the doctrine and in the use of the sacrament of penance no one may deny," he wrote, "[but] whenever growth is admitted, it is in virtue of principles divine which were to be found in the church from the days of the apostles." Most of Hanna's articles were similarly cautious in sketching the lines of historical development of Roman Catholic doctrine.[67]

Other articles, however, enlarged the category of "tradition" to include positions contrary to the received neo-scholastic interpretation. In the "Notes" section, which contained news and commentary, the editors examined particular doctrines and their traditional locus, among them the doctrines of creation and the possibility of developing from the tradition an acceptable presentation of theistic evolution. In an early installment Duffy took up the cause of evolution where John Zahm left off after his suppression. As had Zahm, Duffy argued that Saints Augustine and Aquinas had approved not only of the general evolution of species but of debatable theories supporting it, including spontaneous generation. One could no longer make religion stand or fall with the theory of the immediate creation of life. Rather, Duffy demanded, apologists must incorporate evolutionary principles into Christian proclamation of providence and creation. He was optimistic about the possibilities of such an endeavor:

> The desired reconciliation of theistic philosophy with scientific theories will probably come in the long run through a gradual approximation from both sides. Signs of such a *rapprochement* have not been wanting. Tyndall and Huxley, Wundt . . . of the past generation proved the untenability of the old-fashioned materialistic explanation. The main tendency of present-day philosopher-scientists is to recognize the "increasing purpose" manifested in evolution. . . . We often hear of what St. Thomas would do if he were with us now. . . . The theory of spontaneous evolution and the moderate evolutionism which came down to him from St. Augustine did not disturb him. He found room for them without difficulty in his system of philosophy. Could he find room for a modern theory of evolution? That is a question

which only a [modern] St. Thomas could answer to our perfect satisfaction.[68]

Duffy's appraisal of contemporary philosophy and science moved him to predict, somewhat naively, that the Roman Catholic church would soon embrace it. Writing a year before *Pascendi* precluded that possibility for a generation, Duffy predicted that an imminent reconciliation between theism and evolutionism would be among the brightest moments in the history of the church's relationship to the modern world. His call for a synthesis of theism and post-Darwinism echoed Zahm's:

> the great Pontiff, Leo XIII, who turned us all from logic-chopping textbooks to the broad-minded philosopher-saint of Aquino, has shown how deeply he has imbibed of the spirit of that master by his recommendation "Vetera novis augere et perficere." Our scripture scholars, moreover, have done much to settle difficulties which were thought to exist from the standpoint of religion. The time, therefore, seems ripe for a great synthesis [of evolution and theism] which will "amplify and perfect" the old.[69]

THE CONTROVERSY OVER THE *REVIEW*

Such proclamations were a bit daring in a church that had recently experienced a papal rebuke of the one indigenous pattern of thought to receive widespread attention, namely, the Americanist immanentism associated with the name Isaac Hecker. The *New York Review*'s editors were well aware of the boldness of their prescriptions for intellectual and spiritual renewal in Catholicism, yet they were also merely transitional figures within the larger trajectory of American modernist thought. On one hand, Duffy, Driscoll, Gigot, and the others were, unlike Zahm, fully aware that their efforts at creating a synthesis between ancient faith and modern thought would be considered heretical, not just by an aberrant clique of Jesuits and anti-Americanists in Rome, but by conservative factions within many of the religious orders and within the secular priesthood. They recognized (perhaps in part as a result of observing the experience of their predecessors like Zahm) that the reformulations they proposed on any particular topic—evolution, the Petrine Commission, biblical interpretations, etc.— presumed a more foundational, thoroughgoing reassessment of the religious worldview of medieval Christendom buttressed by the system of neo-scholasticism. On the other hand, they were confident—as events proved, inaccurately so—that such a reassessment could be accomplished within the current structures of thought, even alongside a neo-scholastic paradigm for revelation, religious experience, and ecclesiastical authority. This unfortunate mixture of daring and underestimation of the enemy led to a curiously incomplete self-awareness, reflected in part by the fact that the fate of the *New York Review* itself became something of a cause célèbre in its own pages. Because the "Notes" section kept American priests abreast of contemporary patterns of thought in biblical studies, apologetics, and theology, it returned time and again to the controversy surrounding the *New York Review* itself.

This exercise in self-examination grew particularly intense and anxious during 1907, the year of the condemnations of modernism. In defense of their orthodoxy, the editors reprinted favorable notices from other Catholic periodicals, most of which praised them for striking the right balance between "the guidance of authority" and the opinions of "the most distinguished contemporary thinkers and writers." Immediately after *Pascendi* the editors reprinted an item from the publishers of the *Catholic Encyclopedia* (on which Driscoll and Gigot had worked) "for the compliment it pays to the really remarkable scholarship of a confrere and contributor of our own; as a confirmation from irreproachable sources, of views expressed elsewhere in this issue of the *New York Review*; . . . and most of all, as an inducement to the learned readers of this *Review* to give all possible financial and moral support to that excellent publication."[70]

The editors' response to the condemnation of modernism was telling. As did most progressive American Catholic periodicals, the *Review* printed the encyclical. The editors did not comment upon it directly, but followed it with the aforementioned avowals of orthodoxy. However, unlike other periodicals (see chapter 6), the *Review* did not perform an editorial about-face. The item quoted above asserted that *Pascendi* had confused as many devout Catholics as it had enlightened. And, in seeming defiance of several of the proscriptions of the encyclical, the Dunwoodians continued to publish studies in critical exegesis, immanentist philosophy and theology, and nonscholastic apologetics. Apparently, the editors came to a consensus on the strategy of response to the condemnation of modernism: interpret the encyclical narrowly, disavow the positions it proscribed, and continue to support progressive scholarship and theology. In short: we are not guilty of heresy, so let us not act as if we are. The editors also minimized the scope of the papal condemnation. "Let no good Catholic with this volume [the *Catholic Encyclopedia*, edited by Driscoll] before him," the editors wrote after *Pascendi*, "be afraid that Pius X is going to turn off the light which modern research has afforded to Christian scholarship." The editors then held up *Review* articles by Gabriel Oussani as "assurance that in our day, as heretofore, the Catholic Church can afford to tolerate a proper freedom of criticism in her exegetes in perfect consistency with her own inflexible principles."[71]

The editors pursued this strategy in their interpretations of official teaching. Regarding Pius X's syllabus of modernist errors, *Lamentabili Sane Exitu*, Duffy devoted an article to the praise of the corporate wisdom and patience of the "great wide old Church." As delicately as possible, Duffy suggested that accepting *Lamentabili* was just such an exercise in "patience," as if, given time, the church might accept "the truth amid the error" of modernism. The hope of the modernists in Europe, and their supporters in the United States, was that Pius X was not firmly in the camp of the integralists. "Here and there an ardent member of the Church has shown how much better a Catholic he is than the Pope by extending the condemnation to include, it would seem, everybody who has studied biology or Hebrew," Duffy protested. In fact, the pope "has condemned only extreme views"; the majority of progressive Catholics attempting to reconcile the church to the modern age, such as the priests at Dunwoodie, should still be seen as loyal and devout Catholics. Much of this article reads as an *apologia* for the so-called modernists and for the *New York Review* itself:

> The nineteenth century piled up a vast array of facts, and not a few theories which were in many instances incompatible with the accepted statement of Catholic, or indeed, theistic belief. In response to the needs of the situation learned Catholics took up the work of refutation or the still more delicate task of restatement and reconciliation. From the Catholic point of view as manifested in our history, there is nothing deserving of reproof in this undertaking. To condemn it is to condemn Suarez and Aquinas, Augustine and Clement.

To Duffy's way of thinking, these progressive apologists—be they called "modernists," "developmentalists," or "evolutionists"—represented the highest level of Catholic scholarship. For, in the actual working out of the infallible teaching of the church, "the preliminary work is done by historians, exegetes, philosophers, theologians—any one of whom is liable to be mistaken in the solutions he proposes."[72] Why implicate this grander effort in the misstatements of the minority?

Furthermore, Duffy refused to accept what, in retrospect, appears obvious to the historian, namely, that Rome meant to inhibit or to suppress the larger, more diverse enterprise of modern scholarship in itself—the whole emerging developmentalist agenda—as well as those few individuals who had already abused it. Duffy judged that "this movement of Catholic scholarship has been allowed to proceed almost unchecked by the central authority of the Church." Here and there a book or individual had suffered reprisal or condemnation, "but in the main the settlement of difficulties has been left to the friendly warfare of theological schools within the Church." Duffy sought to soften the impact of the condemnations by limiting them to a few figures and by pointing out that the magisterium had not spoken with full authority:

> And for one who is acquainted with the works of (for example) Cardinal Newman or Father Lagrange, it requires a grotesque twisting of words to find in the Syllabus a repudiation of their positions. Now what strikes the Catholic theologian in this document is its moderation. He knows the strength of the language Rome is not using. He reads a list of false propositions which are gently denominated "errors" even though they deserve in many instances the deeper brand of "heresy." The condemnation is promulgated in a way that is authoritative and effective indeed, but without invoking the infallible magisterium of the Church. And as he reads the lucid and careful statement of the sixty-five propositions that are proscribed, there come up to his mind a number of opinions which the congregation must have considered, and left uncondemned.[73]

Duffy apparently wrote this response to *Lamentabili* before *Pascendi* left no doubt as to the heretical character of the "errors" of modernism. Yet the editors chose to publish his reflections even in light of *Pascendi*. Clearly, the editors refused to accept the implications of the condemnation of modernism. Appended to Duffy's original article was the assertion that *Pascendi* had changed nothing. "The recent official pronouncements" have not impeded Catholic scholarship, and the notion that it must now cease "betrays gross ignorance . . . of the condemned propositions." It was as if the editors of the *Review* could not bring themselves to believe that the substantial work of a generation of Catholic scholars was now in jeopardy. They recited the litany of progressive English-language publications in which the work of these scholars had been published—*Catholic University Bulletin, Catholic Quarterly, Ecclesiastical Review*, the *Catholic World*, the *New York Review*, the *Dublin Review*, the *Month*—and noted that it would not be difficult "to find in any one of these at least some admissions, theories, facts, principles, methods which would sound strange and modern to theologians of the thirteenth or the seventeenth centuries." These journals would continue, the Dunwoodians presumed, as they had before *Pascendi*, to appropriate the

> new facts and theories in physics and astronomy, biology . . . and restricted evolution . . . the results of psycho-physics, the victories of sane criticism, the treatment of the Synoptic problem, the new data in archeology, the study of comparative religions, the use of Newman's theory of development of doctrine, the application of new historical methods to patrology, the handling of obnoxious historical facts, the study of the psychology of religious assent, etc. etc."

They could continue this vast and diverse scholarship and live peaceably in the same church that had produced *Lamentabili* and *Pascendi*—as long as they did not panic and "haul down the standard from territory which has been occupied, and may still be retained, with the blessing and sanction of authority." However, only the *New York Review* continued to pursue these topics.[74]

For Duffy, Driscoll, and Gigot the best evidence for their unique interpretation of the condemnation of modernism was the continuing presence, relevance, and vitality of the *New York Review* itself. It continued to cover topics of contemporary questions resolutely and ". . . in their attitude and conclusions, they [the writers of the *Review*] prove that loyalty to science and to the Holy See is a double, but not a divided duty." Because its contributors hailed from three continents and nine countries, the American journal gave testimony to the true universality of progressive Catholic scholarship. Critics and conservatives might proclaim joyfully the death of such scholarship, the editors acknowledged, but "for our own part, we shall go on about our work, devoted to the ancient Faith and to its living exponent, the Vicar of

Christ; meeting what is false in modern thought with its own weapons; strengthening our souls. . . ."[75]

Within six months this promise was broken. Although financial difficulties was cited officially as the reason for the abrupt termination of publication, the *New York Review* was discontinued by the archbishop of New York because Catholic ecclesiocrats in Rome believed it to be a modernist journal. The *Review* had informed readers of the progress and activities of Catholic modernists, published their articles, and supported their efforts. This overt endorsement of the "movement" ultimately provoked the suppression of the *Review*.

The friendship of the *Review's* editors with Charles Briggs was a case in point. After his trial at Union Theological Seminary, Briggs became convinced that the findings of modern Biblical criticism would open the way to eventual reconciliation with Roman Catholicism on a number of key issues. In 1904 he traveled to Rome to consult with members of the newly established Pontifical Biblical Commission. The *New York Review* reported on the trip and reviewed the article it produced, entitled "Reform in the Roman Catholic Church." The editors acknowledged that the members of the curia "would probably classify his [Briggs's] attitude toward them as polemical" and that the word "reform" carried unfortunate connotations. However, the Dunwoodians endorsed Briggs's call for changes in ecclesiastical procedures "which will lessen the influence of the Roman Congregations and extend that of the bishops of the church"—hardly a *desideratum* of the integralists. Briggs evinced a sincere respect for the Holy Father and an appreciation, if not total acceptance, of Catholic dogmas. "His remarks on Papal Infallibility, the Immaculate Conception, and the theology of St. Thomas Aquinas are interesting—perhaps significant," the editors wrote.[76]

In 1907 the *Review* published opinion dissenting from the Biblical Commission's affirmation of the Mosaic authorship of the Pentateuch. The editors again relied on suspected modernists, in this case Friedrich von Hügel as well as Briggs. Duffy informed *Review* readers that both scholars repudiated the findings of the Biblical Commission. Duffy acknowledged that "at first impluse" a Catholic might be irritated that the views of a non-Catholic were solicited in this matter, but he quoted von Hügel's letter of sympathy to Briggs on the matter:

"When the American Presbyterian Church publicly tried, formally condemned, and crippled you to the best of its ability,
it did so on the double ground of your Pentateuchal positions
and your popish heresies. . . for insisting on a 'Romish' Purgatory. . . . And since then you have moved out of the acuter
Protestantism of Presbyterianism into the *Via Media* of the Episcopal Church with its considerable Catholic affinities. Indeed,
no man, who knows you could doubt the sincerity and generos-
ity with which you recognize. . . many amongst Rome's special
rights and gifts." [77]

And in spite of the ecclesiastical ban, Duffy quoted Driscoll's letter to
von Hügel on the prospect of reunion of other Christian bodies with
Rome. In this letter Briggs expressed his controversial view that, in
spite of the decree of the Biblical Commission, the church "has never
committed itself officially to the Mosaic authorship of the Pentateuch"
and has recognized that Hebrew laws and institutions had developed
throughout history. Duffy judged Briggs's theological position "well
worthy of consideration."[78]

Duffy made it quite clear that the editors of the *New York Review*
took the side of Briggs and von Hügel against the restrictive measures
of the Biblical Commission. With approval, Duffy quoted Briggs's
opinion that the members of the commission "weaken the Catholic
Church in its entire relation to the Bible; they give the adversaries
of the church an opportunity of asserting its antagonism to Biblical
Christianity; they conjure up a fresh conflict with science and erect
another stumbling block to scholars; and build up an additional barrier
to the reunion of Christendom." Furthermore, Duffy enthusiastically
reported Briggs's account of his personal audience with the Pope during which, supposedly, the Holy Father assured the Episcopalian that
neither his signature on the decree of the Biblical Commission, nor
Pius IX's on the 1864 Syllabus of Errors came under the category
of infallibility. On the eve of *Lamentabili* Duffy accepted this as a
positive sign of Rome's increasing flexibility in dealing with Protestants and with the modern world in general and added that "recent
rumors from the Holy City" suggest that Pius X "has put a quietus on
the proposed new syllabus."[79] It was not long before events proved
Duffy wrong.

In this debate over the place of higher criticism in Catholic biblical scholarship, Duffy counselled patience. To soothe Briggs's fears

that Catholicism would ultimately reject all critical methods of modern scholarship, Duffy pointed hopefully to von Hügel's interpretation of the decision of the Biblical Commission. Von Hügel understood the decision less as a matter of dogma, more as a "simple direction and Appeal from scholars to scholars." As such, it welcomed contrary opinions, which "could hardly be taxed as impertinent." Loyalty on the part of Catholic scholars necessitated open speech if the recommendations of authority be found unworkable. Those who truly loved the church would speak out, von Hügel believed, to warn the commission that further accentuation of their position "could not fail to be profoundly damaging to Rome."[80]

Von Hügel reassured Briggs and the Dunwoodians that, in Duffy's words, "Catholicity can and will in the long run find a place for established modern intellectual positions." As an historical religion, Roman Catholicism cannot logically reject historical methods and results; as universal, it must embrace even the world of intellectuals; as a living tradition, an organism, it must possess itself of a principle of development. Most important to Duffy was von Hügel's "formula for patience," for waiting upon the hierarchy rather than despairing of it:

> In conclusion, as a motive for patience he presents a line of thought which, in our opinion, admits of being much more strongly worked out. "I would point out that all Religious Institutions without exception are at their worst in the matter of their relations with Science and Scholarship, doubtless chiefly because they exist, at bottom, as the incorporations and vehicles of requirements and realities, deeper and more important and necessary than are Science and Scholarship. . . ."[81]

Of the coverage and frequent support of Briggs's opinions, perhaps the most injurious to the journal's reputation among the hierarchy was its approval of his debatable views on the papacy. This topic was taken up upon the appearance, in the *North American Review*, of Briggs's article on "The Real and the Ideal in the Papacy." Portions of this article lavishly praised the papacy as the embodiment of the principle of apostolic succession, for its solid scriptural basis, and for governing the "most compact and the best organized body of mankind." On the other hand, Briggs found a number of papal claims "debatable," including the presumed requirement that the successor of St. Peter be also the bishop of Rome, the extent of actual papal jurisdiction, and the preferred monarchical model of church government that unnecessarily and inappropriately excluded the proper participation of both episcopacy and laity in the legislative and judicial functions of the church. Duffy found Briggs's positions "all, theoretically at least, open for discussion." "Indeed," he wrote, "there can be little doubt that in the slow process of time these changes will come to pass, and others, too, of which today we do not even dream."[82]

Here Duffy dallied dangerously close to the issue upon which modernism foundered, namely, the basis and scope of ecclesiastical authority. Duffy desired a greater freedom for debate on this issue than Rome would allow. He wrote:

> The bond of unity is at once so essential and so easily broken that one must not tug recklessly at it wherever it is felt to chafe. On the other hand it must be acknowledged that some would draw it so taut that it is in danger of snapping, and others seem to think that it is intended as a rope to keep out people who are anxious to come in. If due importance be granted to all the practical phases of the problem, we may concede that there are points in our present system of government which are open to discussion and modification. . . . And Dr. Briggs may find some critics who wish to impose as obligatory, points which are merely of theological opinion or of current practice.[83]

The editors of the *New York Review* were not openly disloyal to the ideals of Catholicism nor to the leadership of the pope. Yet they clearly sought to articulate a new framework in which both might effectively permeate the consciousness not only of each Roman Catholic, but of the average Christian as well. For this task both a new apologetics and new ecclesiology were required, as the first issue of the *Review* argued. Unfortunately for these priests, it so happened that Protestant modernists such as Briggs and Catholic modernists such as von Hügel were the most learned, articulate, and devoted of the pioneers of this emerging paradigm. The Dunwoodians did not agree with every stance taken by these men, and in some cases cringed at their excesses, but relied upon their insights and proposals. The Dunwoodians also presumed the good faith of the modernists, their loyalty to the institutional church, and their willingness to compromise in "the wisdom of patience," as Duffy put it.

One may thus begin to understand the Dunwoodians' almost quixotic support for George Tyrrell and his "cause" long after the English Jesuit alienated himself from the institutional church. For example, they blamed the condemnation of Tyrrell's *A Much Abused Letter* and his consequent expulsion from the Society of Jesus on the absence of explanatory preface and notes, and on the poor quality of the Italian translation, rather than on the quality of Tyrrell's thought. On the issue of Tyrrell's orthodoxy, Duffy risked reprisal by declaring:

> when [the reader] asks himself how others deal and how he would deal with the case of a man who is sincerely attached to the Catholic Faith but is worried by intellectual difficulties to which no one can just yet give an entirely satisfactory answer; when he reads in the notes the restatement in orthodox theological terminology of expressions which shocked through their novelty of language, or historical instances which explain the meaning and bearing of vague generalizations . . . he may still be disquieted at a condition of things which would call for such a letter, but he will be reassured . . . as to the loyalty of our foremost Catholic writer to the doctrines and authority of the Church.[84]

Contrary to Archbishop Farley's wishes, Driscoll distributed copies of Tyrrell's *Oil and Wine*, which had failed to earn the *imprimatur*, to his students, and solicited articles from him for the *New York Review*. In one of these articles, "The Dogmatic Reading of History," Tyrrell presented a summary and synopsis of his reflections on theological method. The theologian was dependent upon the prior work of the critic who examined the "facts and events" disclosed by salvation history in light of their probable manifestation in "actual" history. With the "bare" description of the event, the theologian could reflect critically on its "inward meaning." Here as elsewhere in his writing, Tyrrell contended that the arid rationalism of nineteenth-century scholastic theology served to blind the theologian to the true spiritual significance of the event. The introduction of the historico-critical method would counteract the traditionalists' "dogmatic" reading of history and thereby prevent the idealization of the actual fact or event. Tyrrell sought to avoid extremes, he wrote, to navigate "between Scylla and Charybdis" by promoting the historico-critical method so that the "dogmatic reading" would not misconstrue the original fact in order to bring its religious meaning into bolder relief. Neither would the "scientific reading" be allowed to overlook or deny this inward meaning by restricting the analysis of the event to its external aspects. Tyrrell envisioned the process as an ongoing attempt to refine the church's understanding of the correspondence between the external event or fact and its inward meaning. Treating the event as profane, and thus subject to scientific scrutiny, would reveal the life-giving efficacy of faith as it invested the fact with sacred significance. Treating the event as profane would also be in keeping with the long-standing Catholic principle that individuals are free ultimately to reject revelation or to accept it in faith.[85]

In addition to articles by Tyrrell, the Dunwoodians saw fit to solicit and publish articles about him in part to celebrate his position as a preeminent Catholic theologian. For this task they recruited Henri Bremond, who judged Tyrrell to be willing to reshape and adapt new ideas to "the lawful exigencies of modern times" because he knows that "no wealth of dogmatic utterance can ever exhaust the divine fruitfulness of the revelation of Jesus." Most impressive about Tyrrell, and the new breed of apologist he stood as the model for, was his competence in the disparate modern disciplines to which religion must speak a persuasive word. In addition to his facility in contemporary thought, Tyrrell was of course thoroughly versed in ecclesiastical tradition and thus perfectly positioned to effect a reconciliation between the two. Furthermore, he had not rejected neo-scholastic apologetics out of ignorance of them. Tyrrell was a student of the original texts of St. Thomas but felt that thirteenth-century theology were inadequate as an exclusive foundation for twentieth-century apologetics. Bremond found Tyrrell to be a most capable student of the new criticism:

I do not think that the learned in philosophy or criticism will be able to say that he does not know their language . . . he had read them for himself and read them well, with sympathy of comprehension if not always with that of agreement. Without pretending to be a specialist in the History of Religion or in Biblical Criticism, he has assimilated the substance of the best current literature on these subjects . . . this solid and manifold erudition subtly permeating the pages of what is avowed by only a commentary on the Lord's Prayer. . . . On the other hand he faces and discusses as a theologian the problems and conclusions of the various sciences. If at times he wanders beyond the limits prescribed by Scholasticism, he does so with his eyes open, as one who has sojourned long in this land. . . . It is from no neo-scholastic manual that he has learned St. Thomas.[86]

Bremond believed that Tyrrell's critics misunderstood the pastoral character of his writing. He meant not to challenge the dogmas of faith, but to awaken in faithful Catholics an interior life. Had not Pascal, among others, upheld this same tradition? Tyrrell sought a return in modern apologetics to an emphasis on religious experience. "No polemics, no aggressive disputes, no scholastic arguments in favor of dogma, no demonstration of the divinity of the Church," Bremond recounted with approval.

Which method offers the most efficacious means of leading contemporary intelligence to the acceptance of Christian truth? Shall we begin with Christian doctrine or Christian practice? "In truth," Bremond confessed, "the two are one. . . . There is no Christian experience that does not imply a dogma; no dogma which does not express or translate into conceptions some spiritual experience."[87] The adoption of critical methods for the analysis of the "facts" and "events" of God's saving work in history would recall Christians to an interior, vital experience or intuition of the power of these "events" in individual lives. Tyrrell had built a methodological bridge connecting critical science and developmentalist worldview to what Pius X condemned as "vital immanence" and "intuitionism." As we shall see, one of the contributors to the *New York Review*, William L. Sullivan, in turn found correspondence between immanentist theology and the American experience of democracy, individualism, and freedom.[88]

In addition to the exploration of vital immanence through the articles on Newman, Pascal, and Tyrrell, the *Review* included an appreciation of the "New Catholic Apology" by Maude Petre, Tyrrell's disciple and confidant. Ostensibly a report on W. J. Williams's book, *Newman, Pascal, Loisy and the Catholic Church*, Petre's article celebrated the modernist worldview. From the insights of the modernists Williams had developed a

> great apology for the Catholic as opposed to the Protestant idea of religion; it is a profound study of the innermost nature of religious authority as opposed to private judgment; of development as opposed to traditionalism; of the social and corporate life of the Church as opposed to the individualism of mere sects; of true democratic principles as opposed to tyranny on the one side, anarchy and socialism on the other.

Petre applauded Williams's stand against departmentalism in religion, the system by which all facts of experience or knowledge are isolated from communal knowledge and life. Williams's contribution was to return religious experience to its appropriate place as the integrating and unifying factor in one's life—rather than as a "component" or aspect of that life. Ironically, Roman Catholicism, especially as interpreted by the medieval scholastics, had always promoted this integrating activity as the primary thrust of the religious impulse. But such integration would proceed inductively rather than deductively, imposed on the individual not by a hierarchy, not, in Williams's words, by " 'some abstractly perfect proof, not some mathematical demonstration, not some truth behind phenomena, not some fixed idea; but life. . . . ' "[89]

Modern apologetics in the spirit of Newman, Williams, and Tyrrell related the parts to the whole and thus developed a corresponding theory of authority. The limitations and excesses of private judgment must be corrected by religious authority entrusted with the wisdom and experience of the community as a whole. Only the Catholic Church ensured the preservation of this collective wisdom. In Petre's words the church "stands thus for the catholicity of the human mind . . . and for its catholicity in regard to time, representing as she does . . . past, present and future blended into one progressive whole." The church preserves and develops the idea embodied in Christianity and, in this sense, "development becomes one of the very notes of Catholicity, the catholicity of all the ages."

> All this conception of authority is, indeed, democratic, but democratic in no party sense, rather in that sense in which the spirit of man is essentially democratic. There is here no suspicion of subserviency to mere numbers, no divinizing of the people, no setting up of an autocracy of the many over the few. . . . [90]

Like Petre, Rev. Joseph Bruneau, the acquisitions editor for the *Review* before his departure in 1906, also explored the implications of the new apologetics for ecclesiology. He wrote eloquently of the church as a developing organism vitalized by the personal sanctity of individual members. He employed the same images as had his former colleague at the Institut Catholique in Paris, Alfred Loisy.[91] It was David Barry, however, who addressed most directly the question of ecclesial structure and government that would bring the journal to a controversial end. Barry voiced the *Review's* "Plea for a more comprehensive definition of the Church." The Catholic Church had too long relied on the "inadequate, one-sided definition" of itself provided by Cardinal Bellarmine. Bellarmine brought out very clearly the visible element of the church, but not without prejudice to its invisible, supernatural principle.

For Barry the external organization of the church was "only ancillary and complementary to the inner spiritual life of the church which is the pursuit and possession of sanctifying grace." Therefore, the external profession of Catholicity was not essential to unity with the church:

> "Extra Ecclesiam nulla salus" is a hallowed axiom of antiquity, and those who do anything to restrict our notion of church to the external body tarnish the honor due to the church by the suggestion that some of the children of God, perhaps a considerable portion of them, are outside it.[92]

In its place Barry suggested a definition of the church that might incorporate the new apologists' insights regarding the preeminence of the interior life of faith. To underscore the sanctity of its members the church should be seen, Barry suggested, as consisting of those, "still in this life, who are in the state of grace, and of those who are trying to obtain it through the ordinary means appointed by Christ." Perhaps most controversial was Barry's insistence that the importance of the external bonds of the faith—its unity of doctrine, authority, and worship—is not derived from anything intrinsic to themselves, "but from their adaptability as means of grace, without which they would be nothing but weak and beggarly elements." This definition would not find official recognition in Roman Catholicism for half a century. In 1907 Barry invited the charge that his ecclesiology was Protestant in spirit, too openly ecumenical. Few in the curia would endorse a definition of the church that "includes all children of God—all those who worship Him in spirit and truth according to their lights—as well those who are not Catholics, as those who are."[93]

Indeed the *Review*'s coverage of the topics of ecclesiology and authority did not quiet the suspicion among conservative Catholics that the journal reflected heretical views. The majority of the articles on these topics proceeded from the developmentalist and immanentist theologies sketched by authors like Fox, McSorley, and Bremond. The writers on ecclesiology invoked the vital tradition of Catholic theology articulated by Augustine, Pascal, Duns Scotus, and Newman. To these historic figures, and to the authors who invoked them, the church was *not* fixed, static, exclusive, or predominantly clerical. Neither was it primarily a visible and hierarchical reality or society, outside of which there is no possibility for salvation. Rather, these writers invoked most frequently the scriptural image of the Body of Christ to describe the true nature of the church as a mystical and invisible, as well as an institutional and visible, society. If, as the modern theologians affirmed, the Holy Spirit is the dynamic force imbuing with the vitality of faith the life of each individual believer, then the church, so animated, is a vital, living, growing body, influencing and influenced by history, feeding off the indivdual sanctity of its members and feeding them in turn. Such descriptions of the church reflected the unique spirit of their democratic, post-Kantian era, but also anticipated with startling accuracy the major ecclesiological themes of twentieth-century Roman Catholic thought and evidenced an unprecedented sensitivity to ecumenical concerns.

From this summary of the themes of the *New York Review* one may draw certain conclusions and attempt to "locate" the priests of Dunwoodie at a definite point along the trajectory of modernist ideas penetrating the theological sensibilities of progressive American Catholic priests after 1895. First, it is clear that the Dunwoodians possessed in their work a self-awareness and a degree of intentionality largely absent in the previous efforts by John Zahm at a synthetic reconcilation of Catholic faith and modern science. They were aware, to some extent, of the potentially radical implications of their "program of modernism" and of the controversy it might engender. Their calculated departure from the strict vigilance of the Society of St. Sulpice indicated that they anticipated censure at the hands of the Sulpician authorities in Paris. The correspondences of these men during the period when they planned and established the journal and reworked the seminary curriculum reveal their sense that they were inaugurating a bold venture. They approached their teaching and editorial tasks with caution and prudence for the most part, but were not timid in proclaiming, via both organs of dissemination, the dawning of a renewed religious and theological *weltanschauung*.

Unlike Zahm, then, the modernists at Dunwoodie recognized from the beginning that their work would arouse some degree of opposition from the Roman neo-scholastics. Until the disappointing end of his career as an American Catholic apologist, Zahm fancied himself a loyal servant of the church, even in its neo-scholastic incarnation, and held out hope that he would be vindicated by Roman authorities as well as the public that cheered his chautauqua lectures. The relatively narrow scope of his work and its implications for God's governance of the universe perhaps blinded him to the implications of his work, based as it was on a profound shift in paradigm from a classicist to a developmentalist worldview.

The priests at Dunwoodie were attempting, only six years after Zahm's departure from the scene, to provide for the American Catholic church the epistemological, theological, apologetic, and ecclesiological foundations for the new worldview. Had Zahm enjoyed the benefit of that preparatory work—had, indeed, that preparatory work been allowed to come to fruition—he might well have reached a broader public and seen his work take root in American Catholic support for scientific inquiry.

Although the Dunwoodians did not share Zahm's naivete—although they carried the modernist trajectory closer to its radical end—they were not modernists who chose to follow their vision of the new theology where it inevitably led in the years 1895–1910, namely, outside the institutional boundaries of the Roman Catholic communion. They remained ultimately loyal to the Catholic tradition and, what is more, willingly subject to its acknowledged authority—when they could no longer elude the grip of that authority. As obedient churchmen they do not stand as examples of the most radical of American Catholic modernists, those few clerics who, like Tyrrell and Loisy in Europe, could not abide a church that resisted reform so tenaciously and thus ended their association with it. Unlike self-proclaimed modernists (and thus, after 1907, self-proclaimed heretics) William L. Sullivan and John R. Slattery, the priests of Dunwoodie patiently hoped that, though their efforts were doomed to fail, the church would eventually adopt the new paradigm. In any event, they did not welcome censure, or celebrate it when it came.

Nonetheless, they anticipated it even as they resisted it. Their commitment to the new ideas was too open and pronounced, too public, to escape eventual notice and disciplining. In addition to the examples of their modernist program from the journal excerpts and curricular reform analyzed above, there were numerous instances in which Driscoll, Gigot, Duffy, or Bruneau revealed their modernist affinities. Driscoll reviewed favorably Loisy's controversial works, corresponded with him after he suffered excommunication, and disseminated his ideas in print and from the lectern. Historian Michael DeVito somewhat reluctantly concluded that

Driscoll seems, then, to have had a strong penchant for modernist ideas even though ecclesial authority was condemning these ideas . . . he was sympathetic to Loisy's ideas . . . and desirous to propogate [sic] them in the English-speaking world. . . . Driscoll, therefore, seems to have been ambivalent to the official teachings of the Church at that time . . . [not as] the result of prudence but of a conscious deliberation to deceive ecclesiastical authorities.[94]

THE DEMISE OF THE PROGRAM OF MODERNISM AT DUNWOODIE

The existence of such an incipient "program of modernism" under the aegis of the Archdiocese of New York was quite remarkable. William L. Sullivan believed that Archbishop Farley had been duped by the professors at Dunwoodie:

Cardinal Farley of New York was very proud of the *Review* and regarded it as a fine witness to the scholarship of his Seminary. The poor Cardinal had not the least idea what these discussions in criticism were all about; and once in a while he dropped an inept remark concerning them, which his faculty transmitted to us with irreverent delights.[95]

Farley was a cautious man but had a great respect for intellectual achievement and gave Driscoll a free hand in running Dunwoodie. He welcomed the founding of the *New York Review* as an idea whose time had come and lamented "the exaggerated restrictive policy of the ecclesiastical authorities, who, through their unreasonably stringent methods of censorship (Index, etc.) only succeeded in stifling all the initiative on the part of the ablest and best-disposed Catholic scholars."[96]

After the promulgation of *Pascendi*, however, a rumor circulated on the eastern seaboard that Dunwoodie had become a center of modernism. The anonymous author of "Modernism in the American Church," writing in the *American Ecclesiastical Review*, January 1908, concluded that "the evils of which the Pontiff chiefly complains exist to a very large and dangerous extent in the United States."[97] The rumors and the report stemmed from the belief that Edward Hanna was under investigation in Rome for his articles in the *New York Review* on "The Human Knowledge of Christ." That month the Apostolic Delegate to the United States, Archbishop Diomede Falconio, paid a visit to Farley. Why, he wished to know, is the condemned George Tyrrell praised in one issue of the journal under your supervision as the greatest Catholic writer in English since Newman, "in originality of thought, fertility of expression, and an all-pervading sense of religion"? Falconio also charged that the *Review* was a forum for "writers who have a tendency for the condemned doctrines of Modernism." Farley responded with righteous indignation that Tyrrell and Buonaiuti had been priests in good standing when their articles appeared in the *Review*. He also defended four of his diocesan priests traveling in Rome who had stirred up a scandal by their association with Giovanni Gennochi, a priest suspected of modernist sympathies, whom they had first met at Dunwoodie. Falconio's visit, and the investigation of Hanna, a professor of theology at St. Bernard's Seminary in Rochester, was reported in the American press.[98]

Farley's contacts in Rome reported to him the details of the curial suspicions of Hanna, whose series for the *Review* one critic retitled "The Ignorance of Christ." Applying a developmentalist model of human knowledge to the question of Jesus' own self-awareness, Hanna had concluded by 1906 that Jesus grew in knowledge of his divine mission, and implied that he shared the cultural limitations of his contemporaries. He also contended that the apostolic fathers of the church had held these opinions.[99] Alexis M. Lepicier, O.M.I., professor of dogmatic theology at the Urban College of Propaganda in Rome, denounced Hanna and Father Andrew E. Breen, a conservative colleague at St. Bernard's, subsequently delated him to Merry del Val. While in Rome to defend Hanna, Farley attempted to present an angry Pope Pius X with an edition of the *Catholic Encyclopedia* in part prepared, ironically, by the suspect professors at St. Joseph's Seminary. The controversy so tainted Hanna's reputation that his name was eliminated from consideration as coadjutor bishop of San Francisco the first time it was proposed. No less embarrassing to Farley were the duo of self-confessed American modernists, William L. Sullivan and Thomas J. Mulvey, whose dramatic departures from the church were heavily publicized in the local press. Both had direct ties to Dunwoodie and the *New York Review*.[100]

Months before Farley bore the brunt of it, Driscoll had anticipated the controversy. He wrote to Charles Briggs in 1907 to decline an invitation to lecture at Union Theological Seminary and cited ecclesiastical politics as his motivation:

Now my sympathy with Modernism is pretty well known as well as my intimate friendship with several of the most noted of its promoters and so with all this you can readily understand that the Archbishop tho very well disposed towards me and some of my views is at present anxious lest he may be obliged to remove me from my present position and suppress the publication of *The Review*.[101]

Driscoll's predictions were highly accurate. In a swift series of moves in 1908 Farley dispatched Driscoll to the relative anonymity of St. Ambrose Parish in Manhattan. Driscoll's days of influence on the direction of American Catholic thought thus ended rather abruptly. Farley replaced him at Dunwoodie with a man of little advanced learning—intellectualism had proven itself deadly—John P. Chidwick, a former police chaplain. Chidwick implemented Farley's wishes at the seminary. He "monasticized" the seminary, severing its connections with public universities and returning ecclesiastical Latin to the classroom. He restored the former curricular pattern centering on scholastic philosophy and theology, and "The Legend of the Medieval Grail" once again echoed from the corridors. The *New York Review* ceased publication in the summer of 1908, three years after it first appeared. The editors cited financial considerations as the cause of the termination—a justifiable claim, given the limited circulation of the *Review*. Yet the editors also included a questionable, if not forced, explanation for the termination, belied by their enthusiasm of the previous three years: "For the number of Catholics interested in questions which are of importance to the thinkers of the present generation—and which will be vital to all classes in the next—has been found to be so small that it does not justify the continuance of the *Review*." As for the remaining faculty members, John Brady, the managing editor of the *Review*, and Francis Duffy were transferred to parishes in the Bronx and Brooklyn. Those who remained at the seminary—notably, Gigot and Gabriel Oussani—taught and wrote after 1908 from received knowledge rather than from original research. By 1910 all traces of modernism at Dunwoodie had vanished.[102]

For a brief time the program of modernism initiated by Driscoll at Dunwoodie stood as a symbol of the possible future of modernist thought in America. The opponents of that program, first in the narrower Sulpician circles, and then in the broader church, recognized that Driscoll and company had at their disposal the most effective resource for the public conversion of the American priest-hood to the new paradigm in theology, apologetics, and ecclesiology—namely, education—and two of the most effective tools for utilization of that resource—the seminary and the press. Although the program of modernism inaugurated there never reached the level of popular consciousness, the authorities realized that the road to this broader Catholic public ran through the diocesan priesthood. It was this lim-ited "public" that Driscoll wooed and, in the eyes of the traditionalists, threatened. In 1907 Merry del Val, the cardinal Secretary of State of the Vatican, charged that Americanism and modernism were linked and were gaining influence "among the Catholic clergy and laity" in the United States.[103] These fears were confirmed in the case of two American priests, William L. Sullivan and John R. Slattery, who pur-sued the trajectory of modernism from its beginning in liberalism and Americanism to its end outside the Roman Catholic church.

5. Americanism and Modernism as One: William L. Sullivan and John R. Slattery

In the first decade of the twentieth century two American priests, one a Paulist and the other a Josephite, followed the "trajectory of modernism" to its resolution outside of the Roman Catholic church. Both men were initially attracted to Catholicism by the thought of Isaac Hecker and were subsequently encouraged by the public pronouncements of Americanist bishops who called for a synthesis of church and age. And well before the condemnations of modernism in 1907 both the Paulist, William L. Sullivan, and the Josephite, John R. Slattery, had come to reject the neo-scholastic religious worldview after studying the writings of European modernists. Of the Americanists who shared an optimistic assessment of science, a passion for republican ideals, and faith in "the conclusions of the higher criticism," only Slattery and Sullivan followed the full trajectory of Americanist thought to a self-conscious and open identification with the modernists; and only they repudiated institutional Roman Catholicism rather than acquiesce to the terms of *Pascendi*.

MODERNISM AS THE FINAL PHASE OF AMERICANISM:
WILLIAM L. SULLIVAN

The figure of William L. Sullivan, the Paulist missionary and teacher who renounced Roman Catholicism in 1910 and became a Unitarian, poses a challenge for interpreters of American religious history. How is one to understand the spiritual pilgrimage of Sullivan? Was he a reformer whose abhorrence of Romanism in Catholic ecclesiology impelled him towards liberal Protestantism? Was he primarily, as he put it in his unfinished autobiography, "a moral personality under orders," ultimately restless with every institutional expression of the "religion of the Infinite Spirit"? Or does the key to his life and thought lie in a growing patriotism and nationalism expressed, for a time, by his allegiance to the Americanist cause? Was he a modernist? Most provocative, perhaps, is the question linking these two heresies: Does Sullivan's career exemplify the continuity between Americanism and modernism?[1]

When progressive American priests were confronted with the order to renounce programs and methods inspired by the higher criticism, the vast majority did so rather than face expulsion from the church. In his defiance of this order Sullivan emphasized the connection between genuine Americanism and modernism. In this sense his struggle with the church may be seen as the clearest articulation of a modernist sensibility in the American Catholic community between 1895 and 1910.

When referring to Sullivan as a modernist, historians tend to qualify that judgment because modernism is generally understood to be intimately related to the rise, acceptance, and application of the methodologies and conclusions of historical and biblical criticism in the late nineteenth century, and Sullivan is not recognized as a pioneer or first-rate thinker in this regard. Accounts of Sullivan stress his preoccupation with apologetics and moralism, depicting him either as untutored in the critical sciences or as concerned almost exclusively with the liberal Protestant perception of religion as moral formation. In this view Sullivan incorporated insights from critical sciences only when and if they seemed to substantiate a point of apologetics. John Ratté epitomized this approach when he wrote that "the sins of the so-called 'infallible' popes mattered more [to Sullivan] than the critical insights of Weiss or Harnack; and Acton and Martineau and Matthew Arnold were more influential in his intellectual development than Houtin and Loisy."[2]

However, this judgment distorts Sullivan's approach to moral and apologetic questions in that it understates his familiarity with, and appropriation of, the methods and conclusions of European scholarship at the turn of the century. A generalist rather than a specialist, he studied a number of disciplines, especially biblical criticism and comparative religions, and consistently incorporated the critics' findings into his own understanding of the development of religion and religions—much more so than has been previously acknowledged.[3]

Sullivan's failure to produce more than a handful of scholarly articles during his years as a Paulist priest was due neither to a lack of exposure to the new learning nor to a reluctance to identify with the ultimate aims, as he saw them, of the European modernists. Dissatisfied with the quality of scholarship in the American church, he eventually pursued his own course of studies and came under the influence of European modernists.

Sullivan's disappointment in the intellectual sterility of Catholic education began during his seminary years at St. John's in Brighton, Massachusetts, where only John Baptist Hogan seemed to have absorbed enough of the new learning to enable him to develop his own theories of revelation, inspiration, and biblical exegesis.[4] For the most part, the manual tradition, represented by Tanqueray's *Synopsis theologiae dogmaticae fundamentalis*, dominated the curriculum. Sullivan recoiled from this staid approach, describing Tanqueray's work as "trash . . . a violent perversion of proofs . . . outrageous dishonesty to a dissident opinion . . . bad and inconsequent logic . . . nonsense."[5]

However, Sullivan was impressed by Alexander Doyle of the *Catholic World* and joined the Paulists to learn more about modern apologetics and the higher criticism. He hoped to author "a great apologetic work in defense of Christian Revelation—Philosophy, History, Sacred Scriptures, Literature and language . . . cultivated and brought to account in a thorough defense of God's revealed word."[6] His S.T.L. thesis, undertaken at the Paulist House of Studies in Washington, D.C., was an attempt to modernize the philosophical foundations of Paulist apologetics. Entitled "Some Theistic Implications of Modern Philosophy: A Dissertation in Fundamental Dogma," the thesis featured Sullivan's analysis of Bacon, Descartes, Locke, Hobbes, Spinoza, Hume, Kant, Fichte, and Schopenhauer. Although Sullivan turned few heads with his commentary, the range of his reading was itself a departure for the Paulists. Sullivan later described this period of research and writing as "a radiant time."[7]

As his own sophistication in philosophical studies increased, Sullivan grew disenchanted with his Paulist colleagues at Catholic University. He found them woefully unfamiliar with higher criticism and unprepared to teach twentieth-century students.[8] They were, as he described an associate, "muddy, vagrant, and ill-equipped with erudition."[9] Other American orders fared no better in his estimation. Primitive in their various apostolates, they "deem departure from venerable 'Rules' as apostasy from the Lord, [and] are in extreme danger of simply plodding along utterly untouched by modern progress and scientific methods." Some of the most celebrated Jesuits had, he claimed, "made egregious spectacles of themselves in scholarship."[10]

Sullivan's doubts about the "intellectual apostolate" of the Paulists were reinforced when he left Washington for two years (1899–1900) of mission preaching in Tennessee. He considered this assignment to be part of "the grandest work before the church in this country," but discovered that the traditional scholastic apologetic approach was simply ineffective in the American towns and villages he visited. He became convinced that a wholly new apologetic approach was required—one that spoke to the everyday experience and values of Americans. Because his audiences were not receptive to the abstract metaphysics of the manualist tradition, even when expressed popularly, Sullivan perceived the need to develop a new philosophical, historical, and theological context for evangelization. Furthermore, Americans seemed uncomfortable with any system or argument removed from the concerns that they deemed meaningful, practical, and directly applicable to their lives as Americans. The evidence from this period suggests that Sullivan enjoyed his greatest success when he spoke to these basic questions: the nature of right and wrong, the hope for redemption, the immortality of the soul, the dignity of individual conscience. He found Americans to be wary of authority that was not self-authenticating or respectful of cherished democratic values such as freedom of speech and liberty of conscience. These were considered principles of profound moral weight by most Americans.[11]

Coincidentally, though not accidentally, Sullivan began to read Lord Acton and to research the proceedings and debates of the First Vatican Council. Archbishop John Ireland of St. Paul and Bishop Thomas S. Byrne of Nashville befriended Sullivan and recommended that he read the postconciliar correspondence between Acton and Archbishop Peter Richard Kenrick of St. Louis.[12] Thus began Sullivan's obsession with the Inquisition and infallibility, two moments in Roman Catholic history that he came to see as springboards to a new apologetical approach for the American church. Here were moral issues—questions of authority, liberty, and coercion certain to find an audience in the American populace. By arousing the moral indignation of his listeners, Sullivan came to believe, he would open the way for a thorough reform of the institution that had perpetrated such atrocities as Vaticanism, ultramontanism, and religious imperialism. Only after confronting these prior moral questions could the reformer proceed effectively to a critical examination and reconstruction of Catholic ecclesiology and apologetics. [13]

With this in mind Sullivan left Nashville for Washington in 1901 and devoted himself to study of the new critical sciences and their impact upon Catholic philosophical and theological sensibilities. At the same time he communicated with other Americanists, focused his thinking on the moral questions raised by Catholic history and ecclesiology, and attempted to unite these two approaches to reform in a series of articles for the *New York Review*. He still considered himself to be an orthodox Catholic and interpreted any denunciation of critical scholarship in Europe as a temporary aberration caused by "implacable reactionaries."[14] His historical studies had not yet progressed to the point where he perceived such reaction as an episodic, recurring phenomenon, a malaise that threatened in every age to inhibit or stifle the genuine expression of Catholic ideals. From 1901 to 1906 he placed himself at the service of an ideal "unchanging and unshifting Church which is not afraid to proclaim its exclusive truth and its inerrant magisterium in proposing God's word to men."[15]

Toward the end of this formative period a young woman initiated a five-year correspondence (1906–10) with Sullivan after hearing him preach at St. Thomas church in Washington, D.C., sometime in late 1905. Numbering over one hundred letters, this frequent and detailed correspondence with Estelle Throckmorton served for Sullivan as a review of his recent progress, a diary of his current plans for reforming American Catholicism, and an intimate record of his spiritual struggles.[16]

Sullivan saw in Throckmorton an eager student and shared with her his growing knowledge of European scholarship. He believed himself to be intellectually suited for advanced studies and hoped to apply this talent to his pressing concern for reform:

> My mind is most of all speculative and metaphysical. When I began teaching in Washington, I set about selecting a line of special research. There were three inviting fields, philosophy, history, and biblical criticism, plus the history of religions. Natural inclination was toward the first, with No. 2 a good second, but the exigency of present day needs drove me to the third.[17]

Sullivan recommended certain authors to Throckmorton and summarized the work of others. Among those most frequently consulted were Tyrrell, Loisy, von Hügel, Duchesne, and Fogazzaro.[18] He

admitted that at St. Thomas "I did my very best openly and conspicuously, too, to put my students in touch with progressive scholarship."
His own studies led him "fairly deep" into the history of the peoples
that surrounded and influenced the Hebrew state and religion:

> I taught in the form of lectures, as befits advanced studies, and
> was treating of certain religious developments of the Hebrew
> people, and particularly of the history of the Messianic idea. I
> could not retain any self-respect if I simply re-cooked the old, un-
> critical, and absolutely discredited theses of seminary textbooks,
> though I never failed to state fully and adequately the traditional
> opinion. But I simply, out of very truthfulness, had to show how
> slowly Israel struggled into higher religious ideas, and the extent
> to which this advance was indebted in certain instances to the
> religions which surrounded Israel. I had to tell those young men
> who were about to confront a very clever world which is fast
> acquiring an acquaintance with these matters, that the true no-
> bility of prophetism is moral and spiritual, and does not proceed
> from prediction, of which, in the genuine sense, there is very lit-
> tle trace in the prophets. Well, the class took down the lectures,
> and were, and still are, I am sure, thankful for the initiation into
> some of the processes of modern scholarship.[19]

During the period immediately preceding *Pascendi* Sullivan accepted fully "the key to the whole original Modernist movement,"
namely, the notion that individual scholars should respect the facts established by critical scientific investigation of the Bible and of church
history and evaluate for themselves this evidence and its impact upon
faith claims. This enterprise, Sullivan believed, was possible and in
fact encouraged in the context of American freedom of speech and
belief; but it seemed impossible in the context of the "imperialism"
of the Roman hierarchy after 1905:

> A regime of repression set in . . . especially in the field of Bibli-
> cal study. Advanced opinions, it was clear, were to be abolished.
> But what is an advanced opinion? A student of Scripture has
> for his business to understand ancient texts. In so doing he must
> try his best to investigate when the text was written, what in-
> fluences acted upon the author, whether the book showed signs
> of collation, revision or borrowing, and to what extent historical
> sources confirm, fail to confirm, or contradict its statement of

facts. He is, throughout, in the region of accessible data, though often insufficient data. But upon such evidence he has, he must construct his opinions. . . . If an opinion is called "advanced," not in reference to the evidence, but in reference to some official pronouncement which was made independently of the evidence, the student cannot be concerned with that. His one duty is to state facts and to indicate what explanations and interpretations are consistent with the facts.[20]

For Sullivan it was unconscionable for a serious scholar and a person of integrity to overlook indisputable facts as if they did not exist. For one to deny, for example, that Luke manipulated the historical traditions about the behavior of the apostles in order to present them in the best possible light was an act of intellectual dishonesty. That the prevailing dogma of inspiration seemed to exclude such a conclusion mattered little to the scholar in search of objective truth. "If you are to have a dogma of inspiration," Sullivan explained, "it must be elastic enough to cover the facts." Any dogma that "extinguishes the facts" must be "inescapably false" and thereby in need of revision.[21]

As early as 1906 Sullivan was alienated from orthodox Catholicism as proclaimed by Rome. "The Church had been my Absolute," he wrote, "now the Moral Law was becoming my Absolute." His rejection of Newman's defense of inquisitorial practices was "my first *non possum*, the earliest of the absolute affirmations of my moral nature in the face of tradition."

To his ecclesiastical opponents the position of moral absolutism Sullivan adopted after 1906, coupled with his increasing dependence on the "inner leading" of the Holy Spirit, was an uncanny fulfillment of predictions they made about modernism as a series of errors, a "synthesis of heresies": it would feed off Kantian subjectivism, produce a theory of vital immanence, and foster a Protestant disregard for the objective moral order established by God and entrusted for preservation and articulation to the magisterium. To Sullivan it was precisely this hierarchical exercise of authority that often obstructed the creative work of the Spirit in the church. Tragically, Roman institutionalism worked to suffocate individual personality, moral conscience, and "the central organ of right and truth"—the soul of the individual. "I began to see," he wrote in 1906, "that from the very nature of a personality or soul, we incur moral disaster in submitting it without reserve to any institution whatever, civil or ecclesiastical."[22]

Like other Catholic "seekers" of this era, Sullivan was drawn to the writings of the Christian mystics, especially St. John of the Cross. Their rapturous reflections in the liberating and empowering presence of the Divine Spirit in their souls spoke to Sullivan's sense of contentment with the interior life. However, for all their spiritual fervor, several of the mystics failed to speak out during episodes of institutional oppression (here again, the indignities perpetrated by the Inquisition served as Sullivan's primary example). He took their silence as a moral failure of nerve. Thus, because "the moral nature is the supreme dignity of man," even the mystics fell short of his ideal, for they stood idly by as the institutional theologians intellectualized and overanalyzed the faith they possessed as a precious, rich, and impenetrable mystery.[23]

Consequently, Sullivan yearned to be in communion with a certain type of Christian—the moral mystic—who wedded integrity of spiritual vision to a thirst for righteousness. If the institutional church was jealous of inner leading and suspicious of moral individualism, Sullivan's ideal Catholic pursued both. Moreover, the Paulist sought to convince others that his way emerged from the "genuine Catholic past" and would lead to a purified Catholicism:

> Suppose that . . . we learn ever more profoundly that the essentially Catholic habit of adoration must be matched by the essentially spiritual and moral habit of obedience to what we adore and that our adoration is only a formality without it. Then we shall be confronted not with a Categorical Imperative, for that may be an abstraction . . . but with a Will uttering Itself to a soul and waiting for the soul's response. . . . It is to this that Catholic devotion leads the man who has given himself to it. What then must happen when the heavenly Will is found to be in discord with the earthly institutions which led him to It? There is the crisis, such a crisis as tears a man's heart and rebuilds his world. . . . With all its logic Catholicism has no logic for a solution here. No institution has. . . . At last, every philosophy or theology must satisfy naked soul. If it does not, it dies.[24]

Unless institutional Catholicism nurtured within its structures the seeds of its constant reform and rearticulation, it would become obsolete: individual Catholic "seekers" would eventually, perforce, pass out of it. At this juncture Sullivan hoped he had discovered such a company of committed, orthodox Catholics who would craft the theology needed to "satisfy naked soul" and to renew the institutional church. "I was fated, no doubt, to take position with the Modernists," Sullivan recalled. He began "to grasp the idea of the more radical Modernists, that Catholicism, in its essence, was capable of living its abundant life under different formulations."[25]

The modernists Sullivan read from 1901 to 1907 accomplished a fundamental task: they fashioned an objective basis for vital faith. This objectivity depended upon the acceptance of whatever facts and conclusions critical scholarship yielded regarding the doctrines of the faith and their historical transmission. From the collation of these facts the theologian produced a point of departure for the retelling of the Christian story, best understood as the history of the movement of the Holy Spirit in the lives of individuals and groups. If the magisterium is to rely on doctrinal formulas, such formulas must adequately reflect the lived experience of the faithful attested to in Scripture, liturgical life, and history. Dogmas must be articulated within the framework provided by critical scholarship. Sullivan became convinced that "there was no other way of saving the Church; and the Church, as the chief social agency in the moral and spiritual education of mankind could not legitimately imprison itself in so narrow a set of formulas as to be unable to accommodate itself to facts."[26]

In this spirit Sullivan entered into a partnership with the progressive American priests at St. Joseph Seminary who founded the *New York Review*. "It occurred to some of us who were watching the battle abroad," he recalled, "that we should try, however modestly, to prove that American Catholics were not barbarously indifferent to the great problems of expanding knowledge which were agitating the Church in Europe—we saw a chance to light a little candle which might recapture a tiny area from the darkness about."[27]

In his first article for the *New York Review*, "Catholicity and Some Elements in our National Life," Sullivan defended Americanism by an appeal to the results of critical scholarship. The practice of religion, he contended, is determined by "that set of sympathies and prepossessions which come from one's country, age and civilization." In examining the effects of democracy upon the American character and especially upon American religion, Sullivan promoted his own strategy for effective evangelization of the American people. By "falling in with this peculiar temper of a people's mind," he wrote, the preacher will "call with respect and goodwill, and ultimately elicit allegiance and assent." Accordingly, American Catholicism must prove itself to be a guardian of the "just and lawful spirit and aspirations of this progressive, independent and liberty-loving people." There is no animosity whatsoever, Sullivan contended, between "genuine Catholicity" and the spirit of modernity. Herein lay the heart of Sullivan's thesis, namely, that "genuine Catholicity" could never stand in the way of two central features of the national temperament in the United States, freedom of speech and national self-determination in matters of belief.[28] Furthermore, Sullivan located "genuine Catholicity" in the early church, "to which many look back rather than the medieval, as the golden age of Catholicity." In the ancient church, he claimed, "the people were consulted and their racial and national prepossessions deferred to in a manner which could proceed only from the highest conception of the dignity of democracy." Even the ordinary faithful, he exclaimed, had a voice in the election of bishops. This was a significant apologetic strategy. Camouflaged by the larger concerns of the article was a call for a shift in focus from the medieval age of church-state union to the "democracy" of the postapostolic church as a more appropriate model for envisioning genuine Catholicity. "I think our historical scholars could do no greater service," Sullivan suggested, "than by giving us books which would describe those early days and the men who lived them."[29]

If this cultivation and incorporation of public opinion was, in fact, a distinctive element of genuine Catholic tradition, how to explain the apparent scorn for public opinion and for democracy itself exhibited during periods of medieval and nineteenth-century Catholicism? Sullivan answered that these were transitional phenomena, in effect aberrations:

> It may indeed happen that during a period of transition from one model of expressing public opinion to the other, there appears to be some loss and retrogression from a democratic standpoint. Possibly we are in such a period now when civilized mankind want not even a royal spokesman to represent them but prefer to declare their own wishes in their own words. But such transitions the Church has always happily made; and if she is confronting a new one at this moment . . . she will undoubtedly listen again in this age as she listened of old time to the will of the people speaking for themselves.[30]

To convince the modern American that the Roman Catholic church was indeed sympathetic to public opinion, Sullivan argued, church leaders must avoid the exercise of "heedless authority" and allow ecclesiastical minorities the right to speak. Thus Sullivan argued on the basis of practical considerations: without freedom of expression within the church, non-Catholics would perceive the leadership as dictatorial. "It seems proper to say that in questions wherein we are not by the very nature of the case forbidden to speak," he contended, "we should expect and welcome divergent views, and allow them fair expression in a free and fearless press." Sullivan claimed precedent for this argument from John Lancaster Spalding. Speaking before an audience in Rome, the bishop had defended the American Catholic devotion to the U.S. government and constitution, and claimed that they would resist change in either. "Genuine Catholicity," Sullivan added, holds that "there is a sanctity in patriotism."[31]

Sullivan considered his second article for the *New York Review* "daring." It was an exegetical study of the "Three Witnesses" text in the first epistle of John in which, following European scholarship, Sullivan contravened the Roman Inquisition's declaration that the text was an integral part of the inspired original. Instead, Sullivan declared the text was an interpolation of the heretical Priscillianists. With approval Sullivan quoted Bible critic Eberhard Nestle in claiming that efforts to defend the text in supporting the doctrine of the Trinity "have only a pathological interest." Sullivan acknowledged that "the Catholic instinct is to hold fast to the traditional interpretations until the evidence to the contrary is overwhelming." As people "to whom dogma and dogmatic proofs are matters of life and death," Catholics would "hold out against an apparently destructive criticism while an inch of ground remains to be contested." Nonetheless, he argued the "independent attitudes of many theologians" rendered totally irrelevant the words of an 1897 Inquisition decree closing the question.[32]

" 'Loyalty to the Church' is a phrase that should be carefully used," Sullivan continued, "for have we not historic disasters to prove beyond dispute how unwise it is to identify the church with subordinate and reformable decisions, and to stake her authority upon matters which are predominantly within the province of secular science?" Between the "rampant extravagance" of the conservative position and the "candid searching and scholarly criticism" of the progressives, Sullivan wrote, "few intelligent men will hesitate to choose which is the better way of serving Catholicity in these modern days."[33]

In submitting these articles for publication, Sullivan shared the hope of his colleagues on the staff of the *New York Review*, including Driscoll, Gigot, and Duffy, that these advanced positions might find a place within the boundaries of Catholic orthodoxy, even as rather narrowly articulated during the pontificate of Pius X. Indeed, to a man they believed that an honest and sophisticated appraisal of Christian history and Catholic tradition would vindicate them of the suspicion that by adopting modern critical procedures they had abandoned the ancient faith.

> Our purpose was in no sense destructive. We hoped to bring to the knowledge of intelligent priests and lay-folk some of the critical and philosophical questions which, sooner or later, they would have to face anyhow, and to give to these questions such solutions as a liberal and loyal Catholic scholarship could discover. Certainly, at that time, I was orthodox in every article of defined doctrine, and I had no reason to think my associates were not, despite their radical talk from time to time.[34]

The condemnations of modernism shook Sullivan. To escape their effects upon both his health and his standing in the congregation he requested a transfer to the southwest. He met the condemnations with "distrust," he told Throckmorton, and questioned the competence of "the inquisitors." "Among the wilderness of articles, etc., about Modernism, it is extremely rare to discover a statement that is adequate, that appreciates the problems involved, and that carries the question back to its true sources," he complained. No one should comment on modernism, he added, "who does not know biblical criticism pretty thoroughly, possess a good knowledge of the history of theology and doctrine, and enjoy a respectable familiarity with philosophy." He did not abandon his intellectual interests or surrender his hope for eventual reform of Catholic seminary and university curriculum.

Austin, Texas, the site of his new assignment in 1908, offered new opportunities for him, undisturbed as it was by the controversies raging in Washington and New York. En route to Texas he wrote Throckmorton and proclaimed his intention to continue to lecture and to write, for "study is the breath of life to me."[35]

Nonetheless, the condemnations—and the response, or lack thereof, that they provoked in his fellow priests—confirmed Sullivan in his long-standing opinions regarding the condition of the Catholic church in the United States. He suspected that his contributions to the cause of reform would not lie in the area of critical scholarship, and his experience in Austin reinforced this judgment. A mind "most of all metaphysical and speculative" would turn out no substantial scholarly works before Sullivan finally retired from the priesthood and from Roman Catholicism after two years in Austin. Instead, he spent these final months as a Catholic preparing a work of a different order, published in 1910 under the title *Letters to His Holiness, Pope Pius X*. It was hardly what one would expect from the author of several measured, scholarly pieces for the *New York Review* and the *Catholic World*. Scandalized by the book, Throckmorton was troubled by rumors that its anonymous author was Sullivan. How could this scholar and devout Catholic produce such a "blow at Jesus"? "Your informant's impression that I wrote the book is purely inferential," he responded, "[but] I will say that for the book I am principally and primarily responsible—though not wholly so."[36]

Yet this response did not address the more meaningful questions raised by the publication of *Letters to His Holiness*. What line of reasoning compelled Sullivan to shrink from his former resolve to produce significant works of scholarship for his colleagues in the American priesthood and turn, instead, to a sustained polemic bordering on moral fanaticism? If the moral issues raised by Vaticanism came to dominate his reform sensibilities, which events or experiences occasioned his turn from biblical criticism and comparative religion to the moralism of Acton and Martineau? Was *Letters to His Holiness* aptly subtitled "by a Modernist"? How may the work be understood in the context of Americanism and modernism?

The answers to these questions center on Sullivan's analysis of the vitality, or lack thereof, of American Catholic life and thought at the turn of the century. From the beginning of his ordained ministry in 1899, through his missionary work in Nashville and rural Tennessee, during his years of teaching in Washington, and down to his final experience in Austin, one lesson was constantly repeated for Sullivan's edification: Intellectual life in Catholic America was moribund. There was, simply put, no Catholic "audience" for critical religious thought in America. The American clergy, by and large, exhibited the apathy and incompetence in theology and history that Sullivan anticipated, and noted, in the laity.

Coupled with his involvement with the Americanist "movement," this diagnosis of intellectual stagnation convinced Sullivan that he would have to reverse the pattern of European critics of neo-scholastic

Catholicism and ultramontanism. They began with critical studies and were led inexorably to questions of authority and ecclesiology, inspiration and revelation. For the renewal to find a home in America, Sullivan asserted, reformers could not prescind from the essentially moral questions of government, liberty, and authority. Instead, these important issues must be engaged as a prelude and prerequisite to the exploration and acceptance of a new American Catholic understanding of the work of the Infinite Spirit in people and institutions throughout history. In that regard his Americanism was the necessary prerequisite for his modernism. In turn, his modernist program would submit the principal claims and goals of the Americanists in the arena of ecclesiology and church-state relations to the rigorous questions and methods of higher criticism in the arena of the more abstract, intellectual concerns of historical theology, philosophy, and exegesis. As Sullivan perceived Americanism, it affirmed the possibility of options in certain areas of Catholic policy and practice, matters that the Americanists considered to be nonrevealed and thus susceptible to adaptation in history (the proper relationship between church and state, for example). As Sullivan perceived modernism, it supported the pursuit of these reforms or adaptations by demonstrating critically that such reforms were grounded in a non-scholastic yet wholly authentic tradition of Catholic thought. "We know what the American Spirit is in the political and social order," he wrote in *Letters to His Holiness*. "Translate it into the religious order and you have Modernism at its best and purest."[37]

To interpret this final work of Sullivan's Catholic period as incongruent with his prior self-understanding—by suggesting, for example, that *Letters to His Holiness* marks the leap in Sullivan's career from Americanism to modernism—is to ignore the elements of continuity found throughout his life.[38] A shrill polemic indicting Rome for immoral, inquisitorial behavior, the book was a calculated risk, a somewhat naive bid to arouse the moral indignation of American Catholics in the face of the papacy's persistent violation of basic human rights, including liberty of conscience and freedom from state coercion in matters of belief.[39] It represented a shift of strategy rather than purpose. A pattern emerged in Sullivan's thinking that led him to rely more heavily upon an apologetic style fundamentally moral in emphasis as his frustration over the inadequacy of a purely critical, scientific approach intensified.[40]

Accordingly, Sullivan's thoughts turned to matters of national and international politics. By the time he conceived of the idea for *Letters to His Holiness*, his correspondence and essays were peppered with commentary on the intersection of ecclesiastical and international policies. A favorite target was Vatican Secretary of State Merry del Val, who "unfortunately does not love America—his country fared badly at our hands ten years ago; and I know on unimpeachable evidence that he holds us in contempt."[41] In an essay written around the time that *Letters to His Holiness* was published, Sullivan ticked off the diplomatic blunders of the Vatican in Germany, France, Ireland, and the United States, and endorsed the American Catholic Federation, an organization designed to resist the encroachments of Rome upon religious liberty.[42]

In spite of these continuities between his work in Washington and in Austin, it remains true that Sullivan did not jump—he was pushed. What caused him to "go over the top," that is, to abandon entirely the composure of the scholar and assume the posture of the prophet? The answer lies in Sullivan's disenchantment with the American priesthood. As I have noted, he discovered that "few of the younger priests keep in touch with scholarship." "A great many are ordained on extremely slender mental equipment," he confided to Throckmorton.[43] Sullivan was particularly scandalized by the reaction of his colleagues among the intelligentsia when *Pascendi* formalized and enforced the intellectual immaturity of the clergy. When they immediately retracted their opinions or made similar "obscene" gestures of obeisance to Rome, Sullivan was stunned. He characterized them as "moral cowards" devoid of character and integrity. Furthermore, he charged that the Roman system was in fact designed to rob the clergy of individual conscience. It destroyed "personality" by demanding an idolatrous moral submission of individual consciences to the will of the institution. Thereby Rome deprived the priest of his most precious possession, his selfhood.[44]

Sullivan's diaries and correspondence from this period are rife with stories of priests who acknowledged in private, after *Pascendi*, that they had suppressed their questions about the inherited tradition and were, in effect, living a lie. Had not Driscoll, Gigot, and Duffy referred, with "irreverent delight," to Archbishop Farley's unwitting endorsement of their program of critical studies and publications? Of course they had. However, by Sullivan's reckoning, he alone stood firm once the focus of hierarchical suspicion shifted from

Europe to New York and Washington. Two years after *Pascendi* he reflected upon his aversion to clerical groveling: "The usual attitude of priests toward their bishops is somewhat ludicrous. 'No, bishop,' 'Yes, bishop,' is as far toward expressing a personal opinion as they dare to go and even this is spoken with a tremor. I cannot, physically cannot, crawl."[45]

Consequently, Sullivan became somewhat obsessed with his role as a moral prophet to a decaying institution and interpreted its persecution of him as a sign of the righteousness of his cause. It would not be an exaggeration to say that he soon developed a "messiah complex." He identified his own progress with Christ's—the lonely visionary and moral giant who suffered rebuke, insult, and oppression at the hands of the guardians of institutional religion.

> In him [Christ] I saw the historic vocation of personality with an eternal behind it to which none of our low arts can ever approach. . . . If the Ideal enters into history at all, it can have only one place, and that is mastership, and only one residence, the soul of man.[46]

In this frame of mind he retired to Austin only to find more apathy and intellectual immaturity. Finally, his patience at an end, he composed *Letters to His Holiness* as an expression of his moral outrage and in hopes of provoking a confrontation between the ultramontanist and the Americanist-modernist. He depicted Pius X's church as the reincarnation of the Inquisition, a conspiracy of Jesuit intellectuals and curialists seeking to preempt the direct experience of Christ in the lives of the unsuspecting, obedient "Faithful." The modernist sought to return religion to the people and thus sought political and social structures that would facilitate that return. Naturally, therefore, the eyes of many modernists turned to the United States. "Whence could a more zealous advocacy of Modernism have rightly been anticipated?" Sullivan asked.

> Americanism is a word that connotes patriotism. It seems to embrace all that is indigenous to this republic and is typical of it; and whatever becomes of Biblical criticism or the philosophy of dogmatic conformity, the mass of Catholics in this country will not be un-American. So the *Testis Benevolentiae* which laid Rome's solemn disapproval upon Americanism, was not received with enthusiasm, and raised indeed in some quarters a levity not

far removed from disdain. It surely loosened rather than tied more firmly the bonds uniting America to Rome.[47]

As *Pascendi* made obvious, the challenge of modernism as a reform movement within the church was more fundamental and elemental than many acknowledged. Sullivan would not smooth over the obvious and glaring differences in the two orientations to Catholicism, nor engage in the pretense that they could somehow peacefully coexist and complement one another.

A word must be said concerning the magnitude of this question of Modernism. It is not a squabble *intra parietes*, one of the petty ecclesiastical quarrels which the student of large problems can afford to despise. It is fundamentally a great question of spiritual liberty, attended, as advancing liberty nearly always is, with the tragic elements of suffering, as men strive to reach forward to the new light of the intellect while not relinquishing the ancient loyalties of the heart. It has brought a crisis perhaps of life and death to the mightiest religious organization that has ever existed among men. *It aims at a restatement of the creed, a revolutionary change in the external polity, and a regeneration of the inner spirit of the Mother-Church of all Christendom.*[48]

Ironically, therefore, Sullivan agreed with the pope's assessment of the modern conflict within the church. On one side stood the modernists, adherents all of liberalism, democracy, progress, and individual liberty. Adamantly opposed to them were the Romanists, defenders of the church-controlled state. In Sullivan's estimation the absence of coercion of any type under the U.S. Constitution was the truest guarantor of a genuine Catholic value, namely, freedom of choice. The Romanists did not, obviously, believe their own theological claims that human reason, aided by grace, could attain to the good and true without coercion. They perpetuated a system of internal government and a corresponding political philosophy inimical to the true spirit of Catholicism and of the gospel of Jesus alike.

Here then is the Romanized Catholic Church appealing to the American people, asking them to embrace its teachings as the pure Gospel of Christ, and yet saying: "Not only have I a theological, but a political creed. Of that political creed one of the tenets is that church and state should be united. The opposite opinion is a damnable error. . . . Therefore you Americans, ere you perfectly find Christ, must most firmly hold that your Constitution is fatally defective, since it is opposed to the union of church and state." What shall we say of this be we Catholics or not? What can we say except this: that it is akin to blasphemy that a religion should have any political creed whatsoever...that a religion which demands a weakening of loyalty to country before it baptizes us into salvation is obstructing the cause of Christ. . . . To such has the Papacy descended![49]

Sullivan felt that Americans would never fully accept a system in which "the will of people, priests and bishops counts, as such, for nothing." However, this was precisely the insidious way in which the Vatican bureaucrats kept the American church in a perpetual state of dependency and infancy. Sullivan cited a familiar practice: A man not even mentioned in the lists sent by American priests, bishops, and archbishops was appointed to one of the largest archdioceses in the country. "Why?" Sullivan asked. "Because he was an ultra-Roman; because he distinguished himself by taking sides against his country on more than one occasion . . . because he could be depended upon to be a Roman agent here."[50]

Just as the papacy desired to determine state policy and to manipulate ecclesiastical affairs, so did it seek the complete and unquestioning subordination of the processes of critical thought to its own preconceived ends. Thus, anti-Americanism in questions of government manifested itself in anti-modernism in questions of intellectual investigation. The two heresies were not, for Sullivan, disparate phenomena, but two faces of the singular enemy confronting Romanism and Jesuitism.

To Sullivan the "reign of terror" unleashed by Pius X was unprecedented even for the institution had produced the Inquisition. For in the comprehensive crackdown on modernism after 1907 Sullivan perceived the intention to destroy utterly, once and for all, the tradition of intellectual freedom, wedded to the indwelling of the Spirit, which characterized his ideal Catholicism. Sullivan hurled his own anathemas at Pius X:

Under you the Biblical Commission has issued such preposterous decisions, rejected by a practical unanimity of modern scholars, and even by the most eminent members of the commission itself. . . . Under you has fallen an iron age upon Catholic scholarship. You have issued a syllabus, many of whose propositions, rejected by you as false, are part of the very alphabet of critical scholarship. . . . You have left untried no expedient for separating Catholics into a mass of illiterates unacquainted with the scholarship of the last hundred years, and closed in by an opaque curtain of medieval exegesis and scholastic theology. . . . And if we ask who is this Pontiff who defies the laborious acquisitions of four generations of illustrious scholars, we must answer: He is the product of an Italian seminary of fifty years ago, who is an absolute stranger to the sciences he condemns. He knows nothing of biblical criticism. He entered his pontificate ignorant of every modern language but Italian. He is unread in philosophy, in historical theology, in modern psychology.[51]

But in this bleak picture the American Catholic modernist found a place for hope. The reform would survive persecution because the American public simply would not accept the theocratic pretensions of the ultramontanes and would fashion their own vital existence, sooner or later. "A courageous and intelligent laity is the sole hope for a better day," Sullivan wrote. Free-thinking American Catholics would, he was convinced, ultimately reject the pretensions of papalism, along with the distortions they introduced into the Catholic tradition.[52]

Although Sullivan crafted *Letters to His Holiness* to express his outrage over *Pascendi*, he also saw it as a necessary and inevitable moment in a larger historical process of evolution toward a universal religion of the Infinite Spirit. To an inquiring correspondent he explained this strategy:

As you advert to the mood of indignation which the book betrays, let me say that I regret the necessity for it. The academic temper and the scrupulous scientific spirit would have pleased me far more. But so inveterate are the abuses there dealt with, and so scornfully indifferent the attitude of authority towards them, that on reflection I deemed it an urgent necessity to speak with severity, believing this the only way that would make the dead bones bestir themselves.

It has occurred to me for instance that it might be useful to put forth the stages through which a man passes in traversing the ground from the Roman system to the religion of the spirit. This is a pilgrim's progress of which we have too few records.[53]

Sullivan predicted that modernists would soon regain the momentum they had temporarily lost by the condemnations. They would necessarily work outside the institutional church for, as Minocchi had declared, "A genuinely reformative modernism within the Roman Catholic church is now hopeless and impossible." The "finest and noblest phase" of modernism would commence momentarily, Sullivan predicted in 1910.

> Religious criticism once begun is not worthy of itself if it stops half-way in its course. Its duty is to explore the basis of every belief, the natural history of whole religions as well as of individual dogmas, the foundation of morals and the idea of God. . . . It involves retraversing the ground across which the religious history of the race has passed from the earliest days of magic to a worship which is in spirit and in truth. It requires us to search out in the religion of today both what is native to it and what deposits have been left there by past superstitions. . . . A religious thinker who has passed through such a discipline sees the will of the Deity as manifested in the vast purposeful process of things, and not as localized in the Vatican palaces or Delphic caves. He perceives the generic resemblance of all theologies and the similar natural history of all hierarchies, and he becomes less and less disposed to look upon any one system as an exhaustive expression of the infinite Truth-Ideal, or to believe that the Eternal Absolute has delegated as its single oracle any Pontifex maximus whether of old Rome or new. . . . It is toward this intellectually nobler and spiritually simpler outlook that modernists are growing. Disappointed in the hope of winning the age to a particular theology, they are studying the validity of all theologies. Having failed in inducing what they thought was the ultimate religion to adapt itself to the requirements of progress, they are forced to inquire whether, after all, it is the ultimate religion.[54]

Sullivan pursued this dream of a deinstitutionalized religion of Infinite Spirit. On 1 May 1909, the path led him away from Catholicism and to exile in Kansas City, where he was lonely and in ill health. He left the parish in Austin, he told Throckmorton, not only because he could not submit to *Pascendi*, but because the decree had left him friendless and isolated. In 1911 he joined the Unitarian Church in Cleveland, Ohio; in 1912 he was admitted to the Unitarian ministry, serving All Soul's Unitarian Church in Schenectady, New York. For the remaining twenty-three years of his life Sullivan wrote, preached, and ministered in an ultimately futile effort to wed a "catholiciz-ing, supernatural element" to the "moral integrity" of the Unitarian tradition.

In this effort he was joined by his confidant during his years of modernist turmoil, Estelle Throckmorton. They were married in 1913 and lived happily together until Sullivan contracted pneumonia and died while on vacation in Maine in 1935.[55]

Sullivan never repudiated those elements of Catholicism that he believed to be authentically Christian. In fact, he lectured on them fre-quently as a Unitarian. But he was equally fervent in his condemnation of the institutional model for Roman Catholicism that dominated his time and place. Romanism had poisoned the wellsprings of genuine Catholicism, in Sullivan's opinion, by suffocating both the moral sense of the tradition and its authentic supernaturalism.[56]

To the end of his life Sullivan claimed that he had not been taken by surprise by the condemnation of modernism, but understood it as a necessary moment in a larger historical progression to a uni-versal, nondogmatic religion. And it was Sullivan alone who proudly proclaimed himself a modernist, convinced as he was that modernism would reconcile critical science not to "the ancient faith" (committed in his day historically and irrevocably to certain institutional expres-sions) but to a "religion of the Infinite Spirit."

JOHN R. SLATTERY AND THE SURVIVAL OF MODERNISM

John Richard Slattery was born in 1851 to a wealthy family of Irish immigrants in New York. His father, who had exploited his political connections to Tammany Hall in amassing a fortune in the construction business, targeted son John for a career in law and pol-itics. John attended Mass with his parents at the Paulist church on 59th Street in Manhattan and was impressed with the preaching he heard there. Slattery's fascination with Isaac Hecker dated from these days. The model of Hecker's service to the church attracted Slattery, as it had many American Catholic progressives, by its blending of the truths of Christian faith with the purest values of American society. Between stints at the City College of New York and Columbia Law School, Slattery spent a year at St. Charles College, a preparatory seminary in Ellicott City, Maryland, run by the Sulpicians. In 1872

Slattery had what he described as a "conversion experience" while viewing a parade of black members of the Odd Fellows Society. Convinced that he should devote himself to the evangelization of black Americans, Slattery abandoned the study of law and joined the English Foreign Mission Society (Mill Hill Fathers). He was ordained a priest in 1877 at the age of twenty-six and soon thereafter appointed rector of St. Francis Xavier Church in Baltimore. The following year he was named the American provincial of the small society.[57]

As provincial Slattery began to prepare the way for the development of a black clergy. Confronting deep-seated prejudices, from which he was not entirely free himself, Slattery embarked on a campaign to make American Catholicism more responsive to the black community.[58] Like Hecker, he encouraged the assimilation of Catholics into the mainstream of American life. But the situation confronting Slattery was doubly challenging, for he first had to fight for the acceptance of blacks—and for the resources to evangelize them. His religious superiors in England found Slattery arrogant and "undisciplined" in his approach to the problem, and by a vote his brother missionaries in the United States dismissed him from the office of provincial in 1882. Retreating to Richmond, Virginia, at the invitation of Bishop John Keane, Slattery opened a Josephite mission there and wrote numerous articles for *Catholic World* in which he advocated greater institutional support for the Negro missions and battled white stereotypes about blacks.

On the eve of the Third Plenary Council in Baltimore, Slattery sent a memorandum to Herbert Vaughan, his superior in England, with copies to Keane and Cardinal Gibbons. The memorandum made several specific recommendations for the evangelization of black Americans, including the establishment of a Josephite seminary in Baltimore. Although the bishops did not follow this recommendation, they decreed an annual collection for the Negro and Indian missions and formed a Commission for Catholic Missions Among the Colored Peoples and Indians. Despite these gains for his cause Slattery continued to criticize the meager Catholic missionary efforts and published articles documenting the much greater investments of Protestant churches in the evangelization of blacks.[59]

At the same time, Slattery pressed his Mill Hill superiors for an American college to train missionaries. He argued that the seminary in England produced missionaries who understood neither the United States nor the Negro missions.[60] Black missionaries would be much more effective than whites. In this cause Slattery enlisted the aid of Cardinal Gibbons, who intervened with Vaughan, and Bishop Francis A. Janssens of Natchez, who was the first bishop to publicly advocate "colored priests for colored people."[61] Gibbons dedicated St. Joseph's Seminary in 1888. Three years later one of the seminary's first students, Charles Uncles, became the first black man ordained in the United States.

Slattery was encouraged by this success and petitioned Vaughan for the independence of the American Josephites from the English Mill Hill Fathers. Gibbons agreed to accept the new society as a diocesan institute that would choose its own superior but remain technically under the authority of the archbishop of Baltimore. By 1893 the arrangement was finalized and Slattery became the first superior of the Josephites (St. Joseph's Society for Colored Missions).[62]

Encouraged by the recognition and respect that his new post brought him within the American church, and by his friendships with members of the progressive wing of the American hierarchy, Slattery continued his campaign to strengthen Catholic commitment to the black missions. For a time he served as an apologist for Catholicism. In "The Negroes and the Baptists," published in the *Catholic World*, Slattery took issue with an article from "an irresponsible quarterly review published in New York City, and edited by one who claims to be a Catholic." In this article Eugene Didier misrepresented Catholic teaching on slavery. "Everything in Mr. Didier's paper against the Negro is directly contrary to Catholic truth or ethics," Slattery protested, contrasting Didier's statements—for example, that "slavery was a blessing to the slave"—with Leo XIII's condemnation of it as a "dreadful curse."[63] Writing as a Catholic, Didier had slandered the Negro as "a natural born and habitual liar," as "shiftless, shameless, brutal . . . ungrateful, immoral." Slattery was infuriated not only by the language used but by its identification with Catholicism:

> This writer lives in Baltimore—that is, in the same city with the colored Oblate Sisters of Providence, who, since 1829, have been an edifying community consecrated to the cultivation of the highest Christian virtues. . . . How in the face of these good souls any man, Catholic or Protestant, Jew or Gentile, could write as Mr. Didier in last July's *Globe* is simply inexplicable. . . . Mr. Didier's sentiments on the Negro, however, are not those of the white Catholics of Baltimore.[64]

Because he was in direct competition with Protestant evangelists for the souls of black Americans, Slattery was dismayed at any display of Catholic racism. He reported that T. J. Morgan, the corresponding secretary of the American Baptist Home Mission Society, had taken extracts from Didier's article and "with conscious duplicity has made them appear as the teaching of representative Catholics." Unfortunately, Slattery lamented, "some of the more simple of the colored people. . . were inclined to take Morgan's misstatement for the truth, and consequently these least of the kingdom were deeply scandalized at what they in their simplicity believed to be the opinions of the Catholic Church." Slattery responded with a castigation of southern Baptists, who "show no such friendship for the black man."[65]

As superior of the Josephites, Slattery presided over the expansion of the Negro Mission to seven southern states served by twenty-one priests. By 1899 the Josephites had founded churches, a seminary, an orphanage, and an industrial school, and were in need of catechists for the South. Slattery issued a plea for institutional support for a proposed Catholic college for Negro catechists:

> Unless fortified by negro catechists and negro priests, we shall always be at a disadvantage in dealing with the negro millions beyond the pale of Holy Church. The negro looks with suspicion upon white men. The impression left from slavery; the many dishonest tricks upon them; unpaid wages. . . these and countless other wrongs make the negroes suspicious of the whites. . . . How can one say the negroes do not want their own priests since the experiment has never been tried, for we have but two, one of whom is dead?[66]

At this juncture, despite his own misgivings about some of the black students at St. Joseph's Seminary and concerns about the supposed "moral weakness" of blacks, Slattery remained hopeful that the church would provide adequate support for the cause.[67] "The nineteenth century brought them emancipation, right of ownership, education, citizenship," he wrote. "Let the twentieth century crown all by imparting to them the truths of our Holy Religion, in which glorious task, with God's blessed help, no small part shall be played by St. Joseph's College for Negro Catechists."[68] In April 1899 Slattery journeyed to Rome and met with Cardinal Miescylaw H. Ledóchowski and Archbishop Agostino Ciasca, prefect and secretary, respectively, of the Sacred Congregation de Propaganda Fide. Subsequently he submitted a memorial to the Propaganda requesting a grant of funds and farm land for the college. The request was approved and Slattery proceeded with the foundation of St. Joseph's College for Negro Catechists in Mobile, Alabama.[69]

From his ordination in 1877 to 1899, then, Slattery was engrossed in efforts to evangelize black Americans. He traveled extensively, especially in the South, visiting the schools and missions established by the Josephites. Slattery's diverse experiences as an administrator and church leader, and as a missionary to missionaries, shaped his intellectual growth. Like Sullivan, Slattery's observations of the lives and spiritual needs of ordinary Americans, as well as his frustration with the church bureaucracy, convinced him of the irrelevance of neoscholastic apologetics to the vital work of evangelization. He became engaged with the controversial issues of the day that had a bearing on the life of faith.

Slattery's interest in modernism began in 1884, a year that he later described as "the turning point in my life."[70] While lobbying in Baltimore for a seminary to train white and black missionaries, Madame Pvormann, a woman interested in his cause, offered to sell her home for the proposed seminary. Slattery corresponded with the woman and sent her a copy of *The Imitation of Christ*. She returned the courtesy by sending Slattery a copy of Darwin's *On the Origin of Species*. Slattery never met this woman in person but recalled:

> A well-read woman familiar with Haeckel, Darwin, Huxley, Tyndall, and a lot more, she outclassed and outmatched me. But she opened up new vistas. The Bishop of Richmond gave me the help of his own reading and put his library at my disposal. We depended chiefly upon St. George Mivart, Bishop Clifford, of Clifton, England, and the London *Tablet*. This Catholic organ of Great Britain opened—and perhaps still opens—its columns to all sorts of writers who furnished me with divergent views.[71]

Among the "divergent views" suggested to Slattery by his correspondence with Pvormann was the claim that Darwin's theory of evolution had rendered belief in a divine creation untenable. Slattery was troubled by this possibility and authored an essay in 1885 entitled "Contemporary Catholic Thought and Evolution," in which he reported on the theistic evolution of Mivart and sketched ideas that were present in a more developed form in the writings of John Gmeiner and John

Zahm. These ideas included the assertion that Augustine and Aquinas had approved evolution as regards plants and animals, and the notion that God had immediately infused a soul into the human animal.[72]

The encounter with Pvormann and with a body of literature casting aspersions upon doctrines that he held as unexamined assumptions compelled Slattery to engage in a rigorous examination of the conclusions of the higher criticism. In the course of his reading Slattery was greatly influenced by the major proponents of theological modernism, especially Alfred Loisy. He recalled:

> Those years in Richmond saw the first sloughing off [of my priesthood]. I entered the capital . . . with the faith which a devout mother had impressed upon her only child. Upon leaving it my frame of mind may be summed up thus: The story of Adam was a myth; the Pentateuch composite . . . Abraham, Isaac, and other patriarchs, if real personages, were painted in the Bible much as the Lives of Saints . . . no sign of immortality in the Hebrew canon, or of original sin. In a word, the conclusions of higher criticism had found a disciple, who in accepting them might still be called a good Catholic.[73]

Slattery did not move from Americanism to modernism, but embraced both in the same motion. For a decade following his first exposure to the higher criticism he clung tenaciously to the conviction that science and faith could be reconciled within the framework of an updated Roman Catholic theology. He was naturally attracted to the Americanists, who proclaimed a "free church in a free society" and believed in a progressive doctrine of providence by which the emerging American church would become a model for the universal church. Slattery praised his episcopal ally in Virginia, John J. Keane, as a "mystic" and as the embodiment of Hecker's Americanism; he formed a close association with Denis O'Connell, Americanist agent in Rome and later bishop of Richmond; and he corresponded frequently with Archbishop John Ireland, who vigorously supported Slattery's various initiatives regarding the mission to black Americans.[74] Cardinal Gibbons also supported Slattery in these ventures and, as we have seen, intervened with ecclesiastical officials on his behalf on several occasions; Slattery became associated with Catholic University and even contributed a chapter to Gibbons's book *The Ambassador of Christ.* Americanist Alphonse Magnien of St. Mary's Seminary discussed his plans for seminary modernization with Slattery, who sent his own seminarians to take classes there. The Paulist Walter Elliot, Hecker's biographer, published Slattery's articles on the race question and became a close friend.[75]

Slattery shared the enthusiasm of the Americanists for Archbishop Francesco Satolli's speech before the Columbian Catholic Congress in 1893, in which the papal representative blessed the partnership of "the book of Christian truth and. . . the constitution of the United States." As apostolic delegate to the United States, Satolli sought an editor for his speeches, and Ireland and O'Connell, hoping to retain Satolli's favor and to influence his opinions, recruited Slattery for the task. By that time, Slattery's "biography" reports, the Josephite priest had already embraced what he perceived as an integrated program of progressive thought and action, expressed politically in Americanism and intellectually in the stirrings of (what would later be called) modernism at Catholic University. For a time after 1893 Slattery saw Satolli, then a supporter of Keane and Ireland, as the symbol of Roman endorsement for such a program.[76]

By 1895, however, perhaps in response to Pope Leo XIII's encyclical *Longinqua Oceani* cautioning against church-state separation, Satolli had begun to withdraw from the circle of progressive priests and bishops and to gravitate toward the conservatives.[77] Slattery, editing Satolli's speeches at the time, expressed amazement shading into outrage at the "housecleaning" that followed this reversal: O'Connell was removed from his position as rector of the North American College in Rome in 1895; Keane, from his position as rector of Catholic University in 1896. Slattery was devastated by the seeming capriciousness of Satolli, and speculated as to how deeply he could hold *any* position if he was able to reverse himself so arbitrarily and with apparent ease.[78]

As historian William Portier points out, 1895 was the beginning of Slattery's period of profound moral disillusionment, not only with the Roman curia, but also with his fellow priests and the Americanist bishops, who failed to stand by one another in the face of ecclesiastico-political scrutiny following the condemnation of Americanism in *Testem Benevolentiae*. The disillusionment began with Slattery's visit to Rome with Gibbons in 1895. His impression of curial venality and indifference to the needs of the American church and especially of American blacks was reinforced by a second visit in 1899 to secure Cardinal Ledóchowski's support for the catechetical college. Slattery's experiences with Vatican officials convinced him that they were concerned above all with holding on to their privileged positions within an ecclesiastical structure whose supposed divine origin was the subject of the critical work of modernist church historians. During the 1899 visit Slattery met with Ireland and O'Connell to discuss the implications of the recently released *Testem Benevolentiae* and, according to the "Biographie," the three men had a searching discussion of the viability of Catholic doctrine in the light of the findings of historical criticism and modern science. Later, after returning to the United States and hearing Ireland and O'Connell praise the papacy publicly, Slattery decided that they were prone to ecclesiastically induced cowardice and paralysis of intellect. He regarded them as dishonest and ultimately infected with the same strain of ecclesio-political ambition that motivated the curial officials.[79]

Slattery's growing disillusionment with Catholicism was intellectual as well as moral. In 1906 Slattery wrote an article reviewing "how my priesthood dropped from me" during the course of intellectual struggles in the 1890s. As Josephite superior from 1893 to 1903, Slattery recalled, he occasionally taught classes at the seminary and presided over the spiritual formation of the seminarians—two tasks that "tended to peel off [his] priesthood." In teaching the history of the early church, Slattery followed Döllinger's *First Ages of the Church* and Duchesne's work on the origins of the episcopacy. He soon concluded that there was a plurality of polities in the early church and hardly a clear line of development to a hierarchy or papacy. Harnack's *History of Dogma* extended the argument beyond the apostolic age, but Slattery felt that Joseph Turmel's works of critical history were more damaging to the Catholic case for continuity in institutional development.[80] After reading these critical historians Slattery concluded that on contested points concerning institutional development, and especially touching upon the papacy, the Catholic position was untenable. The Roman church had substantiated dubious claims, as often as not, by the use of forgeries and interpolations.

Apart from the question of its historical development the hierarchical church could not withstand the moral force of democracy sweeping the world, Slattery believed. He wrote that ironically, in Pius IX's *Syllabus of Errors*, modern forms of government were condemned, "yet Papal Infallibility was carried in the Vatican Council by a majority vote—an essential element of modern government." Slattery also came to believe that so-called heresies were often simply forerunners of ideas which would soon be adopted as orthodox. "In some way or other, heresies and civil liberty are co-related," he suggested, "heresies first ran afoul of the Church...but in the long run liberty gains the day, and the heresy, its work done, becomes fossilized and useless as Church dogma."[81]

This emphasis on personal liberty was a distinctive characteristic of American Catholic modernism as it manifested itself in the thought of the two priests who confronted the question of the relationship between Americanism and modernism directly, Sullivan and Slattery. They worked independently of one another, but both developed analyses of the question that penetrated to its very core, namely the issue of authority in government. As patriotic Americans, both Sullivan and Slattery were naturally sensitive to the issue and reduced the complicated questions of philosophical paradigms and theological resources to a fundamental struggle over authority: Who shall govern the body, by what means, and according to which standards of accountability? To Slattery especially, movements or individuals had been condemned as heretical primarily because their philosophy or theology or ecclesiology implied uncomfortable political consequences for those in power in the church. If this is indeed the case, Slattery reasoned, let us engage the problem at this fundamental level. Lack of clarity on the interdependency of theology and politics had led to a number of abuses and confusion of priorities. The most grievous of these abuses, Slattery maintained, was the tendency of the government in power to manipulate theological and philosophical reflection, shape it in its own image, and thereby distort it in justifying that governmental model. By focusing on the question of government and its supporting ecclesiology, reform might take root at a substantive level.

As an example of abuses that occur when theology is put to the service of government, Slattery pointed to Jesuitism in the Catholic Church:

> Religious autocracy has gone hand in hand with slavery to government; so much indeed that the absolutism of Ignatius of Loyola has become the norm of church government; save where Concordats protect the hierarchy and clergy; e.g., the removal of Bishop Keane from the rectorship of the Catholic University was simply impossible in France or Spain, or Bavaria. In one word, the Catholic Church has degenerated into the tail of the Jesuit kite. . . . All down the ages what has been condemned at first as

heresy, becomes later on dogma—e.g., Pelagianism stands condemned, yet the Jesuit teaching on the efficacy of grace is Pelagianism. We have heard several professors in Catholic institutes make the same remark.

Slattery noted that the same pattern was apparent in the contest over critical methods and their proper application, for "Loisyism is condemned, yet Loisyism is taught everywhere in seminaries, not openly, but under the cloak of Newman as a rule."[82]

If methods of government carried with them corresponding theologies, Slattery preferred the relationship between the two that had been articulated by Isaac Hecker. Most priests who were trained in the model of Jesuit neo-scholasticism, Slattery observed, "hardly cared a snap about the spiritual life." The writings of Hecker had, however, conveyed to Slattery the insights of Lallemant and Caussade, two great Jesuits "of a school quite outside the drift of Jesuit thought." Lallemant's *Spiritual Doctrine* and the Caussade's *Abandonment to Divine Providence* inspired in Slattery an interest in mysticism that became for him "real life." Upon reading Loisy and von Hügel he was intrigued to learn of the historical antecedents of Christian mysticism in the writings of Pseudo-Dionysius, which in turn were apparently of pagan origin. But this knowledge did not distract Slattery from the life of mystical prayer that he was nurturing in moments of solitude. He was distracted, however, by the "daily experience of the seminary and convents, whose official I was." Slattery was appalled by the quality of seminarians in his charge; the longer one studied under the scholastic regime, "the more careless about his soul's life he grew." The Josephite superior found himself doubting the worth of the priesthood itself:

> Neither Council nor Pope, bishop nor priest, recognizes any self-fault. The reform canons of Council or Synod read alike and fail alike. In fact, the Catholic Church's greatest enemy is her own clergy. . . . A million times better it would be to have them as are other public men, mixing in the public crowd and mart, and taking their everyday chance with the rest. No false halo would surround their heads.[83]

Slattery recalled in 1906 that he had crystallized these growing doubts in one central question, namely, whether Roman Catholicism at the turn of the century embodied the moral ideal of Christianity. He asked himself: "Do morals depend upon religion?" This question led him to study the origins of religion and he read Jastrow, Frazer, and other writers on primitive religions. From a seminary colleague he also learned much about Oriental lore. The result of these inquiries led Slattery to a position similar to the one later condemned by *Pascendi*: the practice of religion was determined exclusively by its social and historical contexts. Much of what passed for religion in the Catholic Church was no more than thinly-veiled rationales for institutional government of the community:

> In the long run I became convinced that morals are the expression of the will of society and not of religion, *qua* religion. The moral principles of Catholicism and Protestantism are Aristotelian. The evangelistic teaching . . . the various other doctrines of the "Sermon on the Mount" have no foothold among either one or the other.[84]

As Slattery's openness to modernist ideas increased, so did his sensitivity to the question of Americanism. During this protracted crisis in his life he was obsessed with the glaring discrepancies between American values and the goals of the papacy. "Like all American Catholics," he asserted, "I believed in a free church, in a free state. . . . But Leo XIII taught that the Church is supreme and the State her handmaid." The more Slattery studied this question, the more "surprised" he was with the official position of the church. He soon recognized that when Archbishop Kain of St. Louis came out publicly for a free Church in a free State, "whether he knew it or not, [he] preached thereby heresy." Accompanying Slattery's decided preference for the American way of government was his increasing intolerance of the authoritarian Roman model, that had stifled every new and innovative idea and spirit in Christendom. The bureaucratization of the church was the reason for its immobility and irrelevance in the modern world. "At work in our own land," Slattery warned, was the same clericalism and autocracy that had driven Tertullian from Rome and the inopportunists from Vatican I. The "insolent minority," in Newman's phrase, continued to dominate church life in the United States, whether it be in "the Corrigan case in Hoboken, the McGlynn of New York, or the Muldoon-Feehan of Chicago."[85]

As we have seen, the Americanists's timid and duplicitous responses to the condemnation of Americanism reinforced Slattery's impression that they were more concerned with ecclesial status than with moral rectitude, and left him with the feeling that he was the only one among them of conviction and integrity.[86] Upon his return to the United States after meeting with Ireland and O'Connell in Rome, Slattery continued his work for the Negro missions and his self-education, a process he reported to O'Connell in a series of letters over the following year.[87] Slattery's essay in the *American Ecclesiastical Review* in November, 1900, entitled "Scholastic Methods, Their Advantages and Disadvantages," suggests the direction his thoughts were taking. Representing what might be termed the first phase of Americanist-modernist thought, the article called for a reconciliation of modern science and Catholic theology and demonstrated how pervasive were the empirical and pragmatic methods of modern science at every level of American society. Just as Aristotelian methods and philosophy inspired a golden age of medieval Catholicism, so should scientific and critical methods inspire a modern Catholic renascence.[88] Slattery sent O'Connell a copy of the essay, and predicted that "curialism" would not be able to withstand the onslaught of "the impetuous sweep of the ever-marshalling hosts of modern studies; evolution, Biology in particular, and the unification of knowledge and methods joined with the uprising of the masses."[89]

The "sloughing off" of Slattery's priesthood continued unabated in 1901, a year that he described as "the most unhappy of my life." At Keane's installation as Bishop of Dubuque, Slattery witnessed Ireland at his most unctuous. And in what was perhaps a final effort to understand and accept the development of doctrine in terms congenial to Catholicism, Slattery studied the writings of John Cardinal Newman, but found them unconvincing.[90] Equally troubling was the diminished episcopal support for the Negro missions, a failure that Slattery attributed to racism in the church. He made this charge explicitly in a vehement 1902 sermon delivered before a black congregation assembled in Baltimore for the first mass of black priest John Henry Dorsey.[91] This sermon reflected the fact that Slattery's intellectual crisis and moral disillusionment had displaced his loyalty to the institutional church. He compared the contemporary hierarchical and dogmatic church unfavorably with the pristine simplicity of the apostolic community and implied that black Americans were discouraged from becoming Roman Catholic by the officiousness of the institution. The sermon incited considerable controversy in Baltimore.[92]

Following the sermon Slattery arranged meetings in Europe with Loisy and Harnack. He apparently hoped to study with Harnack, whose efforts to demonstrate the historicity of institutional Christianity Slattery found appealing. Slattery also read Loisy's *L'Evangile et l'eglise* in December and determined to make it available in English (he later approached Scribner's about the project). The trip to Europe was devoted to studying the claim of the critical historians that external political and ecclesiastical circumstances had consistently determined the shape and content of Christian doctrine. Newman, Loisy, and Harnack each had attempted to reformulate and reinterpret Christianity in light of this insight. Slattery believed that their various philosophical, historical, and religious insights were complementary and conveyed this idea to Loisy himself.[93]

In 1903 Slattery authored a pseudonymous article for the *Independent* entitled "A Root Trouble in Catholicism" which demanded that the papacy and the Catholic hierarchy, mired in an anachronistic ecclesio-political system, "be brought into harmony with modern principles of government." The rejection of the prevailing Roman Catholic ecclesiology, however, also implied a rejection of the theology that undergirded it. Newman's writings on development of doctrine offered the basis for a shift away from neo-scholasticism but, like Sullivan, Slattery deemed it improbable that such a shift would occur. And, like Sullivan, he predicted that the American approach to civil liberties, church-state relations, and the participation of the people in government would ultimately transform the Roman Catholic church. "The alliance [between the Americanization of the world and the Americanization of the church] will not come in our day," he wrote, "but come it must, unless the chiefs of the Church are to be the prime cause why on earth, when he comes, the Son of Man will find no faith."[94]

Slattery's Catholicism was, in his words, "unpeeling." He stepped down from his post as rector of the seminary and in 1903 requested the canonical procedures necessary to be placed *sub titulo patrimonii*, a process leading to retirement. Despite Gibbons's opposition Slattery took a "leave" from the priesthood and enrolled as a law student in the University of Berlin. In 1904 he retired as "superior emeritus" of the Josephites. By 1906 he had renounced the priesthood and Roman Catholicism altogether and denounced supernaturalism, symbolism, and "the whole *modus operandi* of Priestcraft." Rejecting the Catholic doctrine of free will, Slattery adopted a philosophy of determinism. He found the divinity of Christ untenable, for modern criticism demonstrated that there was "no essential difference between His life and that, say, of Francis of Assisi."[95]

In the pages of the Protestant periodical, the *Independent*, Slattery described his disenchantment with Catholic efforts in missionary work among Negroes, and commented upon the true nature of theological modernism. Two years after *Pascendi* he published an article in another periodical interpreting the modernist crisis as but one episode in the ongoing, periodic power struggle within the institutional church, in this case "a victory of the Jesuits, aided by the Franciscans, over the Dominicans." In his analysis the modernist crisis was theological or philosophical in nature only in a secondary, derivative sense. The prior question was political:

> [*Pascendi*] is the formal declaration of war against modern science, not indeed *qua* science, but in all its methods and aims. . . . The Catholic Church may be looked upon as a state . . . or as a society or whatever else we please. She is surely a living witness to her identity. No doubt she has the right to say what she is, what are her parts, what is her constitution, who are her members. Such claims are inherent. Therefore when the Catholic Church by her official mouthpiece—the Pope or his cabinet, the Roman congregations—declares that the doctrine known as modernism is not hers, and adds that its followers are traitors to her cause, we must accept her decision. No court of appeals exists to which we can go.[96]

This was Slattery's most eloquent statement of the reasons motivating his departure from the Roman church, and it echoed a similar declaration of independence by William L. Sullivan. Both priests took the pope at his word, acknowledged that he spoke for that church, and then declared that they could not in good faith remain as members of such a church. Whereas a modernist like von Hügel refused to admit this and pointed to an alternative Catholic tradition, the American modernists recognized that "genuine Catholicity" had always been opposed by the institutionalists. Slattery ruefully quoted Döllinger's axiom that "it is not always the same pope, but it is ever the same papacy."[97]

Slattery maintained that modernism was deemed heretical not because its conclusions were unsound, but because these conclusions followed from principles that were at odds with the neo-scholastic synthesis. He quoted Loisy's insistence that "*modernism*—such as really exists and which is neither *agnosticism* nor the philosophy of *immanence* . . . questions those principles, viz.: the mythological idea of external revelation, the absolute value of traditional dogma, the absolute authority of the church." Rome had decided that scholasticism was the best, indeed the only, system of philosophical and theological reflection capable of preserving papal authority as it had been defined by the First Vatican Council. "Hence, according to Catholic authorities," Slattery wrote, "the antidote of modernism lies in Rome, the episcopate, and scholasticism. To look beyond any one of them is to be a modernist." Slattery admitted that he found this position to be preposterous in light of "the great results of modern scholarship!"[98]

Like Sullivan, Slattery traced the contemporary manifestation of Romanism to "the Italian hatred of democracy." Slattery warned his Protestant readers that "a fact which must be never overlooked in papal documents is that they are also Italian."

> When an Italian says, *Credo in deum*, his god is Imperial Rome, Italy united, and the papacy. Behold his trinity. . . . Papal documents are the charters and by-laws of the theocracy. Through them rings a *note* of religion. The Holy Spirit, Jesus Christ, the blessed apostles, Peter and Paul, the eternal happiness of souls, and so on are the chords upon which, under the stroke of the fisherman's ring, is dinned ever the same theocratical slogan. And it is just this very political aspect which Rome labors to keep hidden from the English, and especially from the American, world.[99]

Slattery's statement of the continuity between Americanism and modernism was even more direct than Sullivan's. Because he valued democracy and freedoms of thought, speech, and religion, Slattery wrote, the Americanist favored a theological model by which revelation was understood as an ongoing phenomenon open to all people and not restricted to a clerical elite. Were it developed sufficiently, the Americanist ecclesiology would be based on the belief in the Divine Spirit as immanent in the community, and would see the church as always engaged in the dynamic process of development. On the other hand the curialists were concerned with preserving the lands and political powers inherited from an age of despotism and monarchy; neoscholasticism provided a theoretical framework in which elitism and the concentration of power in the hands of the few made sense.

Slattery believed that "America is learning [this] lesson" about Rome as a result the Vatican's diplomatic involvement in the Spanish-American War and its aftermath. When William Howard Taft led a

U.S. commission to Rome to discuss the fate of Catholics in the Philippines and in Cuba, Slattery quipped, "there was no question of souls but of property." The curial officials were concerned with the land they might lose and the wealth attendant upon it. Slattery even surmised that Cardinal Satolli, the Apostolic Delegate to the United States at the time, had his sights set on "being an envoy pleni-potentiary to the United States government of the South American republics," presumably to exercise political influence there.[100]

Within this framework of analysis Slattery had little trouble concluding that "the letter on modernism is a political document." He explained that the political theory implicit in modernist philosophical and theological presuppositions was the aspect of the "movement" most insidious in the estimation of the integralists:

> The results of higher criticism had cut the ground from underneath papal pretensions. If scholarship be admitted, Rome's supremacy is gone—a supremacy in the papal eyes of the church over the state, the mistress over the handmaid. There was nothing to do to save this supremacy but to repudiate modernism and modernists, root and branch.[101]

Yet, Slattery believed, the repudiation of modernism had taken the form of "a peevish remedy." Following a period of repression inaugurated by *Pascendi*, he predicted, modernism would reappear with renewed vigor, primarily because it enjoyed the advantage of historical accuracy, science, and progress. The first remedy for modernism proposed by the papacy after 1907—the return to scholastic philosophy exclusively—was inherently flawed, Slattery observed, for modern intellects would quickly discern that St. Thomas's arguments from astrology were irrelevant, and "his sacramental system and his plea for papal primacy rest upon forgeries, which his Dominican brethren in Asia Minor concocted." Slattery found equally feckless a second remedy proposed by *Pascendi*, that priests may take no courses in public universities for which there are chairs in the Catholic institutes, for such chairs were quite limited in number. As though it were self-evidently flawed, he dismissed in one sentence the feasibility of the papal order of vigilance and censorship of condemned writings. And on the matter of "a spy system" created by the pope—the diocesan watch committees—Slattery noted that the German bishops had already refused to promulgate the encyclical unless this requirement be removed— "And out it went for Germany."

Again the reason was political: "Rome wants no trouble with Prussian Germany."[102]

Slattery believed that modernism would survive because it had, in one form or another, entered the mainstream of twentieth-century western culture. He pointed to the abundance of modern novels—which seminarians "love to read"—as part of "an almost universal literary effort" to spread a modernistic, developmentalist worldview. Even the press was suffused with modernism. The world of literature was not unaffected by the world of politics, Slattery realized, and here too the tide of history was against Romanism:

> [Rome] has lost, and lost forever, her once universal hold on the state, the family, the university, the school, and the workshop. Her face is toward the setting sun, and humanity faces ever the morning. She will die hard. . . . in a similar way the old frameworks—law, civilization, Christianity—serve to keep Rome before the eyes of the world. Men put life where there is none. . . . Rome knows full well that she is at least moribund. But she ever looks for that resurrection which seemed in sight under scholasticism, got its first set-back in the Renaissance, its defeat in the Reformation, and its divorce from the state in the American Revolution.[103]

Slattery devoted the remainder of his treatise to detailing the signs of modernist survival despite the intellectual ruin occasioned by *Pascendi*. He noted that Rome had implicated its own bishops and leading scholars in Germany, had attempted to dismantle the Catholic Institute in Paris, and had condemned all positions on the social modernist spectrum in Italy. Yet these actions served, as often as not, to galvanize resistance in these centers and consolidate movements that had been tenuous before the encyclical was promulgated. He took as his chief example of this point the "incisive and no doubt widely read" books of rebuttal to the encyclical, *What We Ask* and *The Programme of Modernism*, and the revival of *Il Rinnovamento* in Italy.[104]

Slattery, like Sullivan, believed that America would be the breeding ground for modernist ideas. The Catholic church there "may be called modern from its cradle"; it blossomed in the American Republic that had "amazed" mankind by excluding the church from its usual status in other governments. And Slattery interpreted the relative silence of the American church after *Pascendi* not as a sign that the church in the United States was intellectually moribund, but as a measure of the disregard with which certain American priests held papal restrictions. When voices were finally raised, he wrote, it was at the instigation of Rome, which silenced Driscoll, shut down the *New York Review*, and denied Hanna the mitre. Rome had, temporarily at least, robbed the incipient movement of its liberal leadership by threatening those ecclesiastics directly in her line of fire—the bishops.[105]

For his part Slattery retreated to Paris where he formed a close alliance with Albert Houtin, possibly influencing his history of *L'Americanisme*, which first expounded the view that Americanism was the "practical preface" to modernism. Slattery spent the last twenty years of his life traveling between France and California, where he practiced law and lived in the comfort ensured by his inheritance.[106]

Sullivan and Slattery were the radicals of the short-lived modernist movement in the United States. They came to similar conclusions as they struggled to make sense of their dual commitment to Roman Catholicism and to the ethos of the United States. Both men studied Roman Catholic institutional development from a historico-critical perspective and concluded not only that political motivations had corrupted the church but also that the neo-scholastic paradigm perpetuated the corruption. Furthermore, for a time both men turned to the mystical tradition as a Catholic alternative to the extrinsicism promoted by Rome. Finally, both men concluded that the progress of vital Christian religion depended in large part on the ability of the progressive thinkers in the United States to survive the modernist crisis, regroup, and continue to pursue their investigations.

There was indeed an intimate relationship between Americanism and modernism. Curial officials were right to fear the entire complex of motivations and aims inspiring their ecclesiastical opponents; and they were also correct in anticipating that modernism would manifest itself politically and socially, as well as theologically and philosophically. To Lemius and his fellow integralists modernism offered no less than the possibility of a comprehensive alternative to the neo-scholastic system of Catholic thought. For a time Sullivan and Slattery agreed with this assessment and were encouraged by the fact that modernist alternatives to neo-scholasticism were beginning to capture the attention of the major institutions of American Catholic intellectual life, as will be evident from the next chapter of this study.

6. The Interrupted Conversation: The Assimilation of Modernist Themes

The story of the impact of theological modernism upon the American Catholic intellectual community is best told by the plotting of a trajectory of thought beginning with the theistic evolution of John Zahm and culminating in the radical Americanism of William Sullivan and John Slattery. However, the full scope of this impact was not confined to the work of these men, their colleagues, and the priest-scholars at St. Joseph's Seminary in New York.

In fact, the most persuasive testimony to the importance of their undertaking, if not the originality of their thought, was the influence they had upon other scholars writing for Catholic America, especially the professors, teachers, and apologists at the fledgling Catholic University of America, and the contributors to major American Catholic periodicals of the day, including *Catholic World, Catholic University Bulletin*, and the *American Ecclesiastical Review*. For example, the editors of these journals welcomed the *New York Review* in 1905, publicized its arrival, shared resources and writers with it, and manifested considerable enthusiasm for its editorial approach to the challenges of reconciling the ancient faith to modern America.[1]

At Catholic University, an institution of considerable importance to the Americanists who intended it to be a center of American Catholic scholarship, the first three professors of theology when it opened in 1889 were European and reflected in their intellectual orientations the polarization of European Catholicism. Peter Joseph Schroeder had been an opponent of the "errors" of Günther and Döllinger at Cologne, and lectured at Catholic University on Vatican I's teaching on revelation, the church, and Scripture. Joseph Pohle, previously a professor at Fulda, also adopted the conservative, neo-scholastic theological line, while Thomas Bouquillon, a Belgian who had taught with Loisy at the Institut Catholique, supported the Americanist party in controversial issues of the day such as Ireland's Faribault-Stillwater school plan. John J. Keane, first rector of the university, taught a course on homiletics, while the apostolic delegate taught a course on "the doctrine of St. Thomas Aquinas."

In 1890 and 1891, two progressive American priests joined the faculty. Church historian Thomas J. Shahan, former chancellor of the Diocese of Hartford, had studied at the Institut Catholique under Louis Duchesne, and had taken courses from Adolf von Harnack at the University of Berlin immediately prior to joining the Catholic University faculty in 1891. From 1895 to his promotion in 1909 to rector of the university, Shahan was editor-in-chief of the *Catholic University Bulletin*, "which acquired a reputation for high standards of scholarship during those years and exercised a widespread influence on Catholic intellectuals."[2] Shahan also became an associate editor of the *Catholic Encyclopedia*, the first volume of which appeared the year of *Pascendi* (1907) and to which he eventually contributed 200 articles. Joining Shahan on the faculty of Catholic University was Thomas O'Gorman, the former rector of St. Paul Seminary and St. Thomas College, a close associate of John Ireland, and a church historian in sympathy with the Americanists. Shahan, O'Gorman, and their progressive colleagues in the university were aware of the work of European modernists in non-scholastic critical thought.[3] They explored these new methods in their teaching and writing occasionally and evinced signs of the self-awareness and sense of commitment to a cause that imbued the efforts of the Dunwoodians. Unlike Driscoll's co-workers, these professors did not adopt a program of modernism, nor were they consistent in their promotion of the new theology. But they were conversant with the ideas promoted by the professors at Dunwoodie and attempted to integrate modernist themes into their own scholarship.[4]

When Schroeder and Pohle supported Cahenslyism and thereby alienated the liberal members of the university's board of directors, they were eventually forced to resign. However, lest the university be seen as a haven for Americanists, Keane was also removed in 1896.[5] Shahan and O'Gorman remained after Keane's departure. Their brief period of creative intellectual activity stood in sharp contrast to the otherwise listless spirit of American Catholic theology in an era of immigrant assimilation, brick-and-mortar bishops, and Roman hegemony over American thought, devotionalism, and scientific inquiry.[6]

In spite of the considerable challenges inhibiting the intellectual life of the young church, there was nothing inherent in the American system preventing the incorporation of modernist ideas and methods into the mainstream of theological and apologetic thought. To the contrary, as Ireland, Keane, Driscoll, Duffy, Slattery, and Sullivan had predicted, the cultural, political, and religious openness of American society provided the context for what may have been an intellectual awakening of the American Catholic community. To a number of the professors at Catholic University, the new non-scholastic modes of thought suggested themselves as a catalyst for such an awakening.

The clearest and ultimately the most controversial statement of the inadequacy of scholastic methods of theology, biblical criticism, and apologetics was published by a European scholar teaching at Catholic University. It appeared in the same year that the priests at St. Joseph's Seminary at Dunwoodie founded the *New York Review*. Henry Poels was a Dutch scholar attracted to the new American university by Father Charles P. Grannan, head of the Department of Sacred Scripture. A respected exegete, Poels was named to the Pontifical Biblical Commission as a consultor. As that commission was considering a number of controverted questions in 1905 and 1906, Poels published a series of articles in the *Catholic University Bulletin* detailing his opinions on the questions. The series examined the relationship of "History and Inspiration" and ran over one hundred pages.[7]

Poels began by acknowledging that modern biblical criticism was seen by many in the Catholic church as a heathen science, inspired by a positivist philosophy. He admitted that modern philosophy was influenced by positivism, but he refused to see this as an undesirable trait solely because it departed from the example of the neo-scholastics. Thomas was a giant of the Middle Ages, but his science was outdated and would not speak to the modern era. "The wall built by the giants of the Middle Ages will weather the storms of time; the men of the 'Dark Ages' used good mortar: but they did not and could not make a bridge between Christianity and modern science," he wrote.[8] Like the Dunwoodians, with whom he consulted, Poels went on to call for a new system of thought spearheaded by modern criticism:

> This union [between science and Christianity] must be effected by the work of Christian *critics*. Critical history is a new-born science; and it must be confessed that present day apologetics feels the need of sound critical studies, which the Fathers could

not furnish. A great amount of new material has been discovered; moreover, history is studied according to new and truly scientific methods. Hence modern unbelief is very largely the work of historians, or at least of those who pretend to be such. They try to show that the history of the world is merely the result of natural evolution.[9]

Poels reminded his readers that biblical criticism was of Catholic origin, and that Catholicism depended upon a critical reading of history to justify its various developments and to evaluate new ideas proposed to the faith for adaptation. He summarized this relationship in the phrase: "History has only to be freed from the slag of false philosophy in the furnace of true criticism."[10] Even though the ancient Christians knew nothing of modern scientific methods, Poels wrote, they were sympathetic to all forms of critical thought, and modern Catholics realized that criticism "is nothing more than a scientific method of bringing forth 'the clear image of truth' and is 'a divine gift' to mankind in more recent times."[11]

The insights of European modernists weighed heavily upon Poels, and in this series he incorporated themes from Loisy's and Tyrrell's work. He believed that many of the cherished "traditions" of pious Catholics would soon be revealed to be grounded in poetical vision rather than in history. This was no cause for concern, he insisted, because there is nonetheless an "abundance of truly and strictly historical events" remaining in the Christian past, and because the poetry itself pointed to the ineffable truths of religion. Historicity and belief were not always compatible. "In the poetry of the semi-historical and religious legends, left by the childlike medieval giants . . . critics admire the divine *beauty*," Poels wrote, "which Christ, the divine author of so many wonderful but not historical parables, has lavished upon His Spouse, the Catholic Church."[12]

Perhaps the most striking aspect of Poels's series on history and inspiration was its level of specificity, its detailed instruction concerning the various methods of biblical criticism and the issues raised by their application to biblical theology. The series took up a significant proportion of the periodical's pages and served as as a primer in the new criticism for Catholic priests and scholars. In discussing the literary criticism of the Bible, for example, Poels reinterpreted the Catholic doctrine on the inerrancy of scripture. Although "it is impossible to admit a single error in the sacred writings," one may understand that

every affirmation of the Bible "must needs be true only in the sense
in which God and the inspired author wish it to be understood." The
literary critic would help in the process of discerning the author's
intention. For Poels "the only way to know the *intention of the author* is to study the *literary character of his writings*."[13] Moreover, he
contended, "we can not expect from those theologians who continue
the work of the medieval scholastics, the solution of the great modern 'biblical question.'"[14] Neo-scholastic biblical study always stood
at the service of neo-scholastic theology and philosophy; therefore,
Poels asserted, this method did not fulfill Leo XIII's demand that
Catholics study biblical history according to a truly critical method.[15]

   In his approach to the particulars of the literary criticism of the
Bible, Poels included "some preliminary questions" and principles that
other progressive Catholics took for granted but that might be new
even to an informed Catholic readership. Among these principles was
the assertion that ancient books necessarily bear the vestiges of common opinions of their time regarding scientific and historical matters, a
point which Gigot had raised in his articles for the *New York Review*.
To preserve the inerrancy of the text, Poels employed a distinction
popularized in European modernist circles:

> The only difference is that, *as man*, the author is of course himself
> part of his generation. But if he does not affirm these common
> opinions as *author*, if he does not affirm *in writing*, explicitly
> or implicitly, that they are true; if he does not guarantee the
> truth of those opinions *personally*; that is to say, if he does not
> affirm them as a man distinguished from and speaking to the
> other members of his generation: *the author, as such*, can in no
> way be considered the *subject* of those errors and *the man*, who
> writes, is their subject only in as far as he is the *representative
> of his generation*.[16]

   In elucidating this and other principles of modern literary criticism, Poels held that these principles of criticism conformed to the
guidelines of *Providentissimus Deus*. As a consultant to the Biblical Commission, Poels was sensitive to Roman opinions and guidelines; consequently, he saw clearly the urgency of the question and
appreciated the ecclesiastico-political repercussions of any statement
of methodological principle. Thus he quoted the encyclical liberally to
establish his conformity with its guidelines.[17] Yet Poels acknowledged
that many questions remained in doubt, and that the new methods

raised as many questions as they resolved. On the matter of the historicity of a particular narrative, for example, he admitted that "the only thing we are not sure of is whether the historical truth of this source or tradition is warranted by *divine* authority." Because large areas of gray remained in the Catholic understanding of the biblical tradition, Poels advised a caution and humility which he seemed to contrast with the "certainties" offered by the neo-scholastics. "To weight Christianity with a view of biblical history, which, when confronted with the facts, is at once seen to be refuted by them," Poels warned, "is a responsibility, which no Catholic would take upon himself, if he realized it."[18]

In the next article in his series Poels demonstrated that the Fathers themselves, even without the tools of criticism, had many "doubts" about the historical character of some biblical passages. Their doubts were different from the doubts of moderns, but Poels argued that each age appropriated the revelation of the apostolic age according to its own horizons of understanding. If nothing else, the doubts of the subapostolic Fathers revealed the great difference of perspective from which Christians of various centuries considered and examined the doctrines revealed to them. This led to important lessons for the Catholic believer:

> But does not history teach an " *evolution*" of Christian doctrine? Is the teaching of the Church at the present day identical with its teaching in the first centuries? If there is a change, how can the interpretation of Holy Scripture in ancient times restrict the freedom of modern Catholic scholars?
>
> There is no Catholic who does not see the great *historical differences* between the Church in the days of the Apostles and the Church of modern times. Although its divine constitution remained unchanged, its form and shape had to be accommodated to the different needs of time, place and peoples. . . . We have no reason to admit that St. Peter knew clearly every dogma held by the Catholic Church after the Council of Trent. There was and is in the Christian revelation an unfathomable depth of meaning, out of which new disclosures may and do from time to time break forth. Therefore history teaches us *different degrees of knowledge*. But all degrees are animated by the knowledge of the articulate *unity* of the teaching of the Church: it is only as a living whole that Christians of all centuries conceive their faith. No doctrine

can retain its place in the Christian creed which is not a branch of the tree of Christ.[19]

Herein Poels provided perhaps the most sophisticated expression of the developmentalist perspective informing American Catholic thought in the first years of the twentieth century. Poels sought to put the best possible face on Loisy's radical ideas, for they were the best defense for Catholicism in an age of historical scrutiny. "Catholics would give a dreadful weapon into the hands of the historians," Poels warned, "if they admitted that in order to know whether teachings are Christian or not, the only question is whether the Church of the first centuries knew and believed them." He borrowed Loisy's image of the gospel as acorn and the church as oak tree: "Those, however, who planted the acorn were sure that whatever might grow from it would be an oak tree, but they could not see the height it afterwards attained, nor the boughs and branches which would crown it. Historically boughs and branches did not exist."[20]

Poels understood that the acceptance of the developmentalist model would require a theology informed by openness to the workings of the Spirit of Truth in the modern era:

This comparison between the natural evolution of living things and the development of the Church will be admitted by Catholic theologians, if, instead of the natural law, and its inevitability, we place the "assistentia Spiritus Sancti" which makes us sure that whatever grows from what Christ has planted is the mustard tree.

Christian revelation did not increase. It is the tree of knowledge which was and still is growing. Since, however, Christian revelation does not exist in the dead copies of Holy Scripture or of the Canons of some Councils, but in the living teaching of the Church, it is often difficult to draw the line between revelation and its knowledge.[21]

The Fathers' imperfect knowledge of science and history thus mattered little for their role as living witnesses to the faith of the Church for their age. Accordingly, their authority rests, Poels contended, not so much on their antiquity as on their consensus as *"proof of the teaching of the Church."*[22] Again, Poels appealed to *Providentissimus Deus* for support, in this case, of his contention that sacred Scripture communicates divine truth only through the constant interpretation of the church. This point underscored the necessity in each age of reaching a consensus upon the revealed meaning of Scripture. In the twentieth century, Poels pointed out, such a consensus would be reached with the benefit of scientific criticism. The method of understanding the religious doctrines of Scripture has changed significantly, Poels averred, for a question now looms large which the Fathers never considered as such: What is the relationship between the human and the divine elements of the Bible? These "new questions suggested by a new science" meant that Catholics of the twentieth century would have to refashion the arguments and ideas of their spiritual predecessors.[23]

Poels sought by this reasoning to justify a shift to a new method of scriptural interpretation. It troubled him that the Fathers had not adopted a critical stance toward scripture. Of course, he reasoned, they could not be expected to, for the religious principles they cherished emerged readily from the written and oral traditions. But for the modern believer, Poels believed, a more subtle method was required in order to discern the same religious principles so evident to the Fathers and expressed in language familiar to them. "The Fathers followed the *theological method* in their study of Scripture," he wrote, "[but] according to [today's] *critical method* modern Scripturists *first* examine what kind of literature has been chosen by the sacred author."[24] The theologian is accustomed to a kind of literature in which every sentence is positively affirmed in its obvious literal sense, whereas the critic has a more flexible and inclusive sense of truth as contained in poetry as well as in literal history.[25]

The theological method of the neo-scholastics was clearly not suited to the critical task. It had been employed, Poels implied, to prevent individuals from gaining new and unprecedented insights from the rich source of Scripture. Such individual initiative might lead to yet another reformation, another schism.

> Nowadays some Catholic scholars seem to consider theology a barn wherein are kept the crops already gathered. They do not seem to realize that the territory of science has an everlasting springtime; although people are not always plowing the same lands. [But] it is not in the barn that theological science is living and working. How, then, must we explain the fact, that some Catholics seem not to like the fresh air of the fields, where— since there are no other fields—the corn is growing among the

weeds? In our opinion, the principal reason is, because in the field of science, everyone has to plow his own little piece of land, and works alone. And wherever some modern Catholics see an individual alone in the fields of theology, they look upon him with distrust.

It stands to reason that we do not wish to be understood as addressing ourselves to Catholics at large. But we cannot help believing that this picture represents the true state of affairs in some of those little Catholic worlds, which their inhabitants easily identify with the one, saving Catholic Church.[26]

In a concluding article of the series Poels invoked Harnack's distinction between two radically different "histories" running parallel to one another, namely, a history of events or facts, and a history of the interpretation of those facts and the consequences of the interpretation given.[27]

Poels's series on history and inspiration suggested that the editors of *Catholic University Bulletin* were open to a variety of opinions and approaches to the new learning. The *Catholic University Bulletin* did not espouse modernist themes systematically, and any editorial commitment to modernism as such was either unclear or disguised. Certain articles, rather than the journal itself, appeared inspired by modernism. That Poels's series was one of the most striking of these is evident from the response that it occasioned among members of the Pontifical Biblical Commission, and, subsequently, in the office of Merry del Val himself. Poels's interpretations of *Providentissimus Deus* were unacceptable to the Vatican, and Catholic University once again came under suspicion of Americanism and, for the first time, of modernism. Poels's sponsor, Charles Grannan, was accused by the trustees, months before *Lamentabili* was issued, of violating the guidelines of the Pontifical Biblical Commission in his teaching. Americanist Denis O'Connell, John J. Keane's successor as rector of the university, vetoed a motion to oust Grannan.[28] As for Poels, his problems with the Biblical Commission's assertion of the Mosaic authorship of the Pentateuch motivated a trip to Rome. There Giovanni Gennochi encouraged him, but apparently Pius X and del Val concluded that his teachings were unsound.[29]

In the meantime the condemnations of modernism were published, and Poels soon faced an ultimatum communicated to him through Cardinal Gibbons: Merry del Val required that he swear a prescribed oath (in Latin) of loyalty to the decisions of the Pontifical Biblical Commission in their precise formulations, or forfeit his chair at Catholic University. With characteristic shrewdness, del Val employed Shahan as the messenger to Gibbons. Shahan had previously shown sympathy for Poels and for progressive Catholic thought; now he was forced to declare allegiances himself. "If Dr. Poels cannot do so [swear the oath], it is impossible for him to occupy the chair of S. Scripture, nor can the Holy See allow him to do so," del Val informed Gibbons, adding significantly that "Dr. Shahan is of course entirely of this opinion and he will fully explain the position to your Eminence."[30] Three months later, on 19 November 1909, Gibbons dutifully reported to the Vatican Secretary of State that, as Poels refused to take the oath "unless permitted to add his own interpretation of the said oath," the Board of Trustees of Catholic University had voted to relieve Poels of his teaching position "being mindful in particular of the recent grave utterances of the Holy See concerning the teaching of professors in ecclesiastical seminaries," namely, the prescriptions against modernism. Gibbons asked only that Poels's dismissal be delayed until the end of the school year due to the "danger of public scandal arising from the sudden cessation of his teaching" and "to avoid the stigma that an immediate removal would put upon this professor."[31]

The periodical to which the Dutch-born scholar contributed fared little better in the years after *Pascendi. Catholic University Bulletin* adopted a radically different format after 1908. It went from a journal of religious thought and scholarship to an almanac of information on Catholic University alumnae.[32]

Yet Poels's articles, however provocative and reminiscent of the work of the Dunwoodians, were only the tip of the iceberg. Poels was certainly not the only member of Catholic University of America's faculty who explored modernist themes and insights in his research. Nor was the *Catholic University Bulletin* the only forum for such exploration.

For example, James F. Fox, D.D., a philosopher-theologian at Catholic University, did not restrict his contributions to the new American understanding of modernist thought to the *Catholic University Bulletin* nor to the *New York Review* to which, as we have seen, he contributed a major article on the pluralism and complexity of medieval scholasticism.[33] He applied certain theological and ecclesiological convictions to the question of church-state relations in a 1907 article published in the third major organ of dissemination of modernist ideas before the fall of that year, the Paulist *Catholic World*.[34]

Troubled by recent responses of the Vatican to the emergence in the West of political liberalism, Fox hoped to counteract the inevitable reaction of modern critics of Roman Catholicism who would exploit these moves by the Vatican and publicize "pernicious misrepresentations" of the true Catholic doctrine on church-state relations. Accordingly, in a didactic series for *Catholic World* he attempted to interpret the Vatican's actions in the most benevolent way possible and to explicate the true and sound Catholic position on the matter.

One of these modern critics, a Mr. Dell, writing for the *Fortnightly Review*, pointed to the Roman condemnation of certain liberal politicians and theologians as ample proof that "we now find ourselves face to face with the claim of the Pope that his authority is absolute and unlimited; that he can and will annul and get aside laws regularly made by the constitutional law-making authority; and that if he annuls them or sets them aside, we are bound to disobey them." Fox responded by arguing that one ought not to read the decrees of modern popes through the lenses of the writings of medieval popes. It is wrong, Fox wrote, to hold "Leo XIII or Pius X accountable for the pronouncements and actions of Boniface VIII or Innocent IV."[35] By comparing decrees of Leo XIII to previous teachings, Fox suggested, one discerns a "clear acknowledgement that in purely temporal affairs the Pope claims no authority." The medieval conception of papacy and state was not to be identified with the modern conception of same. In fact, the entire matter of the papal relationship to temporal power and to heads of state "presents no practical difficulty for Catholics today, who can leave to the historian or the student of law the resolution of the theoretical problem."[36] As if to hedge his bets, Fox also invoked Dupanloup's argument regarding the Syllabus of Errors: even if one insisted that modern popes claimed temporal authority of any kind, this claim must be taken as a hypothesis, an ideal, rather than as a practical political agenda. Furthermore, Fox urged, it is appropriate to take a minimalist position toward the teaching:

> Suppose that it were proved that while the papacy today does not claim, of divine right, any power in temporals, popes in the past have done so, the inerrancy of authoritative, or Catholic, doctrine is not compromised. For no pope has committed the Church to any dogmatic pronouncement on the subject.[37]

Fox believed that the modern age would not accept the temporal claims of the papacy; therefore, he worked to minimize them and substituted in their place his own Americanist evaluation of the question, namely, that the only dogmatic claim of the Catholic Church is "that she received from Christ authority to teach the Gospel to every creature." As a progressive thinker, Fox felt it his right and obligation to prod the church ever forward, especially because official theology "does move, though it necessarily moves slowly." Thus, even if the nondogmatic teaching of Leo XIII (including the encyclical on church-state relations in the United States, *Longinqua Oceani*) did not match the perceptions of modern American Catholics, one may not despair, for this teaching was relative and would soon be outdated:

> When dogmatic doctrine is not involved, the changes, social, moral, intellectual, which take place in the world in which the Church exists, among men, of which she is composed, produce, in the course of time, a revaluation of doctrines, opinions, and attitudes. Before the Encyclical "Immortale Dei" shall be as old as the Bull "Unam Sanctam" is now, future theologians may find that some of its contents too shall have grown obsolete.[38]

Fox concluded with a defense of his right to address such questions so controversially. In this peroration he evinced an optimism about the church and the future which Sullivan and Slattery might not have shared but would have nonetheless applauded:

> The most effective reply to any objections that may be urged, on the plea of prudence or expediency, against drawing attention to the political claims of the Holy See, is that, when those claims are properly understood and their practical import rightly estimated, they need give no apprehensions whatever to Americans, Catholic or non-Catholic. The ideal, or typical, relations of Church and State which Rome insists upon expressing in her canon law presumes a condition, or rather a juncture of several conditions, which is becoming every day more and more theoretical. We need to trouble ourselves only with the actual world in which we live. The Church has lived on through changing centuries by adapting herself to the new demands made upon her. Her fairest triumphs were made before theologians discovered the meaning for the episode of the two swords. While the ancient system of a union between the altar and the throne continues to endure as a

legacy of the days when all Christendom was one family under one common Father, naturally the Holy See will feel called upon to remind us of the excellence of the ideal, even though history proclaims that every attempt made to realize it entailed evil as well as beneficent consequences. Meanwhile the course of events will modify policy, and when policy is long enough established it relegates to oblivion logical and legal conceptions that have no longer any actual application.[39]

One of Fox's colleagues at Catholic University, Father William J. Kerby, also contributed articles to the *Catholic World*, several of which reported on his research in the social sciences. Kerby's even-handed exposition of socialism complemented Fox's treatment of church-state relations in these pages. Kerby refused to "express feeling against it" solely because the Church had condemned it. "The worst that is said against Socialism is undoubtedly true to some degree," he admitted, "but it may be well to remember that that is not stating the whole case as the Socialist sees it."[40] Kerby discredited a number of "myths" about the socialist, pointing out that their opinions on any question were as diverse and broad-ranging as those in any political party. Furthermore, he opined, at least socialists were responding to the needs of the age. Catholic thinkers ought to discriminate between various political manifestations of socialism and its basic aims:

Socialism is what it is because conditions are as they are. It is a reaction as definite in proportions and fixed in its laws as any other great movement that history has seen. That it misunderstands itself, falsely interprets relations to great traditional institutions, errs in analysis, blunders in emphasis, and loses the sense of established facts, does not reduce its vitality, though it adds to its confusion; does not assure its downfall, though it increases opposition. We ought to look behind our institutions into conditions, beneath phenomena to forces, past claims and phrases and illusory hopes to measured statements of carefully ascertained facts, before sitting in judgment. If we study the processes of mind and feeling, the contrasts from which men recoil and the instinct for self-realization that they obey, we find mighty power back of Socialism and independent of Socialists and their mistakes. If we look into our traditional standards of moral judgment, and inspect the sanctions which we attach to transitory aspects of permanently true principles, we may soon learn to question the wisdom of some of the attitudes taken in opposition to the movement and be led to greater care.[41]

Kerby seemed to advocate a type of Christian socialism, but he did not make explicit reference to European modernist movements in Italy and France that were exploring new combinations of religious principles and political ideology. Yet Kerby challenged the neo-scholastic line against socialism as not only ineffective but inappropriate.

> The Church has entered the conflict as the avowed enemy of Socialism. Our colleges teach against it; we lecture and write, preach and publish, against it. We have abundant official pronouncements against it, and an anxious, capitalistic world looks to the Church, nervous with gratitude for the anticipated setback that Catholicism is to give to Socialism. Meantime, we hear complaint on every side that Christianity is losing vigor and Socialism is gaining it.[42]

Kerby promoted a plan for Catholic renewal in a series for *Catholic World* published on the eve of *Pascendi*. In order to "reinforce the bonds of faith" in laymen, the Church would have to recast its self-image; its ecclesiology must be informed by sociological principles. Catholicism in modern America was undergoing a "process of disintegration" because lay Catholics found themselves "in the midst of a conflict between necessary and unavoidable facts of life and actual demands of Church loyalty." This led many American Catholics to frame, on their own initiative, a practice of religion adaptable to current social requirements. This inevitable accommodation, Kerby believed, should be supervised by church authorities lest it lead to error. "Where modification of policy or discipline in the Church may be made without shock to Catholic feeling or sacrifice of vital and essential interests," Kerby suggested, "concessions to great social facts and forces may be advisable." Social reinforcements of the bonds of faith would prove to be most valuable in modern America as they had been for the Catholic Reform Party in Europe.[43]

Kerby acknowledged that this view of the church as a social group, subjected to the action of social forces and limited in natural powers, was new and innovative. Yet, by the all-important criterion of effectiveness, this image of the church was sound. "The Church as a social group, rather than the whole congregation of all the faithful, appeals to our sense of loyalty and enlists our sympathies," Kerby wrote.

This concept of church led Kerby to a number of practical recommendations and reforms in Roman Catholic life, practice and government, including increased lay participation. "Active share in the government of a group is another powerful stimulant of group consciousness and spirit," Kerby wrote, and he saw no specific reason why the great mass of Catholics could not have some control of the institutions of the church. Here the connection between Americanism and modernism manifested itself in American Catholic social thought: Kerby would have American democratic trends guide the reconceptualization of Roman Catholic ecclesiology.

> Among social groups, this share in government by members is of great importance. It is a right jealously guarded, if not always nobly or zealously exercised. Democracy consists largely in this; the vigor of a nation's spirit depends on it. Campaign, election, discussion, party, vote, convention, meeting, all such activities which result from the individual's share in government, foster, in a marked way, political consciousness. It is no shortsighted policy in a great school like Harvard that it permits its graduates to vote for overseers. This share by former students in government plays its part in fostering the spirit of loyalty among them when a hundred other actual interests claim their attention.
>
> Of course the Church is unlike any other group, since the teaching, governing, and sanctifying powers derive from a divine source and are independent of members. However, lay participation in Church affairs, though at present uncalled for in this country except in a minor degree, was not unknown in the past. Attention is directed to the point merely because the age is democratic and practically all great social groups depend on this share in government to foster interest and loyalty among their members.[44]

In the second article in this series, Kerby detailed his vision of the church as a social group in which all members contribute to its internal life and government. He quoted Cardinal Newman on this ideal for the laity as intelligent, well-instructed, and active in the self-determination of the church. Kerby believed that this ideal was possible only to the extent that the sociological model of the Church came into prominence.[45]

Although Fox and Kerby focused on political, social, and ecclesial reform in their work for progressive periodicals, fellow faculty members demonstrated a genuine catholicity of interest by their broad range of contributions to progressive periodicals. These authors adopted the basic strategy of Fox, Kerby, and the editors of the *New York Review*: their articles were instructive and informative, if not openly polemical. By virtue of their subject matter, however, the articles served as introductions to the new methodologies.

For example, Thomas Shahan, recruited to Catholic University by Keane for his sophistication in German and French historical scholarship, used his articles, editorials and book reviews for the *Catholic University Bulletin* and for the *American Catholic Quarterly Review* to promote critical historical methods that he had learned from Loisy's first teacher, Louis Duchesne.[46] Church historian Thomas O'Gorman also discussed historical criticism, and Edward A. Pace investigated modern American philosophies such as pragmatism. Both men were known supporters of the cause of the Americanists before 1899.[47]

George M. Sauvage, C.S.C., authored perhaps the most striking of these articles, a paean to modernist philosophy published in the *Catholic University Bulletin* in 1906. In "The New Philosophy of France" Sauvage introduced Catholic readers to a pattern of thought that "aims to substitute the primacy of life and action" for "intellectualism, the primacy of thought." Characteristic of Catholic modernist thought, these philosophers invoked Duns Scotus rather than Aquinas, Pascal rather than Descartes, and were influenced by Newman. The greatest proponent of this new school, Bergson, intended to expose the irrelevance of intellectualism for the scientific age. The scientific model for the investigation of reality presumed that theories never articulate objective reality, but provide categories to arrange whatever facts are available to the critic. Thus, as experience provides new facts, theories change to accommodate them.[48]

Sauvage pointed out that the starting point of the new philosophy was the data of experience and common sense and the formulas of organized science. It presupposed that reality is known only by intuition, "and intuition consists in living reality . . . all true knowledge, all experienced feeling, all resolutions are of necessity lived actions." For the French school, one knows an idea only so far as one discovers it; a feeling only so far as one has experienced it; an action only so far as one has performed it. Sauvage had no qualms about manifesting his enthusiasm for this new philosophy and accepting its rejection of the static and exterior point of view taken by intellectualism. He concluded that:

> the new philosophy, by its attitude, gives a real view of reality. It is easy to see that the new philosophy is pragmatic. It does not admit, indeed, either the crude pragmatism of common sense which judges the truth and value of things by their utility for ordinary life, or the scientific pragmatism which judges of the truth and value of things by their industrial and purely logical advantages; but it admits that integral and human pragmatism which judges of the truth and value of things by the progress not only material but spiritual, the harmony, the perfection, which they bring into human life.[49]

Sauvage seemed to be endorsing a philosophical system condemned by Rome and to be promoting the work of at least one thinker suspected of modernism, Eduoard LeRoy.[50]

The issues and questions raised by modernism were engaged sporadically from 1900 to 1907 in articles appearing in Catholic periodicals other than the *New York Review*. The attempt to reconcile evolutionary science with Christian theism and the developmentalist understanding of dogma were among the topics discussed by American authors and occasionally by European modernists.[51] The editors of the *American Catholic Quarterly Review*, for example, sprinkled articles advocating a new paradigm for theology and apologetics among the more numerous, non-controversial pieces on Catholic culture and history.[52] Often the authors of these occasional articles had also been published in the *New York Review*. Thomas Gerrard examined "The New Apologetic" in the pages of the *American Catholic Quarterly Review* as he had in the *New York Review*. Developed by Blondel and formulated theologically by Tyrrell, the new apologetic produced no new conclusions, Gerrard argued, but simply demonstrated "a new way of approaching old truths."[53] By focusing on the will and affections of the believer, the "new" understanding of faith avoided the excessive rationalism of neo-scholasticism and comprehended the whole person:

> Again, the faith is not merely an opinion nor yet merely a school of thought; but it is a life and is lived by the whole man. It is not

merely an object of intellectual entertainment and school room disputation...but it is a life which is always with us, which permeates all our actions, which informs every human act, which is lived day after day and all day. Consequently it must appeal to the whole man, not only to his intellect, but also to his heart and affections.

The whole man was made for God and religion was the tie made to bind him to God. Consequently in man is to be found an exigency and a need for God and religion; and this not merely in a vague and general sort of way, but in all the details of the Catholic creed.

Gerrard found this understanding to be particularly suited to modern sensibilities, and in line with previously neglected aspects of the Thomistic synthesis:

> The new method of apologetic, then, engages to point out to the unbeliever this fitness and aptitude of his soul for God and religion. Further, following the theology of St. Thomas, it assumes that we are dealing with human nature as we find it, not as it might have been. Human nature as it now exists is not the technical "status purae naturae" which could have no exigency for a supernatural religion, but it is a nature in which the natural is permeated with and related to the supernatural, and as such it has a need of the supernatural religion for which it was destined, namely, the whole Catholic Faith.[54]

Among its advantages the new method gave the apologist "a due sense of proportion as to the value of scholastic theology." By this Gerrard meant that it would place scholasticism in its proper context and prevent it from dominating Catholic thought. "Scholasticism was ever meant to be and ever will be the handmaid of religion," he wrote, but "the scholastic theologian has need to examine his conscience whether he has not been endeavoring to exalt the handmaid into the position of mistress." As Cardinal Newman had predicted, the new method would balance the use of syllogism and dialectic with a living, organic proof of the truth of faith "more delicate, versatile, and elastic than verbal argumentation." Gerrard reminded his readers that the apologist's mission "is to the present age which present age no longer speaks in Aristotelian terms. And more, not only is scholastic language not current, but scholastic method would seem to have little attraction for the modern spirit."[55]

A second advantage of the new method was the certain inspiration it would provide for the life of faith. Its principles were derived less from dogmatic and moral theology than from Christian mysticism. Its concern for human passions and affections would spur women and men to an active life of service to God:

> Just as the soul looks into itself and finds a need and exigency for God, so also it looks into its higher aspirations and finds that their only chance of realization is in God. Just as in the essence of faith appeal is made to the whole man, so also in the superstructure, namely, the ascetic life, appeal is made to the whole man. The new apologetic sees in all natural loves only so many new ways of loving God. "If a man love not his brother, whom he hath seen, how can he love God, whom he hath not seen?" *i.e.* if a man is void of natural affection, how can he pretend to the supernatural? . . . In this respect it affords a very good corrective to exaggerated ascetics and false conscience. In theory we all admit that human passions and affections are good as entities, and that they are a help to salvation as long as they are kept under the control of reason and do not lead to any breach of the ten commandments.[56]

Gerrard did not seem to recognize that a preference for the tendency toward action and natural virtues had been recently condemned as a dangerous element in Americanism. As readily as Gerrard heralded the advantages of the new apologetic, he dismissed objections against it. To the charge that this "immanentist" method was not a solid foundation for apologetics because it was rooted in the sentiments, he responded by affirming the place of reason in the new method. "The 'affective' apologist does not wish to undervalue the use of reason; nay, rather, he insists upon it as a necessary though secondary factor in the method," he concluded. The new method would not exclude, but complement, the "older and commoner method."[57]

Another article in the *American Catholic Quarterly Review* surveyed the successes and failures of the neo-scholastic movement in the late nineteenth century. It began by praising the intentions of Pope Leo XIII as broad-minded and appropriate for the age. The Thomist revival he envisioned would indeed have fostered a reawakening of sound Catholic intellectualism. Unfortunately, the author noted, Leo's intentions were thwarted by narrow-minded followers who had attempted to impose medieval categories of thought inflexibly upon modern theology:

The call of Leo XIII was to go back to the principles and to the systems of St. Thomas. It was not to move the hands of the clock back through five centuries. That would have been useless as well as retrograde, for the aspect of the problems to be dealt with was a new one. Leo XIII made his appeal to those same perennial principles and luminous truths. The twentieth century was not to be forced back into the twelfth, but the stereotyped, or disregarded, or abandoned principles belonging to no age or place were to be properly reinstated and interpreted anew, and their best extant exposition was to be found in the works of St. Thomas. . . .

Still, though the neo-scholastic movement was a thing to be desired, and, indeed, was in no small measure necessitated by the disintegration of philosophy and the threatened collapse of the social fabric, it has not altogether fulfilled the sturdy hopes that were raised upon it.[58]

The anonymous author shared the modernist critique of the ahistorical character of nineteenth-century neo-scholasticism. Neo-scholastics had almost recklessly entertained a version of Thomistic thought that could only seem anachronistic in an intellectual environment far removed from medieval times:

Instead of reconstructing as did the angel of the schools, drawing the eternal truths of reason into touch with the state of scientific knowledge, such as it was, of his own time; instead of levelling up the products of the Zeitgeist to the principles of the schools, the system of St. Thomas was imported *en bloc* and opened— a black letter page of the Middle Ages in the electric light of the nineteenth century—to the bewildered gaze of inquiring students. The text was in their hands, the professors expounded, but there was no coloring, no context, no adaptation, no framework of historical setting. The student who plodded industriously through his work went out into the world to find that the world spoke a jargon unintelligible to him. . . . But the truest end of the "Aeterni Patris" has, in the main, not been attained. The life-giving touches have been left out, and the real restoration of Catholic philosophy has hardly yet begun.

It is important to note that the author did not suggest that the Thomistic synthesis be discarded entirely and replaced with a system constructed from the findings of historical criticism. Rather, the new learning should inform a revival of Thomism itself:

> If the spirit of St. Thomas is to do the work now that he so ably performed while he lived, it must descend to the arena of twentieth century questions and give them battle on their own ground. The spirit will be the same, living and vigorous. . . . We need the whole framework of the Thomistic philosophy filled in with all the work of modern science. This in itself is no slight task; it is enormous. And it needs an intellect like that of St. Thomas to accomplish it.[59]

This proposed synthesis of Thomistic principles with the scientific worldview was less radical than the reconciliation of the ancient faith and modern thought pursued by the European modernists and the most daring American priests; it seemed, instead to anticipate or foreshadow a neo-Thomist revival in the United States. But the diagnosis of the ills of neo-scholasticism was strikingly similar to the one advanced by the modernists. Other articles in the *American Catholic Quarterly Review* proposed more than a renewal of Thomism, however, and retrieved concepts from modern philosophy and science that might be brought into conformity with a Catholic apologetic. The British writer W. H. Kent plumbed Hegelian philosophy, for example, and rejected as "a sort of intellectual Manicheism" the practice of "treating heterodox systems as something wholly evil." Kent's principle of retrieval presupposed an openness to truth wherever it may be found:

> Unfortunately, controversialists generally lay stress on the errors alone and pay little or no heed to the better elements contained in the systems of their opponents. . . . Who knows or cares what Catholic doctrines were retained by Pelagius or Luther, or what principles of sound philosophy were still preserved by Hume or Hegel. Yet these things must surely be taken into account, if we would fain form a just estimate of the men or their systems. Nor is this all. We may go even further and discern some germs of truth, however disguised and distorted, in the very errors themselves.
>
> It is to be feared that the champions of orthodoxy are too often content to lay stress on the particular dogma which has been denied by the heretic, without paying attention to the

true principles which he has thus misapprehended. For the full and frank recognition of the truth which is held by our opponents would not endanger any Catholic doctrine, while it might do much to provide some common ground and draw us all together.[60]

The question of evolution was featured most prominently in the pages of the *Catholic World*, which solicited from former Paulist superior general and noted scientist George M. Searle an evaluation of the work of St. George Jackson Mivart. Like Gmeiner and Zahm, Searle had been influenced in his studies by the example of Mivart, but the English biologist's last article had earned him condemnation. Searle was thus placed in a precarious position. He refused to discredit Mivart's life work, but could not exonerate Mivart from the charge that his final words made faith seem less an assent to authoritative teaching and more a harmonizing of intellectual opinions.[61] Mivart had suggested that Roman theologians should relinquish the idea of an infallible Church, for it stood in the way of scientific progress. "To my mind," Mivart had written, "it was clear that unless the infallibility of the Church could be seriously disclaimed, and the possibility of error in past conciliar decrees allowed, the needed evolution of dogma was impossible."[62]

Searle took two tacks in his response to this situation. First, he disagreed with Mivart's assertion that all religious truths must be submitted to scientific scrutiny. Without clarifying the principle of discrimination he followed in this, Searle argued that Mivart had misinterpreted the teaching of the church in order to have an easier target for his bitter attacks. Second, Searle explained that Mivart's mental state was affected by the placing of his books on the Index, leading him to exaggerate the implications of his scientific theories in such a way as to warrant charges of heresy. Searle was not prepared to acknowledge the troubling possibility that Mivart had simply been consistent in his application of scientific method to Catholic doctrines.[63] Perhaps Searle's caution on this matter was inspired by the example made of John Zahm, the first priest to face condemnation by Rome precisely because he had appropriated elements of Mivart's thought in an imprudent manner. In any case, the articles in Catholic periodicals that focused on evolution were similarly cautious.[64]

In the months preceding the condemnation of modernism there were, however, a number of articles published in American Catholic periodicals that explored the thought of the European modernists. In 1906 the *Catholic World* published a series in l906 devoted to Antonio Fogazzaro's modernist novel *Il Santo*.[65] In the same year the editors ran a series by American modernist William L. Sullivan on theology and inspiration that reflected the influence of George Tyrrell.[66] And Tyrrell's own proposals for the renewal of Catholic theology appeared in the publication.[67] Tyrrell predicted that Catholic thinkers would eventually adopt a developmentalist model for theology, apologetics, and ecclesiology, but posed the difficult questions to be answered by the proponents of the model. "Does the 'deposit of faith' and do the infallible definitions of the Church bind us absolutely to the categories and thought forms of the age in which they were framed?" he asked "If, as it seems, we are bound to them as of absolute value, as finally true for philosophy, science, and history, then we have a new brood of problems, for we must show that those of different ages are consistent with one another, and that those of all the ages together are still valid and furnish collectively a rule by which modern thought should be corrected." On the other hand, he warned, "if we deny that past forms are to be the criterion of present and stand by all the implications of that denial, we not only contradict tradition in a substantial point, but we shall find it hard in many ways to erect a secure barrier against liberal theology."[68] In this article Tyrrell repeated his distinction between Catholic theology and Catholicism, refusing to identify neo-scholastic theory with the fullness of Catholic reflection on the experience of God.[69]

As this brief survey of articles appearing in American Catholic periodicals prior to the condemnations of 1907 suggests, the *New York Review* and the writings of Gmeiner, Zahm, Slattery, and Sullivan were not the only means by which the developmentalist model adopted by the modernists in Europe was introduced to the American Catholic community. None of these periodicals could actually be called "modernist." Neither did the progressive faculty of Catholic University deserve the label. The editors of the *Catholic World*, the *Catholic University Bulletin*, and the *American Catholic Quarterly Review* did not follow a program designed to implement modernist methodologies. The proportion of articles devoted to modernist themes was much smaller in these periodicals than in the pages of the *New York Review*. The professors at Catholic University who contributed many of these articles did not recognize the heretical implications of these ideas in the same way that a priest like Slattery did. On the contrary, these American Catholic thinkers were experimenting with the new paradigm and in a less systematic fashion than Driscoll and Gigot, Sullivan and Slattery.[70]

Differences in the level of commitment to the task of exploring modernist ideas and methods was illustrated by the variety of responses to the condemnation of modernism in 1907. As we have seen, the priests at Dunwoodie continued their program for almost a year, aware of the precariousness of their situation but hoping to escape reprisal. Sullivan and Slattery understood and accepted the fact that Rome would stand for no compromise; and because their consciences would not allow them to submit, they left the church. Zahm chose to abandon his research rather than to face the charge of heresy and ecclesiastical censure. The professors at Catholic University and the editors of the *Catholic World* and the *Catholic University Bulletin* were evidently alarmed by the condemnations. Almost overnight these priests made a complete about-face, vigorously renouncing positions that they had previously endorsed with equal fervor. In response to *Pascendi*, the Board of Trustees at Catholic University established a committee "empowered to make a survey of modernistic books in the library of the University and to make recommendations on the matter."[71] Poels's resignation was accepted when his contract expired at the end of the 1909–1910 term. Others fell in line behind the encyclical in a ecclesiastical climate in which "certain persons, in public controversy against modernism, in brochures, newspapers, and other periodicals, go to the length of detecting the evil [of modernism] everywhere, or at any rate of imputing it to those who are very far from being infected with it."

For example, in 1906 William Turner had written in the pages of the *New York Review* that Kantian philosophy had led to the recovery in the church of the principle of divine immanence and was capable of inspiring a wealth of good in Christian theology.[72] By May 1908 Turner had experienced an intellectual conversion. He wrote an article for the *Catholic University Bulletin* that was designed to vindicate that periodical's orthodoxy. "The doctrines now known as Modernism, which are explicitly condemned in the encyclical *Pascendi Dominici Gregis*, have lost in the eyes of Catholics whatever claim they may have made to be regarded as contributions to philosophical truth," he proclaimed.[73] He denounced "the philosophical bases of modernism" and described Kantian epistemology, as *Pascendi* had, as little more than "philosophical agnosticism." Turner now professed to abhor the very thought of opposing neo-scholasticism:

> Among the causes which the Encyclical assigns for the prevalence of Modernism is the "ignorance and contempt of scholasticism." The contempt is openly proclaimed in books, reviews, pamphlets and even in the daily press. . . . Even those who owe less to the scholastics than the Modernists do are ready to testify at least to the relative worth of what, after all, was at one time the dominant system of thought in the world of Western Christendom.[74]

Thomas Shahan, the editor of the *Bulletin*, added his submission to Turner's. In an editorial published four months after the promulgation of *Pascendi* he acknowledged that, given the firm teaching of the encyclical, there could be no doubt as to the inadequacy of the model for theology that the modernists had introduced. "Henceforth," Shahan wrote, "these opinions, in the eyes of believing Catholics, are reprehensible errors."[75] He continued with a full-fledged defense of the papal prerogative to speak clearly and authoritatively on such matters. From that moment the *Catholic University Bulletin* devoted itself to explication of the errors of modernism and to noncontroversial, often esoteric articles. By 1910 the new editor, William Turner, dropped all pretense to academic inquiry: the format of the periodical changed entirely, and topical articles disappeared altogether.

Similar reversals were occurring at the *American Catholic Quarterly Review* and the *American Ecclesiastical Review*, both of which avoided scrupulously any further treatment of critical studies in archaeology, history, biblical science, and theology. The Paulist *Catholic World* was perhaps most obvious in its haste to acquit itself of heresy or of sympathy with a heretical movement. The issue of February 1908 was devoted almost exclusively to a repudiation of each and every modernist error named in *Pascendi*. George Searle attacked an article published in the December 1907 issue of the *North American Review* entitled, "The Catholic Reformation and the Authority of the Vatican." Its author, Charles Johnston, had suggested strongly that the Roman Catholic church might learn something from, and be renewed by, the men it condemned as modernists. Johnston scoffed at the pretensions of the Holy Office—the "Holy Inquisition"—that presumed to declare what shall or shall not be held true in criticism, history, science "Nothing is more certain," Johnston concluded, "than that a candid study of the Scriptures, and a sincere examination of early history, will cut at the root of the Vatican's assumptions."[76] Searle responded with righteous indignation. The Catholic recognized that the truths of the deposit of faith were not to become the object of scientific scrutiny and possessed in themselves more certainty than any scientific endorsement could award them. Searle suggested that Protestants could not comprehend this simple article of faith:

> It is, no doubt, rather hard for non-Catholic Europeans or Americans to realize what the position of the Catholic Church is with regard to the matter of religion. . . . Accustomed as they are to regard religion as merely a matter of speculation, in which no definite and certain results can ever be obtained, they seem to fail even to conceive the position of those who maintain and really and thoroughly believe that certain facts in the domain of religion are known with absolute certainty, though many of them are entirely unattainable by abstract reason, and in no way verifiable by experiment or observation. Of course the method by which these facts have been ascertained is different from that employed in scientific research . . . but we regard them as having a higher degree of certainty than that possessed by any of those of experimental science. We believe them to have been revealed by God himself. . . . The system—if it may be so called—of Modernism is in itself entirely irreconcilable with the fundamental Catholic position.[77]

The *Catholic World* also published a series of sermons preached in St. Patrick's Cathedral on the errors and causes of modernism. Upon the insistence of Farley, Cornelius Clifford, who had discussed the various new Christologies in the pages of the *New York Review*, offered a reflection on "The Obediences of Catholicism."[78] In another sermon Thomas Burke, a Paulist priest, explained that the modernists were excommunicated because they had in effect repudiated the teaching of the First Vatican Council that God can be known with certainty by means of things that are made.[79] In yet another sermon Father Joseph F. Mooney admitted that "the symptoms [of modernism] have in a measure manifested themselves in this favored land of ours" but, he hastened to add, the symptoms were "so vague and faint that they passed well-nigh unheeded." Who, after all, would be attracted to a system that holds that the proof of God is a matter of sentiment, that the Sacred Scriptures are human experiences that could have happened in any religion, and that Christ was not always conscious of His Divine Mission?[80]

In this as in the other denunciations of modernism that echoed the papal condemnation, the preachers presented modernism as a set of erroneous conclusions rather than as a method, or set of methods, of approaching the questions raised by scientific criticism. The one exception to this trend was Father Joseph W. Daily, perhaps the most insightful of the St. Patrick's preachers. He interpreted the controversy as finally centering on the question of authority. "We must maintain that it is most essential to acknowledge and to follow authority in matters of dogma," he said, "[and], in fact, any man who thinks he assimilates knowledge without the assistance of another deceives himself."[81]

The *American Catholic Quarterly Review* also adopted a submissive tone in reporting on *Pascendi*. Its editorialist, John T. Murphy, praised Pius X for his vigilance, insight, and erudition in identifying the heresy. Murphy followed the encyclical's definitions closely by linking modernism with the errors of rationalism, agnosticism, and psychologism, and by suggesting that the modernist sought the "subordination of Catholicism to the progress of modern, naturalist science."[82] After expressing concern at the extent of modernism's influence, Murphy briefly surveyed its manifestations in France, Germany, England, and Italy. Regarding the presence of modernism in the American Catholic Church, he made a prediction that was to prove prophetic:

It has been said that in other countries, too, including our own, there have been and are certain upholders of the Modernist's methods and errors. We know not to what extent this statement is correct; if it be well founded, the encyclical "Pascendi" will effectively stop the emanations and squelch the very germs of the disease.[83]

In a sense, then, the vigilance committees and anti-modernist oaths were unnecessary in the American church. With a few notable exceptions, each of the priests who had dabbled in modernism before 1907 was cured of this curiosity by the encyclical: further warnings and implementation of the ban were superfluous in most cases. In the few cases in which American clerics persisted in their commitment to the dissemination of the new thought, the actions of the American episcopacy were sufficient to enforce the ban on modernism. As if to make reparations for the embarrassment, the Archbishop of New York accorded the priests at his diocesan seminary at Dunwoodie the honor of translating into English the work that explained the errors of modernism to the American clergy, J. B. Lemius's *A Catechism of Modernism*. Thus ended the short-lived conversation begun in the American Catholic intellectual community by the proponents of modernism and their liberal colleagues in the priesthood.

Conclusion: On the Significance
of American Catholic Modernism

In each event in which the spirit of modernism manifested itself, Roman ecclesiastical authorities, working through the American hierarchy, moved to silence the offending parties. Under threat of censure Zahm halted the distribution of *Evolution and Dogma* and turned to writing travelogues. Driscoll was forced to discontinue the *New York Review* and was removed from his position as president of St. Joseph Seminary; Gigot was effectively silenced; Sullivan and Slattery moved beyond Roman Catholicism. After the syllabus of Modernist errors *(Lamentabili Sane Exitu)* and the condemnation of modernism *(Pascendi Dominici Gregis)* were promulgated by Pius X in 1907, progressive theological and philosophical scholarship vanished from the pages of American Catholic journals.

What, then, is one to make of the brief appearance in certain American Catholic seminaries, universities, and publications of an inchoate program of modernism? We have seen that this program never reached fruition and was adopted piecemeal by its various proponents: Zahm applied modernist arguments and attempts to reconcile faith and science to the restricted topic of evolution, Sullivan focused on Americanism and vital immanence, the Dunwoodians placed these and other concerns in the context of the battle to supersede neo-scholastic categories of thought. Furthermore, none of these figures, Zahm included, was an altogether original thinker or a first-rate theologian. At best they presented European ideas in a fresh and creative way, tailoring them to the needs of the American situation. For the most part, however, their contribution to American Catholic intellectual life, preempted as it was by the Vatican in 1907, lay in their fairly unsystematic, unorganized attempt to disseminate and popularize the ideas of European Catholic scholars on the cutting edge of a revolution in Christian thought.

Furthermore, it is apparent that the scope of the American Catholic modernists' influence on their colleagues in the priesthood, on the laity, and on the life of the American Catholic church was limited. The periodicals that disseminated modernist themes enjoyed a collective readership of no more than a few thousand Catholics, many of whom were not trained in such a way as to be able to absorb the nuanced positions of the European and American authors.[1] The seminarians who matriculated from St. Joseph's in New York and St. John's in Brighton, Massachusetts, from 1900 to 1908 were, to a greater or lesser degree, exposed to the new critical methods and theological and ecclesiological insights during their training, as were certain graduate students at Catholic University, but it is impossible to determine the extent of that influence or how closely those ideas were applied in later pastoral work and preaching—if at all. John Zahm attracted sizable crowds to his chautauqua lectures, and William L. Sullivan gained some attention by his exposé of the failings of Roman Catholicism and the papacy, but the long-term impact of such public demonstrations was undetermined by the condemnations of modernism.

Nonetheless, the episode of American Catholic modernism was significant for the history of the church in this country in that it demonstrated the intellectual appeal of non-scholastic modes of Catholic thought and, in so doing, exposed the limitations of Roman neo-scholasticism in the American context. Modernism's strongest advocates insisted that the new apologetics be attuned to the particular interests, needs, and sensibilties of the American people. Thus the brief prominence of Zahm, Sullivan, Slattery, Poels and the Dunwoodians is noteworthy in an environment that has been described as intellectually sterile. The judgment that the church in the United States lacked an intellectually vital community of scholars, philosophers, and theologians is beyond argument; but the conclusion that this was so because of a lack of curiosity or spirit of inquiry among clergy and laity does not follow. After his return from mission work in the South, an enthusiastic William Sullivan called for a new, modern American Catholic apologetic, informed at least in part by the insights of modernism. Before his priesthood "dropped" from him, John Slattery also argued that a renewed Catholic approach to evangelism, more responsive in idiom and content to the patterns of American Negro spirituality, would find a receptive audience in the United States. And, given John Zahm's popularity on the lecture circuit and in the secular press, the enthusiastic welcome extended to the *New York Review* by

Catholic editors and educators, and the tentative appropriation of the new thought by Catholic University professors, Sullivan's claim that "the very air and soil of America are favorable to Modernism" is worthy of consideration.

A partial explanation for the influence of the American Catholic exponents of modernism, however short-lived, lies in the sense they had, or acquired, of their potential audience. To their credit the priests addressed topical issues in a nonspeculative fashion, always sensitive to their practical applications and to the needs of their audience. Zahm attracted enthusiastic crowds, considerable press coverage, and a certain degree of celebrity because he spoke to an issue of contemporary interest—the origins of man—clearly and authoritatively. The American public, Catholic and non-Catholic alike, was struggling at the turn of the century with the theory of evolution and the shadow of doubt it cast upon traditional theism. When a figure of religious authority—a Roman Catholic priest, no less—proclaimed from podium and periodical that there was nothing inherent in the theory of evolution, properly understood, that eclipsed a sound and vital Christian faith, a segment of that public was intrigued. After all, that assurance had been provided on a more general level by liberal bishops such as Spalding and Ireland who had made the reconciliation of church and age, Catholicism and science a cause celebré. Targeting a different and much smaller audience, the editors of the *New York Review* strove to present innovative and sometimes esoteric material to a readership composed primarily of novices in the field of modern critical religious thought. Accordingly, many of the articles and essays began with a review of the received teaching of the scholastic manuals, proceeded to a critical treatment of historical antecedents, and concluded with a sustained discussion of both the inadequacies of the inherited wisdom and the advantages of the new methods. More complex topics were treated in a series of articles. Sullivan contributed technical treatments of specific questions to the *New York Review* and the *Catholic World* but later turned to the treatise, the popular novel, and the autobiography to promote a message blending elements of individualism, patriotism, Catholicism, and universalism.[2]

Furthermore, these progressive priests articulated a view of religion and religious life that made a place for individual experience and encouraged Catholics to adopt a critical, ends-oriented approach to their understanding and appropriation of the faith. The intended audience of a wider revival of Catholic thought—primarily immigrant

Catholics faced with the challenges of assimilation into the American mainstream—could find in the new apologetics a view of Catholicism designed to reduce the inevitable tension between the requirements of American citizenship and those of religious faith. Indeed the proponents of this new apologetic were condemned in part because Rome believed that by considering the needs of their audience they were compromising the essentials of the faith.

Yet the American priests also spoke to the need, experienced by many liberal Catholics, for an intellectual system, a theology and ecclesiology, that provided a theoretical framework for their faith in the *American* Catholic Church. How could democratic values mesh effortlessly with Catholic faith? the Americanists asked. To some it seemed that the new theology, purified of its corrupt elements, might be capable of providing the answer. These American Catholics did not seek to deny their religious heritage, nor even, in most cases, to purge it of Roman influence. Yet they were open to the possibility of a synthesis between Americanism and Romanism, to a renewal of the church inspired by the work of the Holy Spirit in history—and, for many Americans, modern history resolved itself into the drama of the emergence and victory of liberties of thought, speech, and religion, and the rise of self-governing peoples. For a brief time at the turn of the century, certain American Catholics held out hope that the new critical scholarship begun in Europe might provide the impetus, and perhaps the framework, for such a renewal. Thus, Americanism sought expression in new forms of theology, apologetics, philosophy, and ecclesiology—and Zahm, the Dunwoodians, Slattery, and Sullivan, among others, identified this expression with various forms of thought that Rome later, to their chagrin, conflated and condemned as modernism.

In the decades immediately following the promulgation of *Pascendi* the charge of "modernism" became a term of opprobrium in Catholic circles; in the aftermath of the Second Vatican Council, it has been revived as a staple of ultraconservative Catholic rhetoric. Many of the contemporary Catholics who continue to identify the Tridentine liturgy as the essential and irreformable expression of Roman Catholic orthodoxy believe that the Council was convened by a modernist pope and that its various decrees gave official voice to an insidious conspiracy by an "underground" network of modernists.[3]

Responsible comparisons between historical periods require careful and sustained attention to the nuances and details of each period under consideration. Such a comparison is beyond the scope of the present study. Nor is it within the author's competence to survey and pronounce upon the complex and resourceful arguments made on both sides of the current debate between the Vatican's Congregation for the Doctrine of the Faith (the institutional successor to the Holy Office whence came the condemnations of modernism) and the American Catholic theologians who have been temporarily silenced and/or removed from teaching positions and their many supporters in the American Catholic community.[4] Reflection on the contemporary situation does, however, bring the turn-of-the-century controversy into sharp relief and may serve to illustrate the distinctiveness of that period.[5]

There are notable similarities between the two situations. Borrowing the Weberian concept of "elective affinities," sociologist Lester Kurtz studied the interaction of turn-of-the-century Vatican bureaucrats and modernists ("bureaucratic insurgents") and found that the worldview of each group was developed and sustained in direct relation to and coordination with the particular personal and social interests of the group.[6] Such affinities continue to exist today and have been reinforced by the "professionalization" of American theologians; i.e., by their increased identification with the academy and its hallowed principles and procedures. Catholic scholars of religion are now organized in various independent academic councils and societies that provide fellowship and a kind of protective cocoon that Driscoll, Zahm, Gigot, and others did not have.[7] Thus the "divide and conquer" strategy of the curia that was effective in their day is at least partially countered in our own.[8] The American episcopacy, then as now, implements curial directives against recalcitrant theologians, but its actual ability to ensure widespread conformity to ecclesial norms has been severely compromised, if not altogether abolished, by the contemporary theologian's awareness and acceptance of his responsibilties to the various publics of church, academy, and society—and his awareness of the pluralism of meanings of "ecclesia" itself.[9] Although Zahm, Driscoll, Sullivan and Slattery were among the first American Catholic thinkers to recognize the need and desirability of appealing to these various publics, they could not rely upon a similar consensus among their brother priests, especially when the storm came, and thus found only fleeting and strictly conditional institutional support.

The professionalization, increased self-awareness, and greater solidarity of American theologians as a distinct class of scholars has served in recent years to further institutionalize a fundamental disagreement between bishops and theologian-apologists in the United States that was at the heart of the initial controversy over modernism. This long-standing disagreement first emerged in the aftermath of the Enlightenment and concerns the proper sphere of rational critical inquiry and the limits of the scientific method. In describing this clash of worldviews, sociological constructs such as "elective affinities" or "sociological ambivalence" provide only a partial explanation for the actors' motives and behaviors and must be informed by an awareness that personal belief has an integrity all its own and, in certain individuals at certain times, leads to action uncompromised by social or political considerations.

The American priests sympathetic with what they understood to be the modernist program were, as this study has shown, mere novices at the game. Indeed, even the European modernists they admired were themselves the first generation of Catholic scholars to confront directly and comprehensively the most radical implications of the new learning. In this sense both the Europeans and their American proteges were Catholic pioneers. Some testified to moments of personal crisis and "conversion experiences" as they gradually assimilated the insights of non-scholastic philosophies or the discoveries of the higher criticism of the Bible or the findings of the natural sciences.[10] Compelled to subject once-cherished beliefs, now recognized as embarrassingly naive, to a searing examination, the early modernists entered upon their new awareness with the stark absolutism of the convert. Stranded between the radical skepticism or agnosticism of the secular rationalist on the one hand and the uncritical fideism of the supernaturalist on the other—"between Scylla and Charybdis," as both Tyrrell and Sullivan described it—they struggled to fashion a *via media* that would satisfy modernity's most rigorous intellectual criteria for the examination and expression of religious faith.

Perhaps it is not surprising, then, that John Henry Newman was invoked frequently by both the Americans and the Europeans; indeed, one may almost trace an individual's movement along the modernist trajectory at given times according to his opinion of the English cardinal's attempt to outline this desired *via media*. As if to avoid the Scylla of unbelief, Newman opposed "the spirit of liberalism in religion" manifested in "the doctrine that there is no positive truth in religion, but that one creed is as good as another." He refused to allow Christian doctrine to be reduced to fit within the scope of human knowledge and experience. As an "objective fact" divine revelation is subject neither to the latest conclusions of scientific research nor to the changing contents of public consensus; and its internal consistency and objectivity is properly guarded by the Roman church's hierarchical authority and powerful traditions.[11] At the same time Newman anticipated and inspired much of the ground-breaking work of the modernists. His *Essay on the Development of Doctrine*, for example, undermined the notion that doctrinal integrity rests on doctrinal immutability. To the philosophical eclecticism and historical ignorance of Roman theologians he offered the *Grammar of Assent* as a specifically theological contribution to a "true philosophy of religion." By providing an analysis of the concrete processes of reasoning and believing through a sustained consideration of the subjective experience of faith, Newman laid the foundations for subsequent explorations of vital immanence—and steered clear of the Charybdis of extrinsicism.[12]

Students of Newman such as Blondel and Tyrrell in Europe and Zahm and Driscoll in America applied in their own disciplines his general principles concerning the problem of faith in a scientific age. Those such as Loisy and Sullivan who despaired of the solutions promised in Newman's broad charter followed their sense of moral outrage over Rome's capricious authoritarianism out of the church. Both men acknowledged (with a degree of pride) that they had followed the trajectory of modernism with utter honesty to its final unfolding beyond Catholicism. In this they proved Pius X prophetic and at least partially correct in his analysis of the dangers inherent in an unbridled appropriation of critical methods and "vital immanence."

Theologically, the Second Vatican Council provided a kind of official endorsement of the mediating enterprise of Newman and his twentieth-century followers. The council fathers invoked the historic "both/and" of the Catholic tradition (in this case, room within the church for *both* rational critical inquiry concerning doctrine *and* the ahistorical and supernatural character of divine revelation) in the hope of easing the Scylla-Charybdis tension of the "either/or" that had dominated Catholic self-understanding since Vatican I (*either* noncritical acceptance of the objective fact and particular expression of divine revelation *or* complete and absolute perfidy). The resulting paradigm for Catholic self-understanding stressed the ongoing human experience of the divine and incorporated the results of modern biblical and historical criticism.[13]

Catholics on both sides of the contemporary controversy over the limits of critical inquiry and academic freedom argue within the framework established by Vatican II and appeal to conciliar documents. Thus it is not surprising that those who call the American theologians "modernists"—and thereby overlook their oft-stated acceptance of the church's dogmatic teaching and its basis in supernatural revelation—happen to be those Catholics who are most uncomfortable with the council itself. These traditionalists imply that the mere appropriation of the new paradigm is in itself constitutive of the condemned "synthesis of all heresies."[14] To many American theologians the most troubling aspect of the contemporary situation is that certain bishops, taking their signals from Rome, seem to be adopting the same position.[15]

To invoke "modernism" today however, is to return to a time in which the dominance of neo-scholastic thought precluded the possibility of a careful and gradual appropriation of the findings and methods of the critical sciences and post-Kantian philosophies. Were these findings and methods to gain currency in the wider church, the integralists supposed, the hegemony of neo-scholasticism would be seriously challenged. Rather than identify Catholic orthodoxy with any single system of thought, the modernists experimented with various methods that might be employed to scrutinize and recover the apostolic sources and expressions of the faith. This was, as we have seen, a characteristic theme of the *New York Review*.

The condemnation of modernism led to a systematic repression of the experiments. American Catholic "experiments" in the ensuing decades were conducted within the epistemological framework of scholasticism; given this qualification, it was possible for the subsequent neo-Thomist revival to serve eventually as a bridge between the received scholastic orthodoxy and the new systems of thought that emerged in the years preceding Vatican II. Neo-Thomism enjoyed papal and episcopal endorsement and the proper theological pedigree; it was integrated into the sacramental and devotional life of church and was accessible to the laity; and it was thus a more measured way by which historical and critical reflection upon the experience of believers might enter the theological mainstream.[16] What is important for the present analysis is that the basic assumptions of the scholastic world view were gradually modified and nuanced by the infusion of historical and critical studies—but never abandoned. Despite the different issues upon which it turns, the contemporary debate concerning the definition of orthodoxy and the limits of public dissent is in part a reprise of the turn-of-the-century confrontation between defenders of scholastic thought and advocates of pluralism in theological method. Those who seem to condone the displacement or even abandonment of the basic worldview of the manual theologies are associated with modernism.[17]

The sterility of thought and the lack of creativity that characterized American Catholic theology and apologetics for decades after the initial condemnation of modernism and the subsequent imposition of anti-modernist oaths were neither accidental, nor, as some have suggested, due to an inherent incompetence of American Catholics in matters intellectual. Instead, they were the unfortunate result of a studied decision taken by Rome in the years after *Pascendi*: it is best to abandon innovation and original research, lest the specters of Americanism and modernism reappear and thus scandalize the faithful.

NOTES

INTRODUCTION: THE TRAJECTORY OF MODERNISM IN AMERICAN CATHOLIC THOUGHT, 1895–1910

1. John A. Zahm, *Evolution and Dogma*, reprint edition (New York: Arno Press, 1978).

2. William L. Sullivan, *Letters to His Holiness Pope Pius X* (Chicago: Open Court Publishing Co., 1910), p. 75.

3. Ibid., p. xviii.

4. William R. Hutchison, *The Modernist Impulse in American Protestantism* (Cambridge, Mass.: Harvard University Press, 1976), pp. 2–9.

5. Since the formation of a Roman Catholic modernism working group in conjunction with the American Academy of Religion, a good deal of research has been conducted on the parameters and "definition" of this movement. There are broad areas of consensus on the question of a definition of modernism, but the study is still in a stage of development as new materials become available and archival sources are penetrated. See, for example, Gabriel Daly, "Defining Modernism," in Ronald Burke, Gary Lease, and George Gilmore, eds., *Modernism: Origins, Parameters, Prospects* (Mobile, Ala.: Spring Hill College, 1984), pp. 3–13.

6. Michael V. Gannon, "Before and after Modernism: The Intellectual Isolation of the American Priest," in John Tracy Ellis, ed., *The Catholic Priest in the United States: Historical Investigations* (Collegeville, Minn.: St. John's University Press, 1971), pp. 337–39.

7. "Notes," *New York Review* 1, no. 1 (June-July 1905): 25.

8. Francis E. Gigot, "The Higher Criticism of the Bible: Its Constructive Aspects," *New York Review* 1, no. 4 (January-February 1906): 303.

9. John Ratté, *Three Modernists: Alfred Loisy, George Tyrrell, and William L. Sullivan* (New York: Sheed and Ward, 1967), pp. 318–29.

10. See Chapter 1 of this study for a discussion of this debate.

11. James J. Fox, D.D., "Scotus Redivivus," *New York Review* 1, no. 1 (June-July 1905): 22–46; Thomas J. Gerrard, "Dichotomy: A Study in

Newman and Aquinas," *New York Review* 3, no. 4 (January-February 1908): 380–83.

12. William Turner, "The Philosophical Bases of Modernism," *Catholic University Bulletin* 14, no. 2 (May 1908): 443.

13. See, for example, John R. Slattery, "How My Priesthood Dropped from Me," *Independent* 61 (6 September 1906): 565–70.

14. John Tracy Ellis, "The Formation of the American Priest: An Historical Perspective," in Ellis, ed., *The Catholic Priest in the United States*, p. 69.

15. John Ireland, "The Church and the Age," in his, *The Church and Modern Society* (Chicago: D. H. McBride, 1896), p. 97.

16. See Sullivan, *Letters to His Holiness,* and Slattery, "The Workings of Modernism," *American Journal of Theology* 13 (October 1909): 555.

17. Gannon traced the aftereffects of the modernist condemnation in "Before and after Modernism," pp. 350–59.

18. For example, Nicholas Lash analyzes the modernist controversy as indicative of a "transformation of consciousness" in "Modernism, Aggiornamento, and the Night Battle," in Adrian Hastings, ed., *Bishops and Writers: Aspects of the Evolution of Modern English Catholicism* (Wheathampstead, Hertfordshire: A. Clark, 1977). The concept of "paradigm shift" is formulated in Thomas S. Kuhn, *The Structure of Scientific Revolutions* (Chicago: University of Chicago Press, 1962).

19. Lester J. Kurtz, *The Politics of Heresy: The Modernist Crisis in Roman Catholicism* (Berkeley: University of California Press, 1986), pp. 167 ff.

20. Christopher J. Kauffman, *Tradition and Transformation in Catholic Culture: The Priests of Saint Sulpice in the United States from 1791 to the Present* (New York: Macmillan, 1988); Gerald P. Fogarty, S.J., *American Catholic Biblical Scholarship: A History from the Early Republic to Vatican II* (San Francisco: Harper and Row, 1989).

1. JOHN ZAHM AND THE CASE FOR THEISTIC EVOLUTION

1. *Reynolds Newspaper,* London, 29 August 1897; *Catholic Review,* July 1894, p. 19; *Catholic Times,* 5 May 1894, pp. 15–16; *Catholic Citizen,* May 1894, p. 22. Citations in this chapter are taken from copies made from the collection in the Congregation of Holy Cross archives, Notre Dame, Indiana (hereafter cited as CSCA-ND).

2. John L. Morrison, "A History of American Catholic Opinion on the Theory of Evolution, 1859–1950" (Ph.D. diss., University of Missouri, 1951), pp. 79–110, chronicles the debates in America up to the time of Zahm's involvement.

3. Zahm was preceded by Paulist George M. Searle and Rev. John Gmeiner, among others, in supporting evolution. But neither of these priests received the acclaim awarded Zahm. "The wide advertisement you receive in the secular and religious press has added wonderfully to your drawing power and you are now one of the *cards* of the lecture platform," a reporter from Cincinnati's *Catholic Telegraph* cabled Zahm; Thomas F. Hart to John Zahm, CSCA-ND.

4. See Richard Hofstadter, *Social Darwinism in American Thought, 1860–1915* (Philadelphia: University of Pennsylvania Press, 1945).

5. See Cynthia Eagle Russet, *Darwin in America: The Intellectual Response, 1865–1912* (San Francisco: W. H. Freeman, 1976).

6. Ibid.

7. On Abbot, see Sydney E. Ahlstrom, *A Religious History of the American People*, 2 vols. (Garden City, N.Y.: Image Books, 1975), 2: 226; and, William R. Hutchison, *The Modernist Impulse in American Protestantism.* Hutchison builds upon the work of Lloyd J. Averill, *American Theology in the Liberal Tradition* (Philadelphia: Westminster Press, 1967).

8. Hutchison, p. 33.

9. On the Free Religious Association, see Octavius Brooks Frothingham, *The Religion of Humanity* (Boston: David G. Francis, 1873).

10. Ibid., pp. 16–17.

11. For a careful treatment of Bushnell's theological work, see Claude Welch, *Protestant Thought in the Nineteenth Century, 1799–1870* (New Haven, Conn.: Yale University Press, 1972), pp. 258–68. Welch stops short of terming Bushnell's method a "synthesis." But he employs Bushnell's own self-description as one pursuing "Christian comprehensiveness." One of his central theological intentions was "the desire to recognize and reconcile at a higher level the truths present in the varieties and antitheses of sects and dogmas. . . . The decisive elements in Bushnell's methods are hinted at when he speaks of the way the truth is uncovered—by 'dissolving' the form of a dogma and viewing its content 'historically', by taking down the 'drapery of language,' and thus by separating out the 'real truth of feeling' " (pp. 258–59).

12. *A Genetic History of New England Theology* (New York: Russell and Russell, 1963), quoted in Hutchison, p. 45. The Bushnellian legacy to later modernism lay in two areas. In "Dissertation on Language" he explored the language of the creeds, concluding that it was more poetic than denotative and could be sacrificed to the task of creedal reconstruction. In *Christian Nurture* (1847) he departed from many tenets of Calvinist orthodoxy, especially those related to total depravity, in favor of a corporate view of salvation more congenial to Catholicism.

13. Ahlstrom, *A Religious History of the American People*, 2: 232.

14. Hofstadter, *Social Darwinism*, p. 14.

15. Joseph LeConte, *Religion and Science* (New York, 1873). LeConte stressed the theistic possibilities of science, which he saw as a rational, empirical natural theology.

16. Lyman Abbott, *The Evolution of Christianity* (Boston: Houghton Mifflin, 1892) and *The Theology of an Evolutionist* (Boston: Houghton Mifflin, 1897).

17. Newell Dwight Hillis, *A Man's Value to Society* (New York: Fleming H. Revell Company, 1899), p. 70.

18. Newman Smyth, *Old Faiths in New Light* (New York: Charles Scribner's Sons, 1879) and *Through Science to Faith* (New York: Charles Scribner's Sons, 1902).

19. F. P. Garesche, *Science and Religion: The Modern Controversy* (St. Louis: n.p., 1876), pp. 8–9.

20. "Draper's Conflict between Religion and Science," *Catholic World* 21 (May 1875): 179.

21. Camillus Mazella, *De Deo Creante. Praelectiones scholastica dogmaticae* (Woodstock, Md.: n.p., 1877), p. 344. In similar fashion an anonymous reviewer of *The Descent of Man*, writing for the *Catholic World*, described as "nothing but claptrap for the ignorant" Darwin's reasoning that variations in the human species led to the conclusion that the human had evolved from a lower species. Taking umbrage at Darwin's interpretation of his own data, the author argued that the animal-like composition of human embryos at certain stages of development did not necessarily yield a theory of human evolution from animals; it only proved that God's creative design was uniform throughout the animal kingdom, and that animals and men shared the same creator. Furthermore, the author concluded, publications that supported Darwinism, such as *Popular Science Monthly* and *Nature*, were thus "degrading humanity and destroying the bases of morality, religion and civilization," "The Descent of Man," *Catholic World* 26 (January 1878): 508, 511.

22. Mazella, p. 307.

23. Morrison, pp. 102–103.

24. Garesche, *Science and Religion*, pp. 20–21.

25. Michael Gannon, "Before and after Modernism," p. 314.

26. Henry F. Brownson, ed., *The Works of Orestes A. Brownson*, 20 vols. (Detroit: Thorndike House, Publisher, 1884), 9: 520–25.

27. *Freeman's Journal*, 28 May 1898, p. 4; "A Protestant View of Christianity," *Catholic World* 55 (August 1892): 770. See also: H. H. Wyman, "Science and Faith," *Catholic World* 71 (April 1900): 5, 8; George McDermot, "Spencer's Philosophy," *American Catholic Quarterly Review* 26 (October 1901): 658; and William Poland, "Modern Materialism and Its Methods in Psychology," *Ecclesiastical Review* 17 (August 1897): 150.

28. Morrison, pp. 181–82.

Notes 249

29. Arthur Preuss, "Darwin's Unprovable Theory," *Fortnightly Review* 5 (29 September 1898): p. 3.

30. Morrison, p. 183.

31. "Catholicism, Protestantism, and Progress," *Catholic World* 62 (November 1895): 145–53.

32. Quoted in Morrison, p. 70.

33. Morrison notes, pp. 152–53, that there was at least one American Catholic Darwinist, William Seton, grandson of Elizabeth Bayley Seton, novelist, philanthropist, and paleontologist. He formed a close friendship with fellow Darwinist Dominican Pere LeRoy, and with Zahm and Mivart. Even after certain of their works had been condemned, Seton continued to quote these works to substantiate his endorsement of Darwin. His own book, *A Glimpse of Organic Life*, explained to Catholic school children the operations of natural selection. He went beyond radicals Mivart and Zahm by defending the "survival of the fittest" version of evolution. Seton wrote primarily for *Catholic World*: "The Hypothesis of Evolution," *Catholic World* 66 (November 1897): 201; and "How to Solve One of the Highest Problems of Science," *Catholic World* 58 (March 1894): 788, were two exemplary efforts.

34. Augustine F. Hewit, "Scriptural Questions," *Catholic World* 44 (February 1887): 660.

35. Ibid., p. 677.

36. "Evolution and Darwinism" *Catholic World* 56 (November 1897): 227.

37. "Science or Bumblepuppy?" *American Catholic Quarterly Review* 12 (October 1887): 636–46.

38. Rev. John Gmeiner, *Modern Scientific Views and Christian Doctrines Compared* (Milwaukee: J. H. Yewdale and Sons, Printers, 1884), pp. 3–4.

39. Ibid., p. 15.

40. Ibid., p. 157.

41. Ibid., pp. 51–52.

42. Ibid., p. 159.

43. Ibid., pp. 157–58.

44. Ibid., p. 211.

45. Ibid., pp. 165–70.

46. Historians and scientists agree that the 1880s was the turning point in the debate over the scientific validity of the evolution theory. Evidence was obtained and experiments conducted that confirmed the basic framework of the Darwinian theory. See St. George Jackson Mivart, *Contemporary Evolution* (London: Henry S. King and Co., 1876), for a view before this decisive decade; and, for a more modern view, see William E. Agar, *Catholicism and the Progress of Science* (New York: The Macmillan Company, 1940).

47. Gmeiner, "The Liberty of Science," *Catholic World* 48 (November 1888): 149.

48. Quoted in the *Catholic Citizen*, 24 August 1896, CSCA-ND.

49. Ralph E. Weber, *Notre Dame's John Zahm: American Catholic Apologist and Educator* (Notre Dame, Ind.: University of Notre Dame Press, 1961), p. vii.

50. Ibid., pp. 10–19.

51. Ibid., p. 11.

52. Ibid., pp. 18–19.

53. Ibid.

54. John Zahm to Albert Zahm, 1883, CSCA-ND.

55. The Bloomington *Progress*, 1895, CSCA-ND.

56. An impression that was no doubt buoyed by responses such as that of the *Freeman's Journal* of 3 August 1895, which termed Zahm "a sensation"; or the letter from Dr. Thomas F. Hart of the *Cincinnati Catholic Telegraph* that confirmed "The wide advertisement you received in the secular and religious press has added wonderfully to your drawing powers and you are now one of the *cards* of the lecture platform," CSCA-ND.

57. John Augustine Zahm, "The Catholic Church and Modern Science: A Lecture" (Notre Dame, Ind.: Ave Maria, 1886), pp. 6–7.

58. See, for example, John Zahm, *Moses and Modern Science*, (D. J. Gallagher and Publishers, 1894), a reprint from the March 1894 issue of the *American Ecclesiastical Review* which developed the position on the deluge and on Augustine, pp. 36–42.

59. Zahm, "The Catholic Church and Modern Science," p. 19.

60. Ibid., p. 21.

61. Ibid., pp. 22–23, 24.

62. Ibid., pp. 42–44.

63. Ibid., p. 25. St. Thomas Aquinas and the Jesuit theologian Suarez followed Augustine's teaching on derivative creation, Zahm asserted, and he could produce voluminous evidence to support his general point that evolution enjoys a rich lineage in Catholic tradition.

64. Ibid., pp. 30–31ff.

65. Ibid. Zahm was in touch with Mivart; excerpts from their correspondence are available, CSCA-ND.

66. John A. Zahm, *Catholic Science and Scientists* (Philadelphia: H. L. Kilner and Co., 1893).

67. Ibid., pp. 127–28.

68. Ibid., p. 128.

69. Ibid., pp. 133–35, passim.

70. "Religion can dispense with science, but science cannot progress without religion, cannot ignore revelation—only under the fostering care of the religion of our fathers, only under the patronage of the Catholic

Church, therefore, can science find that stimulus or experience, that energizing influence that favors the development of which she is capable. . .," quoted in Zahm, *Catholic Science and Scientists*, pp. 216–17.

71. Quoted in Zahm, *Evolution and Dogma*, "Introduction," by Thomas J. Schlereth, n.p.n. Zahm was encouraged in this view of his role as Catholic apologist for science and religion by a spate of favorable reviews of *Bible, Science and Faith*, including one by Cardinal Gibbons contending that Zahm's work would "dispel prejudice" by clarifying the relationship between the new science and faith. These reviews are on file at the Holy Cross archives at Notre Dame (CSCA-ND).

72. Mivart to Zahm, postcard, 18 May 1896, CSCA-ND.

73. Weber, pp. 16–28.

74. Zahm received the most intensive press coverage of his career during the chautauqua lectures. See, for example, "Dr. Zahm Denies the Universality of Noah's Flood—An Interesting Lecture Delivered before the Catholic Summer School at Plattsburgh," the *Sun*, July 1893, pp. 13–14, CSCA-ND.

75. John Zahm to Denis O'Connell, 13 February 1893, O'Connell, "Roman Correspondence 1890–1894," Catholic University of America Archives (hereafter cited as CUA).

76. John Zahm to Albert Zahm, 22 July 1896, John Zahm Collection, University of Notre Dame Archives (hereafter cited as UNDA).

77. John A. Zahm, *Bible, Science and Faith* (Baltimore: John Murphy and Co., 1894), pp. 60–69.

78. Ibid., p. 78.

79. Ibid., p. 80.

80. Ibid., pp. 84–91, 313–16.

81. Ibid., p. 77.

82. Reprinted in "Opinions of the Press," the *Tablet*, December 1824, p. 28, copy in CSCA-ND.

83. Ibid.

84. Ibid.

85. Ibid.

86. Reprinted in "Review of *Bible, Science and Faith*," the *New World*, 12 January 1895, pp. 30–31, CSCA-ND.

87. Ibid., p. 31, CSCA-ND.

88. Ibid.

89. "The Bible and Science:—Review of *Bible, Science and Faith*, " the *Tablet*, December 1824, p. 27, CSCA-ND.

90. Ibid.

91. John A. Zahm, *Evolution and Dogma* (reprinted, New York: Arno, 1978), pp. 435–38.

92. Quoted in James R. Moore, *The Post-Darwinian Controversies* (Cambridge: Cambridge University Press, 1979), p. 194.

93. Quoted in ibid., p. 196.

94. Zahm, *Evolution and Dogma*, p. vii.

95. Ibid., p. v.

96. Ibid., pp. xvii, 69–70.

97. Ibid., p. 433.

98. Ibid., pp. 50–53.

99. Ibid., p. 75.

100. Ibid., p. 83. On this point note the similarity of approach in John Gmeiner, *Modern Scientific Views and Christian Doctrines Compared* (Milwaukee, 1884), pp. 3–4.

101. Zahm stated this point unequivocally in *Scientific Theory and Catholic Doctrine* (Chicago, 1896), p. 9.

102. Zahm, *Evolution and Dogma, pp.* 162–63.

103. Ibid., p. 83.

104. Ibid., p. 370.

105. Ibid., pp. 200–201.

106. Moore, *Post-Darwinian Controversies*, elaborates the categories I have drawn upon in this section.

107. Ibid., p. 142. See also Bowler, *Evolution*, pp. 186–89.

108. Neal C. Gillespie, *Charles Darwin and the Problem of Creation* (Chicago: University of Chicago Press, 1979), pp. 1–18, 85–108. See especially John C. Greene, *Darwin and the Modern World View* (Baton Rouge, La.: Louisiana State University Press, 1961); and id., *The Death of Adam: Evolution and Its Impact on Western Thought* (Ames, Iowa: Iowa State University Press, 1959).

109. See John D. Root, "The Final Apostasy of St. George Jackson Mivart," *Catholic Historical Review* 71 (1985): 1–25, for a statement of Mivart's development, and especially for his reaction to Leo XIII's encyclical on biblical interpretation which, Root argues, "provided a sharp impetus" to Mivart's final break from the church (pp. 7–8).

110. Zahm was in correspondence with Mivart, who thanked him for "carrying on my work in the United States"; Mivart to Zahm, 18 May 1896, CSCA-ND.

111. Zahm, *Evolution and Dogma, p.* 70.

112. Ibid., p. 416.

113. Ibid., pp. 71, 354.

114. Ibid., p. 122.

115. Ibid., p. 71.

116. Zahm, *Bible, Science and Faith*, pp. 121–22; *Evolution and Dogma*, pp. 388–90.

117. Zahm, *Evolution and Dogma*, p. xiv.

118. Ibid., p. 141.

119. On this point see George M. Searle, "Dr. Mivart's Last Utterance," *Catholic World* 71 (1900): 353–65; and Searle, "Evolution and Darwinism," *Catholic World* 66 (1897):227–38. Also compare Weber, *Notre Dame's John Zahm*, pp. 109–12.

120. On responses to *Providentissimus Deus*, see Roger Aubert, ed., *The Christian Centuries*, vol. 5: *The Church in a Secularized Society* (New York: Paulist, 1978), pp. 164–203.

121. *Catholic Citizen* (24 August 1895).

122. Hewit to Zahm, 7 October 1895, John Zahm Collection, UNDA.

123. "Mind in Action," *Ave Maria* 63 (9 February 1946): 145. The article on Zahm appeared in the *New York Herald*, 4 August 1895, p. 1.

124. John Zahm to Albert Zahm, 11 November 1896, John Zahm Collection, UNDA.

125. A periodical that otherwise supported Zahm, the *Colorado Catholic*, admitted as much: "when Fr. Zahm tells us that St. Augustine was an incipient evolutionist. . . he doubtless shocks some good people. . . who resent as impious any attempt to connect sacred names with so irreligious a thing," pp. 16–17, CSCA-ND.

126. Sebastian Messmer to Thomas O'Gorman, 20 January 1896, CSCA-ND.

127. O'Gorman quoted this rebuff in an angry letter seeking Zahm's support, O'Gorman to Zahm, 27 January 1896, CSCA-ND.

128. Sebastian Messmer to John Zahm, 20 January 1896, CSCA-ND.

129. Edward Pace commented upon this trait in Messmer rather caustically in a letter to Zahm: "I have not yet replied to Bishop M. He was more severe upon me than upon Dr. O'Gorman. It seems, according to his account, that in order to relieve you from your awkward position, a compromise was made to the effect that I would be allowed to lecture only on the express condition that I should not transgress the bounds of orthodoxy. This 'compromise' Bp. M. regretted and begged me to cancel the engagement made with you. You do not seem to be in the cancelling mood just at present. All in all the episode is a nice introduction to lectures on Messmerism," Pace to Zahm, 2 February 1896, CSCA-ND.

130. Sebastian Messmer to Thomas O'Gorman, 20 January 1896, CSCA-ND. John Zahm to Bishop Messmer, 1 February 1896, CSCA-ND. Ibid.

131. John Zahm to Bishop Messmer, 1 February 1896, CSCA-ND.

132. Zahm, *Bible, Science and Faith*, p. 170.

133. "Dr. Zahm," the *Review*, 23 April 1896.

134. Ibid., p. 2.

135. *New York Journal*, 12 November 1896.

136. Weber, *Notre Dame's John Zahm*, pp. 93–94.

137. Salvatore Brandi, S.J., to Archbishop Corrigan, 13 June 1896, John Zahm Collection, UNDA.

138. John Zahm to Albert Zahm, 6 December 1896, John Zahm Collection, UNDA.

139. John Zahm to James Cardinal Gibbons, 9 March 1897, copy in UNDA.

140. John Ireland to Denis O'Connell, 1897, copy in UNDA.

141. Quoted in Weber, *Notre Dame's John Zahm, p.* 107.

142. Zahm to Ireland, 5 March 1899, copy in UNDA.

143. "Father Zahm Submits to Rome," *Daily Tribune*, 2 July 1899.

144. Français to Zahm, 10 November 1898, John Zahm Collection, UNDA.

145. For a thorough discussion of the neo-scholastic worldview and the ways in which it was threatened by reliance on secondary causes in the manner described by Zahm and others, see Gabriel Daly, *Transcendence and Immanence: A Study in Catholic Modernism and Integralism* (Oxford: Clarendon Press, 1980).

146. "Leone XIII E L'Americanismo," *La Civiltà Cattolica*, ser. 17, vol. 5, 18 March 1899, pp. 641–43.

147. "Evoluzione e Domma," *La Civiltà Cattolica*, ser. 17, vol. 5, 7 January 1899, pp. 34–49.

148. Ibid., pp. 40–41: "Dopo d'aver ripetuto col Mivart, che, 'Dio creo l'anima dell'uomo direttamente, e il suo corpo *indirettamente*, ossia per l'operazione delle cause secondarie,' il Prof. Zahm, con una disinvoltura veramente americana, scrive, 'Quest'opinione della origine derivativa del corpo di Adamo e pur essa in perfetta armonia con altri principii emessi dai due grandi luminari della Chiesa, Sant' Agostino e San Tommaso.'. . . Evidentemente, quale che siasi questo 'aspetto,' se crediamo al Prof. Zahm, bisognerà dire che l'angelico Dottore fu illogico e incoerente."

149. Ibid., p. 41. It should be noted that the condemnation of Zahm was intricately connected with Bishop Hedley of England, who supported Zahm and wrote similar opinions on evolution. The "Zahm affair" was meant to make an example of the American.

150. Ibid., pp. 42–48.

151. On the connection between Americanism and modernism, see Margaret Mary Reher, "Americanism and Modernism: Continuity or Discontinuity?" *U.S. Catholic Historian* 1 (1981): 87–103.

2. THE SIGNS OF THE TIMES:
MODERNISM AND ANTI-MODERNISM

1. See Josef L. Altholz, *The Churches in the Nineteenth Century* (New York: Bobbs Merrill, 1967), pp. 59–89, for a discussion of the context and

content of the decree of infallibility and the larger battle against liberalism in all its forms.

2. Pope Pius X, *Pascendi Dominici Gregis*, quoted in Amanda Watlington, ed., *Official Catholic Teachings* (Wilmington, N.C.: McGrath, 1978), p. 103.

3. On rationalism as it was perceived by nineteenth-century Roman Catholicism, see Edgar Hocedez, *Histoire de la théologie au XIX e siècle*, 3 vols. (Paris: Desclee, 1948), 1: 8–9. On the reaction of the Tübingen School to rationalism, see Alexander Dru, *The Contribution of German Catholicism* (New York: Hawthorn Books, 1963), pp. 41–47.

4. The following discussion of the rise of neo-scholasticism relies on two sources: Roger Aubert, *The Christian Centuries*, vol. 5: *The Church in a Secularized Society* (New York: Paulist, 1978), pp. 164–203; and Gerald A. McCool, *Catholic Theology in the Nineteenth Century: The Quest for a Unitary Method* (New York: Seabury, 1977), pp. 129–215.

5. Although at first neo-scholasticism relied on an eclectic philosophical base strongly influenced by the rationalizing tendencies of Suarezian Thomism, as time passed more voices advocated a return to authentic Thomism. Among these were the two Jesuits who were to dominate Roman theology in their lifetimes: Mateo Liberatore, the major contributor to the restructuring of the scholastic philosophical synthesis; and Joseph Kleutgen, whose enduring work lay in the rearticulation of Thomistic systematic theology. Liberatore helped to move the Roman College from Suarezianism to the more authentic Thomism promoted in the pages of *La Civiltà Cattolica*. Kleutgen's erudition graced the pages of two seminal Vatican documents, Vatican I's Apostolic Constitution on Faith, *Dei Filius*, and Leo XIII's academic call-to-arms, *Aeterni Patris*. See McCool, pp. 216–40.

6. Gabriel Daly, *Transcendence and Immanence: A Study in Catholic Modernism and Integralism* (Oxford: Clarendon Press, 1980), pp. 175–76.

7. James J. Fox, D.D. "Scotus Redivivus," the *New York Review* 1, no. 1 (June-July 1905): 30.

8. Aubert, p. 169.

9. Maurice Blondel, *L'Action: Essai d'une critique de la vie et d'une science de la pratique* (Paris: Felix Alcan Editeur, 1893). For an insightful treatment of the stages of the reform movement inspired by Blondel, see Roger Haight, "Three Modernists: Blondel, Laberthonniere, and LeRoy," *Theological Studies* 35 (1974): 632–66.

10. Quoted in Daly, p. 14.

11. Daly, pp. 19ff.

12. Aubert, pp. 179–82.

13. George Tyrrell, *Medievalism: A Reply to Cardinal Mercier* (London: Longmans and Co., 1908), pp. 123–24.

14. Loisy insisted that the beliefs of Catholicism had become "an abstract system which no longer had any hold on intelligent minds, even

among believers, and which were in defiance of what is most certainly known about the origins of the Bible and of the Jewish and Christian religions." In *My Duel with the Vatican: The Autobiography of a Catholic Modernist*, trans. Richard Wilson Boynton (New York: Greenwood Press, 1968), p. 95. Recent sociological studies of the nineteenth-century scholastics and their repudiation of the modernist paradigm stress the role played by heretical movements in the maintenance of institutional hierarchies. The social organization of these groups solidify when threatened by a common "enemy." See Lester R. Kurtz, *The Politics of Heresy* (Berkeley: University of California Press, 1987) on the integralists' "elective affinity" to the cognitive orientation undergirding their social grouping. See also Charles Talar, "Paradigm and Structure in Theological Communities: A Sociological Interpretation of the Modernist Crisis" (Ph.D. diss., Catholic University of America, 1982).

15. George Tyrrell, *Christianity at the Crossroads* (London: Longmans and Green, 1909), pp. 25, 30.

16. Rev. J. B. Lemius, O.M.I., *A Catechism of Modernism, founded on the encyclical Pascendi Dominici Gregis by Pope St. Pius X* (Rockford, Ill.: Tan Books and Publishers, 1981), translated at St. Joseph's Seminary, Dunwoodie, New York, pp. 27–32.

17. Pope Pius X, *Lamentabili Sane Exitu*, quoted in Bernard M. G. Reardon, *Roman Catholic Modernism* (Stanford, Cal.: Stanford University Press, 1970), p. 211.

18. In fact, this was a common strategy in combatting modernism: attack the character of the most prominent modernists. On this point see Alec R. Vidler, *The Modernist Movement in the Roman Church: Its Origins and Outcomes* (Cambridge: Cambridge University Press, 1934), pp. 120–25. Vidler accepted Albert Houtin's contention that "Loisy abandoned Christian theism and belief in the Incarnation," but adds, "it does not follow that such abandonment was required or implied by the argument of *L'Evangile et l'église*. It is, on the contrary, to be understood that this was not so." (p. 125). See Loisy, *Memoires pour servir à l'historie religieuse de notre temps* (Paris: Emile Nourrey, 1931) 3: 260.

19. *Pascendi Dominici Gregis*, p. 68.

20. Lemius, *A Catechism of Modernism*, pp. 29–32.

21. Ibid., pp. 27–32, passim.

22. Daly, p. 189.

23. Pope Pius X, "Contra neo-reformismus religiosum," *Acta Sanctae Sedis* 4Q (Rome, 1907): 266–69, passim.

24. Lemius, p. 24.

25. Friedrich von Hügel, "Loisy," *The Encyclopedia Britannica*, 11th ed., vol. 16 (New York: Encyclopedia Britannica, Inc., 1911): 927.

26. *The Programme of Modernism: A Reply to the Encyclical of Pius X, "Pascendi Dominci Gregis,"* trans. Alfred L. Lilley (London: n.p., 1908), p. 171.

27. Ibid., p. 177.

28. Quoted in Daly, p. 192. Italics mine.

29. Ibid.

30. See, for example, Mary Jo Weaver, ed., *Letters from a "Modernist"* (Shepherdstown, Pa.: Patmos Press, 1981) for the correspondence between Tyrrell and Ward; Lawrence F. Barmann, ed., *The Letters of Baron Friedrich von Hügel and Professor Norman Kemp Smith* (New York: Fordham University Press, 1981); and the correspondence between von Hügel and Blondel published in R. Marlé, *Au de la crise moderniste* (Paris, 1962). Also, consult John Root, "The Correspondence of Friedrich von Hügel and Clement C. J. Webb," *Downside Review* 99 (1981): 288–98.

31. Maurice Blondel, *The Letter on Apologetics and History and Dogma*, trans. Alexander Dru and Illtyd Trethowan (New York: Rhinehart and Winston, 1964), p. 24.

32. Ibid., pp. 386–88.

33. Barmann.

34. George Tyrrell, *Christianity at the Crossroads*, p. 25.

35. Maurice Blondel, *Lettres philosophiques* (Paris, 1961), p. 10.

36. Ibid., pp. 33–37 passim. Blondel, *L'Action*, pp. 110–11. See also Jean Lacroix, *Maurice Blondel: An Introduction to the Man and His Philosophy* (New York, 1968), p. 45; and Henri Bouillard, *Blondel and Christianity*, trans. James M. Somerville (Washington, D.C.: Corpus Publications, 1969), pp. 15–25.

37. See Lucienne Laberthonniere, "Le Dogmatisme moral," *Annales de philosophie chrétienne* 136 (1898): 531–62; 137 (1898): 27–45, 146–71; and other essays collected in *Essais de philosophie religieuse* (Paris, 1903). For commentary see Haight, pp. 640–42.

38. "L'Apologetique et la methode de Pascal," *Revue du clergé français* 25 (1901): 472–98.

39. Friedrich von Hügel, *The Mystical Element of Religion: As Studied in St. Catherine of Genoa and Her Friends* (2nd ed., London, 1923), 2: 338. Joseph P. Whelan discusses von Hügel's immanentism in *The Spirituality of Friedrich von Hügel* (New York: Newman Press, 1971), pp. 66, 92, 198.

40. Ibid., pp. 15–25, passim.

41. George Tyrrell, "The Relation of Theology to Devotion," *Month* (November 1900). See David Schultenover, *George Tyrrell: In Search of Catholicism* (Shepherdstown, Pa.: Patmos Press, 1981), p. 98. See also George Tyrrell, *Through Scylla and Charybdis: The New Theology and the Old* (London: Longmans and Green, 1907), p. 122.

42. George Tyrrell, *The Church and the Future* (London: Longmans and Green, 1910), p. 25. See Schultenover, p. 299.

43. See Paul Misner, "Social Modernism in Italy," in Ronald Burke, Gary Lease, and George Gilmore, eds., *Political and Social Modernism* (Mobile, Ala.: Spring Hill College, 1988), pp. 18–35.

44. Darrell Jodock, "Liberal Catholicism—Reform Catholicism—Modernism: A Critical Discussion of Thomas Michael Loome's Agenda for a New Orientation in Modernist Research," *Downside Review* 100 (1982): 176.

45. Thomas Michael Loome, *Liberal Catholicism—Reform Catholicism—Modernism: A Contribution to a New Orientation in Modernist Research* (Mainz, West Germany: Matthias-Grunewald, 1979), p. 169.

46. Tyrrell, *Christianity at the Crossroads*, p. 25.

47. Jodock, pp. 172–77.

48. Zahm fit Tyrrell's definition of a modernist: "By a Modernist I mean a churchman, of any sort, who believes in the possibility of a synthesis between the essential truth of his religion and the essential truth of modernity," *Christianity at the Crossroads*, p. 30.

49. Ibid., p. 25.

50. Tyrrell, *Christianity at the Crossroads*, p. 33. See also Gabriel Daly, "Defining Modernism": " 'Modernism' was the term employed by Pius X and his senior curial advisers in their attempt to describe and condemn certain liberal, anti-scholastic, and historico-critical forms of thought occurring in the Roman Catholic Church between c. 1890 and 1910."

51. Those individuals implicated by *Pascendi* became the prototypes for the public and official image of the modernist, especially Alfred Loisy. Loisy and Tyrrell felt compelled to test the limits of authority. Those, like von Hügel, who did not confront authority but worked within the system as much as possible, were not formally condemned; nonetheless, scholars have recognized that these figures belong in any consideration of the phenomenon of Catholic modernism. This is simply to say that the open repudiation of ecclesiastical authority on the hierarchical model was not a characteristic of all of the Roman Catholic modernists; in fact, many abandoned their original research altogether when authority spoke, and hoped for a better day for the ecclesial community to which they were devoted. On this point, see Baron von Hügel, "Official Authority and Living Religion," reprinted in *Essays and Addresses on the Philosophy of Religion*, second series (London: J. M. Dent and Sons, Ltd., 1926).

52. Robert H. Wiebe, *The Search for Order, 1877–1920* (New York: Hill and Wang, 1967), pp. 133–55, discusses the revolution in values accompanying these transitions.

53. See Henry Steele Commager, *The American Mind: An Interpretation of American Thought and Character Since the 1880's* (New Haven, Conn.:

Yale University Press, 1960); see also Sidney Mead, "The American People: Their Space, Time, and Religion," in *The Lively Experiment: The Shaping of Christianity in America* (New Haven, Conn.: Yale University Press, 1960).

54. William James, *Pragmatism* (New York: World Publishing Company, 1955), p. 33.

55. Ibid., p. 42.

56. Ibid., pp. 59–60, passim.

57. See John K. Roth, *Freedom and the Moral Life: The Ethics of William James* (Philadelphia: Westminster Press, 1969) for an example of James's influence on modern ethics. In fact, James was more concerned with the psychic state of man than with socio-political applications of pragmatism. See William James, *The Varieties of Religious Experience: A Study in Human Nature* (New York: Collier Books, 1961).

58. William R. Hutchison's "Cultural Strain and Protestant Liberalism," *American Historical Review* 76 (1971): 386–411, adds to this skein of challenges by reaching certain conclusions about the influence of 250 American Protestant leaders' social and intellectual background on the way they perceived modernity and theology.

59. See Jerry W. Brown, *The Rise of Biblical Criticism in America, 1800–1870: The New England Scholars* (Middletown, Conn.: Wesleyan University Press, 1969) and Allan Nevins, *The Emergence of Modern America, 1865–1878* (New York: n.p., 1928), pp. 264–89.

60. William Adams Brown, *The Essence of Christianity: A Study in the History of Definition* (New York : Charles Scribner's Sons, 1902), pp. 6–7.

61. George A. Gordon, *The Christ of Today* (Boston: Houghton Mifflin, 1895), p. 63.

62. Brown, p. 23.

63. Gordon, p. 6.

64. Ibid., pp. 28–29.

65. Newman Smyth, *Passing Protestantism and Coming Catholicism* (New York: Charles Scribner's Sons, 1908), pp. 169–71.

66. Charles A. Briggs, *Church Unity: Studies of Its Most Important Problems* (New York: Charles Scribner's Sons, 1909), pp. 435–42, passim.

67. Each of the American Catholic modernists was conversant with Protestant and Jewish modernist thought. John Zahm read, for example, Lyman Abbott's *Theology of an Evolutionist* (Boston: Houghton Mifflin, 1897) and *The Evolution of Christianity* (Boston: Houghton Mifflin, 1892), and quoted Protestant geologist Joseph LeConte, among others, for support on the theory of evolution. The editors of the *New York Review* invited Charles Briggs to lecture at St. Joseph's Seminary, reviewed his books, and reported on his travels and lectures in the "Notes" section of the periodical. They also reported on the activities of Felix Adler and the Ethical Culture Society. Sullivan and Slattery cited Protestant theologians and both were eventually

drawn away from Roman Catholicism to communion with liberal Protestant churches; Sullivan even became a Unitarian minister (see chapter 6).

68. Hutchison pointed to three characteristics shared by Protestant modernists that set them apart from other liberals: 1) their conscious, intended adaptation of religious ideas to modern culture, 2) the idea that God is immanent in human cultural development and revealed through it, and 3) the notion that human society is moving toward a realization in full of the Kingdom of God. In William R. Hutchison, *The Modernist Impulse in American Protestantism*, p. 2.

69. Two important works crystallized this hope. Baptist minister William Newton Clarke at Colgate Theological Seminary published *An Outline of Christian Theology* (New York: Charles Scribner's Sons, 1899), the first such survey of Christian theology written from a thoroughly modern perspective. In it he adopted a developmentalist worldview and emphasized the historical approach to Scripture. He also elevated piety and religious experience to an unprecedented prominence. Among liberal Protestants this work was extremely influential. Similar themes appeared with greater evangelical bent in Henry Churchill King's *Reconstruction in Theology* (New York: Macmillan, 1901). On the wedding of social justice programs to the higher criticism, see Washington Gladden, *Who Wrote the Bible? A Book for the People* (Boston: Houghton Mifflin, 1891) and *How Much Is Left of the Old Doctrines?* (Boston: Houghton Mifflin, 1894), in which he popularized the new theology in its practical applications. One must also mention in this regard William Rainey Harper, who worked in Chicago to gain acceptance for the scientific understanding of the Bible, especially in the periodical he founded, the *Biblical World*.

70. The best account of the Americanist episode remains Thomas T. McAvoy, C.S.C., *The Great Crisis in American Catholic History, 1895–1900* (Chicago: Henry Regnery Co., 1957). See also Margaret Mary Reher, "Americanism and Modernism—Continuity or Discontinuity?" *U.S. Catholic Historian* 1, no. 3 (Summer 1981): 86–100.

71. James J. Hennesey, S.J., warned historians not to expect American Catholic intellectual movements to conform to European patterns: "the Roman Catholic Church in the United States developed in a political and social climate radically different from the European. Its unique development affected its theological thinking in ways that we can scarcely understand if we attempt to fit them into categories conditioned by the European experience." In "Papacy and Episcopacy in Eighteenth-Century American Catholic Thought," *Records of the American Catholic Historical Society*, 1966, p.175.

72. John Farina, *An American Experience of God: The Spirituality of Isaac Hecker* (New York: Paulist, 1981), p. 131.

73. Ibid., pp. 95, 131, 167.

74. Quoted in Robert D. Cross, *The Emergence of Liberal Catholicism in America* (Cambridge, Mass.: Harvard University Press, 1958), pp. 171–72.

75. Quoted in Walter Elliott, *The Life of Father Hecker* (New York: Columbus, 1894), p. 292. Hecker tended to see Protestantism as homogeneous, especially in its central error, the doctrine that human nature is "utterly worthless." Those Protestants who modified the doctrine of total depravity, he argued, are in fact abandoning Protestantism and moving toward a Roman Catholic position. Isaac Hecker, *The Aspirations of Nature* (New York: Kirker, 1857), p. 147.

76. At times, Hecker understated and underestimated the strength and dominance of the neo-scholastic leadership in Rome. For example, his interpretation of Leonine restrictions on individual liberty as directed not to Americans but to easterners did not stand up to the test of *Longinqua Oceani*, promulgated six years after his death and repeating these restrictions to American-bishops. For the relevant text of the encyclical and an introductory comment, consult John Tracy Ellis, ed., *Documents of American Catholic History* (2nd ed., Milwaukee: Bruce Publishing, 1962). The pope praised the growth of the church in the United States, grateful that "unopposed by the constitution and the government of your nation, fettered by no hostile legislation... [Catholics are] free to live and act without hindrance." However, he warned, the separation of Church and State was not a desirable model for other societies. Indeed the Catholic Church of the United States "would bring forth more abundant fruit if, in addition to liberty, she enjoyed the favor of the laws and the patronage of public authority."

77. Farina, p . 124.

78. See, for example, Joseph p. McSorley, C.S.P., "The Church and the Soul," the *New York Review* 1, no. 1 (June-July 1905): 68.

79. Hecker distinguished between the aridity of medieval scholasticism and the authentic neo-Thomism that did not gain momentum in the church until after his death. Farina, pp. 95, 167.

80. Quoted in Farina, p. 124.

81. John Tracy Ellis, *The Life of James Cardinal Gibbons, Archbishop of Baltimore, 1834–1921*, 2 vols. (Milwaukee: Bruce Publishing Company, 1952), 2: 101. In the book, di Bartolo applied Cardinal Newman's *obiter dicta* theory—that all scientific and historical comment in the Bible not bearing directly on dogmatic truth was subject to correction at the hands of modern criticism—to the concept of the teaching authority of the church. Consequently, he argued for a minimalist interpretation of ecclesiastical inerrancy, limiting it to certain spiritual truths clearly contained in the deposit of faith. Most controversial were his assertions that popes had seldom taught with infallible authority and that the church had mistakenly canonized numerous individuals. Di Bartolo also seemed to argue that Catholic scientists need not abandon hypotheses that contradicted revealed truths, for science was always revising its theories and progressing towards greater veracity.

82. Quoted in Cross, p. 124.

83. On the relationship between Ireland and Spalding, see Marvin O' Connell, *John Ireland and the American Catholic Church* (St. Paul: Minnesota Historical Society Press, 1988), pp. 131, 365, 370–71.

84. "The Church and the Age," in John Ireland, *The Church and Modern Society* (Chicago: D.H. McBride and Co., 1896), p. 95.

85. Ibid., pp. 97–98.

86. Ireland's introduction to Elliott's *Life of Father Hecker* was reprinted in Felix Klein, *Americanism: A Phantom Heresy* (Crawford, N.Y.: Aquin Book Shop, 1951), pp. xiii-xxi.

87. Reher cited this correspondence, p. 101.

88. O' Connell, *John Ireland and the American Catholic Church*. Also see James H. Moynihan, *The Life of Archbishop John Ireland* (New York: Harper and Brothers, 1953), p. 110. Loisy reflected on Ireland in *Memoires*, 1: 563.

89. David Francis Sweeney, *The Life of John Lancaster Spalding, First Bishop of Peoria, 1840–1916* (New York: Herder and Herder, 1965).

90. Spalding's teacher at Louvain was Canon Gerard Ubagh. From traditionalism he derived the dictum that the acquisition of metaphysical truths depends upon a primitive divine teaching and its oral transmission; thus, the individual depends on faith and the authority of others as bases for religious certitude. From ontologism Ubagh taught that necessary and immutable ideas can be known only by an intuition of God present to the mind and perceived by the intelligence. Spalding wrote to Orestes Brownson on one occasion, confessing that "I was brought up in a school which did not admit that [the existence of God] can be proven in a strict and logical sense." Quoted in Sweeney, p. 83n. Sweeney, pp. 78–90, details the controversy.

91. Quoted in Sweeney, p. 93.

92. John Lancaster Spalding, "Catholicism and A.P.A.ism," *North American Review* 154 (September 1894): 284.

93. Related in Sweeney, p. 267.

94. Spalding, "Address at the Dedication of Catholic University," quoted in Sweeney, p. 171. On O'Connell's role in the Americanist crisis, see Gerald P. Fogarty, S.J., *The Vatican and the Americanist Crisis : Denis J. O'Connell, American Agent in Rome, 1885–1903* (Rome, 1974).

95. Quoted in Sweeney, p. 265.

96. Quoted in John Tracy Ellis, *The Formative Years of the Catholic University of America* (Washington, D.C.: American Catholic Historical Association, 1946).

97. See Baron von Hügel to Percy Gardner, April 25, 1903, in Baron von Hügel, *Selected Letters 1896–1924* (London: n.p., 1927), pp. 120–21.

98. Reher, p. 99.

3. THE PROGRAM OF MODERNISM AT DUNWOODIE

1. "The Pastoral Letter of 1884" in Peter Guilday, ed., *The National Pastorals of the American Hierarchy, 1792–1919* (Washington, D.C.: National Catholic Welfare Council, 1923), p. 239.

2. See Ellis, *The Formative Years of the Catholic University of America*, especially chapter 1, pp. 15–86. O'Connell's tenure as rector was disastrous. The university's broker declared bankruptcy and two-thirds of the investment portfolio was lost. Like Ireland, O'Connell felt compelled to prove his orthodoxy and, after *Pascendi*, even went to the length of delating his scriptural scholar at CU, Charles Grannan, to Rome for questionable exegetical tendencies. See Hennesey, *American Catholics*, p. 216, and Colman J. Barry, O.S.B., *The Catholic University of America, 1903–1908: The Rectorship of Denis J. O'Connell* (Washington, D.C.: Catholic University Press, 1950).

3. Gannon called the *American Catholic Quarterly Review*, published by Archbishop Patrick John Ryan of Philadelphia, "the foremost exemplar of clerical intellectualism at the onset of the century." Authors Walter Elliott, William Kerby, and Thomas Shahan, among others, reported on recent advances in exegesis of Scripture, historical science, and evolution studies. "Before and after Modernism," p. 327 (see Introduction above, n. 6).

4. Christopher J. Kauffman, *Tradition and Transformation in Catholic Culture: The Priests of Saint Sulpice in the United States from 1791 to the Present* (New York: Macmillan, 1988), pp. 29–30 describes the *esprit ecclésiastique* informing the Sulpician ideal of the "priest-victim" and "ecclesiastical servant."

5. Quoted by Ella M. E. Flick, "John England," *Records of the Catholic Historical Society of Philadelphia* 33 (1927): 374.

6. Kauffman, *Tradition and Transformation in Catholic Culture*, pp. 154–60, provides the details of Magnien's career. See also Michael Charles Neri, "American Suplicians and the *New York Review*," *Bulletin de Saint Sulpice* 5 (1978): 254–60.

7. Hogan is quoted in Kauffman, *Tradition and Transformation in Catholic Culture*, pp. 172–73.

8. "Each of the doctrines has a history . . . they have been developed . . . as germs of necessity become successfully in time doctrines." "It is clear that one cannot demonstrate the church in scripture . . . [but] the world is not ready for these facts—it is necessary to form a synthesis of the facts to make them acceptable." Hogan to Loisy, 18 April 1898, quoted in Kauffman, p. 173. Kauffman described Hogan as "utterly free from the grip of apriori beliefs" but reluctant to publicly articulate a new apologetic according to the modern methodologies until a synthesis was fully developed by other scholars. While the theologians and exegetes were pursuing that end, Hogan urged seminaries to introduce their students to the defects of *a priori* reasoning so current

among the neo-scholastics; he also promoted the historical understanding of biblical criticism, and critiqued the ahistorical neo-scholastic synthesis.

9. John Hogan, *Clerical Studies* (Boston: Marlier, Callahan, and Co., 1898), pp. 461–64. See Fogarty, *American Catholic Biblical Scholarship*, pp. 73–74.

10. Hogan, *Clerical Studies*, pp. 471–72, 473, 474; Fogarty, *American Catholic Biblical Scholarship*, p. 74.

11. Fogarty, pp. 73–74.

12. Kauffman, pp. 158, 168. Most distressing to these polemicists was the widespread dissemination of these ideas among the future leaders of the church in America. For example, John Ireland did come under the influence of Branchereau during his seminary days in Paris. Years later, enemies of the archbishop of St. Paul traced his Americanism, with its tendency to stress human intuition of the dynamic activity of the Holy Spirit, back to his studies with the Sulpicians. Their pedagogy produced such distortions, it was contended, precisely because it deviated from the standards set by the Roman manuals.

13. Ibid., p. 160.

14. Gannon, "Before and after Modernism," p. 332.

15. These quotes, and a biographical sketch of Driscoll, are found in Michael DeVito, *New York Review, 1905–1908* (New York: United States Catholic Historical Society, 1977), which fails to place the events at Dunwoodie in their proper perspective. DeVito leads the reader clearly to the conclusion that a modernist impulse emerged in the efforts of the scholars, teachers, and journalists assembled there before 1909, but refuses himself to confirm it, thus, in a sense, "wasting" much of the material he presents. A characteristic passage: "the correspondence of [the *Review's* editor, James F. Driscoll] reveals that he was very close and friendly with prominent modernists. He exchanged ideas with them, offered to collaborate with them; invited them to write for the *Review*; published their writings; and accepted their suggestions and criticisms of his Journal. When these thinkers were beginning to be suspected and oppressed by the Church authorities, his correspondence shows support for them and his sympathy with their debatable views. Driscoll's associations with the modernists were of such a caliber that one would think that he too was a modernist. . . . But, there is no available evidence that would corroborate the thesis that Driscoll himself was a modernist" (pp. 237–38). By "available evidence" DeVito meant a written affirmation of the "anti-Christian conclusions" of the modernists. Accepting *Pascendi*'s claim that the modernists shared a developed system and set of conclusions, DeVito based his evaluation of Driscoll and his colleagues on the premise that "One could accept [modernists's] methodology and their orthodox views while still rejecting their anti-Christian conclusions. . . . A modernist. . .was one who affirmed anti-Christian conclusions by the use of the new scientific methods of the day." Incredibly, DeVito concluded that

only two figures, Loisy and Turmel, fit exactly the criteria of *Pascendi*. Thus, there were only two modernists; the rest, progressives: "The few modernists who eventually arrived at these theses in their thought were Loisy and Turmel, whereas people like Tyrrell, von Hügel, Petre, and Bremond did not. Heretical modernism should not be taken in such a way as to include relatively progressive Catholic opinion," (p. 191). Ironically, the encyclical is here used to narrow rather than to expand (as was the pontiff's intention) the possible scope of the heresy. In his provocative essay, "Before and after Modernism," Michael Gannon placed only the three self-confessed American Catholic modernists—Thomas Mulvey, William L. Sullivan, and John R. Slattery—into this interpretative framework. Contrary to the argument of this thesis, Gannon concluded that "Indeed there was probably no real connection between the Americanist and modernist movements either by way of cause or practical preface" (p. 337).

16. Driscoll to Dyer, 30 September 1901, Sulpician Archives, Baltimore (SAB). Driscoll predicted that he would attempt to impede Sulpician Americanization and inhibit Sulpician scholarship. "Well, at times it is refreshing to think that Paris is a couple of thousand miles away," he confided to Dyer.

17. Driscoll to Dyer, 5 October 1901, SAB.

18. Driscoll to Dyer, 9 October 1902, SAB.

19. Francis F. Gigot., S.S., *A General Introduction to the Holy Scriptures* (New York: Benziger Bros., 1900), pp. 553, 555.

20. Ibid., pp. 556, 557.

21. Francis Gigot, "Authorship of Isaias XL-LXVI," *New York Review* 1, no. 2 (August-September 1905): 180.

22. Francis Gigot, *Special Introduction to the Study of the Old Testament*, Part I: *The Historical Books* (New York: Benzinger Brothers, 1901), p. 32.

23. "Evidently someone, perhaps Fr. Collin—has denounced Fr. Gigot at headquarters and they are after him. Should Levisque and Touzard, the actual scrip. professors at S. Sulpice, be asked to examine the books, all would be well, Fr. Gigot having already received a letter from the former fully endorsing the Sp. Introd. (one of Gigot's books)—and styling it a model textbook. But in the present circumstances, it is much more probable that the books will be submitted to Vigoroux or Fillion. With the latter there is *no possibility* of their passing muster and only a doubtful one with the former," Driscoll to Dyer, 26 February 1902, SAB.

24. Ibid.

25. Driscoll to Dyer, 11 April 1902, SAB.

26. Ibid.

27. Gigot to Dyer, 19 January 1905, SAB.

28. Gigot to Dyer. 14 January 1903, SAB.

29. Gigot to Dyer, 13 February 1905, SAB.

30. Maher to Dyer, 11 January 1903, SAB.

31. Both sides in the matter argued that the other made the first move. Farley to Dyer, 28 January 1906, SAB.

32. DeVito cited a number of instances in which the editors of the *New York Review* misled Farley; for example, when ordered to cease publication of articles by Tyrrell after his dismissal from the Society of Jesus in 1906, they countered with an article by Henri Bremond, "Father Tyrrell as an Apologist," that acclaimed the orthodoxy and balance of Tyrrell's apologetic writings. Tyrrell wrote to von Hügel that Driscoll "is full of youth and enthusiasm and seems to inflict his alumni with his spirit. How the Archbishop of N.Y. trusts his seminarians and why I do not know. Probably, he [Farley] does not know enough to be frightened," p. 109.

33. Driscoll to Dyer, 11 January, 1905, SAB.

34. Dyer's mood changed from disbelief to anger to disappointment. He was obsessed with the betrayal and, months later, wrote to Joseph Bruneau, S.S., the only Sulpician at Dunwoodie who did not secede with the others but chose to move on, asking him to find out how early, and by whom the defection was planned. "My contention," he wrote, "is that they had [Farley's] assurance before ever they decided to leave St. Sulpice at all. Please tell me whatever you may know . . . that may throw light upon the matter—I wish to make use of what you will send me," Dyer to Bruneau, 14 April 1906, SAB.

35. Edward R. Dyer, *To the Sulpicians of the United States*, a privately printed letter (Baltimore: St. Mary's Seminary, 1906).

36. James F. Driscoll, R. M. Wakeham, Francis E. Gigot, John R. Mahoney, and Timothy P. Holland to E. R. Dyer, 9 January 1906, SAB.

37. Dyer to Driscoll, 11 January 1906, SAB.

38. Dyer to Farley, copy, 11 January 1906, SAB.

39. Farley to Dyer, 28 January 1906, SAB.

40. Dyer to Farley, 6 February 1906, SAB.

41. Dyer, *To the Sulpicians of the United States*, p. 55.

42. Ibid., pp. 148–49.

43. DeFoville to Dyer, 13 March 1906, SAB.

44. Arbez to Dyer, 30 January 1906, SAB.

45. Maher to Dyer, 21 January 1905, SAB.

46. Price to Dyer, 10 January 1908, SAB.

47. "Editorial," *Boston Evening Transcript*, 13 January 1906; "Editorial," *Boston Evening Transcript*, 3 February, 1906. More embarrassing, however, was the article in the *Western Watchman*, which identified the Dunwoodie professors as modernists: "More Potemkinizing," 1 February 1906. A sample passage: "In the Scriptures we are bound to follow the lead of conservative European thought. There is a school in Europe that is as restless as the American wing of the orders; a school that does not hesitate to say that the apostles were only partially responsible for the faith of our day, and that Our Lord Himself was mistaken in some things. In a showdown between

the exegesis of the Sulpicians and the professors of Dunwoodie we do not hesitate to declare ourselves on the side of the former," p. 90, copy in SAB. Driscoll wrote a letter to the editor of the *Transcript* in which he denied that the editors of the *Review* sought to inaugurate a movement of "new Catholicism." The secession, Driscoll argued, was not due to controversy concerning his orthodoxy nor to disagreements over censorship policy; the former Sulpicians "simply availed themselves of the liberty guaranteed to them when they entered the society; and in doing so they have been actuated by the sole motive and desire of rendering the most efficient service in their power to the cause to which they had devoted their lives, viz: that of ecclesiastical education."

48. Michael Gannon, "Before and after Modernism," p. 335.

49. Driscoll to Dyer, 4 June 1902, SAB.

50. Ibid.

51. DeVito, pp. 25–28, fills in the details of Duffy's career.

52. Duffy to Dyer, 21 January 1898, SAB.

53. Quoted in DeVito, p. 29.

54. Quoted in Arthur J. Scanlan, *St. Joseph's Seminary, Dunwoodie, New York, 1896–1921* (New York: The United States Catholic Historical Society, 1922), pp. 109–11.

55. Gannon, p. 334. Apparently, Farley was not aware of the content or syllabus of the guest lectures. DeVito reported that he was surprised and chagrined to hear that, for example, Gennochi had played so prominent a role in the lecture series.

56. For a thorough treatment of Giovanni Gennochi's career and correspondence with Loisy, see Francesco Turvasi, *The Condemnation of Alfred Loisy and the Historical Method* (Rome: Edizioni Di Storia E Letteratura, 1979).

57. Ibid., p. 169.

58. For a comprehensive survey of the emerging alternatives to the traditional "inspired and inerrant" formula for biblical texts, see James T. Burtchaell, *Catholic Theories of Biblical Inspiration since 1810* (Cambridge: Cambridge University Press, 1969). Literary and historical criticism of scriptural texts does not imperil the authority of dogmatic statements or implications contained therein, for the proper object of such criticism is not the supernatural and transcendent aspect of Holy Scripture, Gennochi contended. Science studies phenomena of the natural world; faith in the divinity of Jesus, for example, is a supernatural gift of God and the "evidence" that generates that faith cannot be demonstrated by mere science or by natural history. This is not to say, however, that science disproves or excludes the evidence or discredits the faith that the evidence excites. This last affirmation set Gennochi apart from Loisy's position in *Autour d'un petit livre*.

59. See Gigot's ongoing series, "The Higher Criticism of the Bible," in *New York Review* 2, no. 2 (September-October 1906), no. 3 (November-December 1906), and no. 4 (January-February 1907).

60. Diomede Falconio to Archbishop John Farley, 15 January, 1908, 1–11, Archives of the Archdiocese of New York.

61. See Mark Stephen Massa, *Charles Augustus Briggs and the Crisis of Historical Criticism* (Minneapolis: Fortress Press, 1990).

62. Charles A. Briggs, *Biblical Study: Its Principles, Methods and History* (New York: Charles Scribner's Sons, 1883), pp. 9, 10, 16.

63. William R. Hutchison, *The Modernist Impulse in American Protestantism* (New York: Oxford University Press), pp. 92–94, provides an excellent synopsis of Briggs's work and his place in liberal Protestantism.

64. Quoted in Max Gray Rogers, "Charles Augustus Briggs: Hersey at Union," in George Shriver, ed., *American Religious Heretics* (Nashville: Abingdon Press, 1966), p. 94.

65. Charles A. Briggs, *Whither? A Theological Question for the Times* (New York: Charles Scribner's Sons, 1889), p. 44. See also Briggs, *The Authority of Holy Scripture: An Inaugural Address* (New York: Charles Scribner's Sons, 1891), p. 24. Reaction to Briggs's conviction of heresy before the presbytery of New York reflected the widening gap between old and new in Protestant theology. The response of the periodicals that considered themselves liberal revealed how incomplete was their grasp of the implications of Briggs's modernist version of the new theology. None of his defenders in the liberal press seemed to anticipate that their particular tradition might be threatened by the critical methods of Briggs. Nearly all non-Presbyterian reviewers of Briggs's books and inaugural address found him forceful and sound in pointing out how modern Presbyterianism had drifted from its standards.

66. Briggs's articles for the *North American Review*, such as "Reform in the Roman Catholic Church," (July 1905) were reviewed favorably in *New York Review* 1, no. 2 (September-October 1905): 239–40. These were written at the same time he was speaking at Dunwoodie and might reflect his comments to his Dunwoodie audience, but this can only be speculation.

67. Father Terrance F. X. O'Donnell, Church of St. Barnabas, Bronx, New York. Scanlan, *St. Joseph's Seminary*, p. 110, reported that Abbe Felix Klein approved of Driscoll's revised curriculum.

68. Gannon, p. 335.

4. THE *NEW YORK REVIEW:*
A JOURNAL OF MODERNIST THOUGHT

1. The evidence is simply too abundant and convincing to argue otherwise, although at least one historian has done so. DeVito included in his thesis a chapter (pp. 187–248) on "Modernism and the *New York Review*"

in which he provided abundant evidence of the modernist ethos of the review; intriguingly, however, he refuses to see the journal as a modernist effort, in part because he accepted Lemius's definition of modernism and concluded, on that basis, that the Dunwoodians did not accept the "anti-Christian conclusions" of the modernists. But this evaluation of modernism was based on no consensus of "anti-Christian conclusions." Driscoll, "shows his support for [the modernists] and his sympathy with their debatable views," but he was not a modernist, for "One could accept their methodology and their orthodox views while still rejecting their anti-Christian conclusions. A modernist. . . was one who affirmed anti-Christian conclusions by the use of the new scientific methods of the day," DeVito (pp. 237–39).

2. For example: Ernesto Buonaiuti, "St. Francis of Assisi in Modern Critical Thought," *New York Review* 2, no. 4 (January-February 1907): 459–78; and Maude D. Petre, "A New Catholic Apology," *New York Review* 2, no. 5 (April-May 1907): 602–9.

3. See James F. Driscoll, S.S., "Recent Views on Biblical Inspiration I," *New York Review* 1, no. 1 (June-July 1905). Gigot penned twenty-one articles on criticism for the *Review*, for example, "Abraham: A Historical Study," *New York Review* 2, no. 1 (July-August 1906): 37–48.

4. Francis P. Duffy to Edward J. Hanna, 8 January 1905, copy, from Archives of Diocese of Rochester, St. Bernard's Seminary.

5. This announcement was reprinted in *New York Review* 1, no. 4 (January-February 1906): 132–33. "The strides made in scientific and historical research during the past half century have forced upon us the consideration of new problems, and have rendered necessary the restatement of many theological positions," the editor wrote. "The new issues thus raised cannot without ever increasing harm continue to be ignored by Catholics as has too generally been the case in the past."

6. "Editorial," *Boston Evening Transcript*, 13 January 1906, p. 2.

7. Fogarty, *American Catholic Biblical Scholarship*, pp. 51–55.

8. On his regrets at leaving Dunwoodie Bruneau wrote to Dyer that Driscoll "does not seem to understand my position well and how I am really in the impossibility of remaining with them at Dunwoodie in their actual situation. This pains me. . . . I will never again find what I had here," Bruneau to Dyer, 15 January 1906, SAB.

9. "Editorial," *Catholic World*, June 1905.

10. Wilfrid Ward, "The Spirit of Newman's Apologetics," *New York Review* 1, no. 1 (June-July 1905): 4–5, 8, 11.

11. Ibid., p. 10.

12. George Fonsegrive, "Catholicity and Free Thought," *New York Review* 1, no. 1 (June-July 1905): 21.

13. Ibid., pp. 22–28.

14. James J. Fox, D.D., "Scotus Redivivus," *New York Review* 1, no. 1 (June-July 1905): 30.

15. Ibid., p. 32, 35, 36.

16. Ibid., p. 36.

17. Ibid.

18. Ibid., p. 37.

19. Ibid., p. 41, 42.

20. Ibid., p. 44.

21. Ibid., p. 45, 46.

22. Ibid., p. 46.

23. Joseph P. McSorley, C.S.P., "The Church and the Soul," *New York Review* 1, no. 1 (June-July 1905): 68, 69.

24. According to the editors of the *Review*, Gerrard was "a close student of . . . not inimical to the progressive movements in Christian apologetics . . . sensitive to the 'new and moving spirit' of moderns like Newman . . . [who] has added from his own research and intuition a word here and there, "Notes," *New York Review* 3, no. 4. (January-February 1908): p. 578.

25. Thomas J. Gerrard, "Newman and Conceptualism," *New York Review* 2, no. 4 (January-February 1907): 430, 431.

26. Ibid., p. 432.

27. Ibid., pp. 433, 440.

28. Ibid, p. 440.

29. Ibid., p. 441.

30. Thomas J. Gerrard, "Dichotomy: A Study in Newman and Aquinas," *New York Review* 3, no. 4 and no. 5 (January-February, March-April 1908): 381.

31. See Wilfrid Ward, "The Function of Intransigeance," *New York Review* 2, no. 1 (July-August 1906).

32. Gerrard, "Dichotomy," p. 389.

33. David Barry, "The True Function of Experience in Belief," *New York Review* 3, no. 3 (November-December 1907): 258.

34. Ibid., pp. 258, 259, 266.

35. George Tyrrell, *Lex Orandi: or Prayer and Creed* (London: Longmans, 1903) and *Lex Credendi: A Sequel to Lex Orandi* (London: Longmans, 1907).

36. William Turner, "A Contemporary French School of Pragmatism," *New York Review* 2, no. 1 (July-August 1906): 36.

37. "Reviews," *New York Review* 3, no. 6 (May-June 1908): 727.

38. Ibid., p. 728.

39. Ibid., p. 729.

40. Cornelius Clifford, "Holtzmann's Life of Jesus," *New York Review* 1, no. 1 (June-July 1905): 48.

41. James Driscoll, S.S., "Recent Views on Biblical Inspiration I, *New York Review* 1, no. 1 (June-July 1905): 48.

42. Ibid., p. 84.

43. Vincent McNabb, "The Petrine Texts in the Fourth Gospel," *New York Review* 3, no. 6 (May-June 1908): 606.

44. Ibid., pp. 606–8.

45. Francis E. Gigot, D.D., "The Higher Criticism of the Bible: The Name and the Thing," *New York Review* 1, no. 6 (May-June 1906): 723, 724.

46. Ibid., p. 725.

47. Francis E. Gigot, D.D., "The Higher Criticism of the Bible: The Name and the Thing," p. 727.

48. Francis E. Gigot, "The Higher Criticism of the Bible: The Nature of Its Problems," *New York Review* 2, no. 1 (July-August 1906): 68, 69, 70.

49. Ibid., pp. 68–69.

50. Francis E. Gigot, D.D., "The Higher Criticism of the Bible: Its General Principles," *New York Review* 2, no. 2 (September-October 1906): 158.

51. Ibid., pp. 159, 160.

52. Ibid., p. 161.

53. Francis E. Gigot, D.D., "The Higher Criticism of the Bible: Its Constructive Aspect," *New York Review* 2, no. 3 (November-December 1906): 302–5.

54. Francis E. Gigot, D.D., "The Higher Criticism of the Bible: Its Relation to Tradition," *New York Review* 2, no. 4 (January-February 1907): 442–43.

55. Ibid., p. 444, italics added.

56. Ibid., p. 444.

57. Francis E. Gigot, D.D., "The Higher Criticism of the Bible: Its Objective Aspect," *New York Review* 2, no. 5 (March-April 1907): 587, 588.

58. See for example, Gigot, "Leading Problems Concerning the Book of Job," *New York Review* 1, no. 4 (January-February 1906): 579. Gigot also penned a series of noncontroversial articles on the teaching on divorce in the New Testament.

59. Gigot, "The Higher Criticism of the Bible: Its Constructive Aspect," p. 303.

60. Pope Pius X, *Pascendi*, pp. 96–98.

61. James F. Driscoll, D.D., "Recent Views on Biblical Inspiration II," *New York Review* 1, no. 3 (November-December 1905): 198.

62. Ibid., pp. 199–201.

63. Ibid., p. 201, 204.

64. Ibid., p. 205.

65. F. Hugh Pope, O.P., "The Historical Geography of the Greek Bible," *New York Review* 3, no. 6 (May-June 1908): 687–88, 691, 702, 703.

66. See Gabriel Oussani, "Archaelogy and the Higher Criticism," *New York Review* 2, no. 6 (May-June 1907): 719–48; Oussani, "The Code of

Hammurabi and Mosaic Legislation," *New York Review* 1, no. 4 (December-January 1905–1906): 488–510; and, Oussani, "The Administration of Law and Justice in Ancient Israel," *New York Review* 1, no. 6 (April-May 1906): 739–61.

67. Edward J. Hanna, "The Power of the Keys," *New York Review* 3, no. 4 (January-February 1908): 561–65.

68. "Notes," *New York Review* 1, no. 2 (September-October 1905): 238.

69. Ibid., p. 239.

70. *Catholic Weekly*, 15 November 1907, quoted in "Notes," *New York Review* 3, no. 4 (January-February 1908): 356–57. In praising the journal, the author commented on the "Notes" section: "of the 'notes,' however, it ought to be said that they are worthy of a better name. They are unsigned. We suggest to the writer that his work is of an importance which should justify him in coming to the front with his name. Practically every recent event worth speaking about which has happened in the world of religious thought is recorded with suitable, and sometimes very vigorous, comment. It is largely through 'notes' of this kind that general opinion is formed. . . . It is here that an attitude is taken towards orthodoxy and unorthodoxy. It is here that we find an indication of that spirit of true progress which pays due regard to the guidance of authority and to the choice of the most distinguished thinkers and writers" (pp. 357–58).

71. "Notes," *New York Review* 3, no. 3 (November-December 1907): 359.

72. "The Syllabus of Pius X," *New York Review* 3, no. 3 (November-December 1907): 342, 343.

73. Ibid., pp. 343–44.

74. Ibid., pp. 342, 345, 346.

75. Ibid., p. 348.

76. "Notes," *New York Review* 2, no. 2 (September-October 1906): 239–40.

77. Baron Friedrich von Hügel to Charles Augustus Briggs, as quoted in "Notes," *New York Review* 3, no. 4 (January-February 1908): 517–18.

78. Ibid.

79. Ibid., pp. 518, 519, 520.

80. Ibid., p. 519.

81. Ibid., pp. 519–20.

82. "Notes," *New York Review* 2, no. 5 (March-April 1907): 650–53.

83. Ibid., p. 653.

84. "Notes," *New York Review* 2, no. 4 (January-February 1907): 520.

85. George Tyrrell, "The Dogmatic Reading of History, " *New York Review* 1, no. 3 (October-November 1905): 269–76.

86. Henri Bremond, "Father Tyrrell as an Apologist," *New York Review* 2, no. 6 (May-June 1907): 763.

87. Ibid., pp. 768, 769.

88. William L. Sullivan, "Catholicity and Some Elements in Our National Life," *New York Review* 1, no. 1 (June-July 1905): 259.

89. M. D. Petre, "A New Catholic Apology," *New York Review* 2, no. 5 (March-April 1907): 602, 603, 604, 605.

90. Ibid., pp. 607–8.

91. See *New York Review* 1, no. 4 (December 1905–January 1906): 540; see also Scanlan, pp. 92–111.

92. David Barry, "A Plea for a More Comprehensive Definition of the Church," *New York Review* 2, no. 5 (March-April 1907): 691–97.

93. Ibid., p. 697.

94. DeVito, p. 197.

95. William L. Sullivan, *Under Orders: The Autobiography of William Laurence Sullivan* (Boston: Beacon Press, 1944), p. 107.

96. Driscoll reported this conversation with Farley to Dyer in a letter, 11 January 1905, SAB.

97. "Modernism in the American Church," *American Ecclesiastical Review* (January, 1908): 44.

98. "Report to Pope on Hanna," *New York Times* (January 15, 1908): 3. Also see Falconio to Farley, January 15, 1908, Archives of the Archdiocese of New York; and Farley to Falconio, January 22, 1908, quoted in Gannon, "Before and After Modernism," pp. 341–42.

99. Edward Hanna, "The Human Knowledge of Christ," *New York Review* 3, no. 4 (January-February 1908).

100. Mulvey's defection was reported in the *New York Sun*, 18 July 1908. See Thomas Mulvey, "Review of Francis G. Peabody, *Jesus Christ and the Social Question*," *New York Review* 2, no. 6 (May-June 1907): 696–98. See Fogarty, pp. 132–35, for a recounting of the relevant correspondences concerning the Hanna affair.

101. Driscoll to Charles A. Briggs, 8 December 1907, copy in SAB.

102. "Editorial," *New York Review* 3, no. 6. (May-June 1908). DeVito, pp. 272–77.

103. Merry del Val to Archbishop Diomede Falconio, 12 December 1907, quoted in Fogarty, p. 135.

5. AMERICANISM AND MODERNISM AS ONE:
WILLIAM L. SULLIVAN AND JOHN R. SLATTERY

1. John Ratté argues that Sullivan's development "confirmed the orthodox interpretation of Modernism as a rite of passage to Liberal Protestantism," *Three Modernists* (New York: Sheed & Ward, 1967), pp. 260–62. Thomas T. McAvoy argued against a connection between Americanism and modernism

in "Liberalism, Americanism, Modernism," *Records of the American Catholic Historical Society of Philadelphia* 63 (1953): 225–31. Michael B. McGarry, C.S.P., "Modernism in the United States: William Laurence Sullivan, 1872–1935," *Records of the American Catholic Historical Society of Philadelphia* 90 (1979): 33–52, and Margaret Mary Reher, "Americanism and Modernism: Continuity or Discontinuity?" *U.S. Catholic Historian* 1 (1981): 87–103, argue for the connection.

2. Ratté, *Three Modernists*, p. 264.

3. This oversight is due largely to the previous unavailability of the Sullivan-Estelle Throckmorton correspondence that has recently been coded and filed in the archives of the Harvard Divinity School (AHDS). I am indebted to Alan Seaburg, the archivist of the Andover-Harvard Theological Library, for making this correspondence available to me. Many of these letters describe the works of scholarship and spirituality most influential on Sullivan.

4. Sullivan, *Under Orders: The Autobiography of William Laurence Sullivan* (Boston: Beacon, 1944; revised ed., 1966), pp. 50, 54, 63, 64, 66. On Sullivan's own progress in critical studies, see Warren E. Duclos, "Crisis of an American Catholic Modernist: Toward the Moral Absolutism of William L. Sullivan," *Church History* 41 (1972): 370.

5. Diary entry of 15–17 January 1897 (Sullivan papers, AHDS). Ibid., 24 January 1897.

6. Ibid., 24 January 1897.

7. William L. Sullivan, C.S.P., "Some Theistic Implications of Modern Philosophy: A Dissertation in Fundamental Dogma" (Washington, D.C.: Archives of the Catholic University of America, 1900).

8. Sullivan, *Under Orders*, p. 75.

9. Sullivan to Estelle Throckmorton, 3 September 1910 (AHDS).

10. Sullivan to Throckmorton, 2 March 1910 (AHDS); also see Sullivan to Throckmorton, 16 August 1910 (AHDS).

11. On the impact of his mission work in Nashville, see McGarry, "Modernism in the United States," p. 36, and Duclos, "Crisis," p. 370. For a statement by Sullivan on the American ethos, see "Protestantism and Catholicism in a New Age," a sermon delivered by the Rev. William L. Sullivan at the First Congregational Church, All Souls, 6 April 1919 (AHDS), and idem, *Under Orders*, pp. 64 –70, 90 –95.

12. Duclos, "Crisis," p. 376.

13. Sullivan also contended that inquisitors first sought to question the moral integrity of theological dissenters. "Even in cases where the man's life had been conspicuously blameless . . . the horrid, irreligious, utterly un-Christian and criminal axiom, *Cherchez la femme* is considered ample to cover the incident," Sullivan to Throckmorton, 30 May 1910 (AHDS). Other correspondence indicates that Sullivan felt that his moral character, while in truth above reproach, would be a target for his ecclesiastical opponents once he was identified as a modernist.

14. On Sullivan's connection with the Americanists, see Sullivan, *Under Orders*, pp. 65, 90. On his comparison of the Americanist ethos with French republicanism, see William L. Sullivan, "Montalembert and Lammenais," *Catholic World* 76 (1903): 468.

15. Sullivan, *Under Orders*, p. 66.

16. Most of the letters are typed and bound in chronological order in the William Laurence Sullivan Papers, AHDS.

17. Sullivan to Throckmorton, 11 September 1910 (AHDS).

18. Sullivan to William Wendte, 4 September 1910 (AHDS); Sullivan to Throckmorton, 9 June 1906 (AHDS); Sullivan to Throckmorton, 30 January 1910 (AHDS).

19. Sullivan to Throckmorton, 1 1 December 1909 (AHDS).

20. Sullivan, *Under Orders*, pp. 70–71. See also Sullivan, "The Future of the Christian Religion," *Catholic World* 70 (1899): 157.

21. Sullivan, *Under Orders*, p. 73.

22. Ibid., p. 66.

23. Ibid., p. 89.

24. Yet Sullivan perceived in the mystical tradition of Roman Catholicism an important emphasis he found lacking in Unitarianism; see Sullivan, "Is Protestantism in Decay?" an unpublished essay, 19 November 1933 (AHDS).

25. Sullivan, *Under Orders*, p. 79.

26. Ibid., p. 88. See also two articles Sullivan wrote at this time on the necessity of incorporating the methods of higher criticism into Catholic biblical and historical studies: "Fr. Hogan and the Intellectual Apostolate," *Catholic World* 75 (1903), and "The Latest Word on the Theology of Inspiration," *Catholic World* 84 (1905).

27. Sullivan, *Under Orders*, pp. 105–6.

28. William L. Sullivan, C.S.P., "Catholicity and Some Elements in Our National Life," *New York Review* 1, no. 2 (November-December 1905): 262–63.

29. Ibid., p. 264.

30. Ibid., p. 265.

31. Ibid., p. 267. See also David Sweeney, *The Life of John Lancaster Spalding: First Bishop of Peoria, 1840–1915* (New York: Herder & Herder, 1965).

32. William L. Sullivan, C.S.P., "The Three Heavenly Witnesses," *New York Review* 2, no. 2 (September-October 1906): 175–88.

33. Ibid., p. 188.

34. Sullivan, *Under Orders*, p. 106.

35. Sullivan to Throckmorton, 15 May 1908 (AHDS).

36. Sullivan to Throckmorton, 14 June 1910 (AHDS). Also, on *Letters to His Holiness*, see Sullivan to Wendte, 4 September 1910 (AHDS). Francesco Turvasi believes that Sullivan copied the style and much of the

substance of *Letters to His Holiness* from a similar work by Italian modernist Ernesto Buonaiuti entitled *Letters from a Modernist.*

37. William L. Sullivan, *Letters to His Holiness Pope Pius X* (Chicago: Open Court, 1910), p. xvii.

38. See Duclos, "Crisis," p. 371, and Ratté, *Three Modernists*, p. 289 as examples of this flawed interpretation.

39. Sullivan articulated this strategy in a letter to Throckmorton. The book's "concessions to criticism shock those that have never known the processes of criticism. . . . To such, the book will be merely a scandal. But to those in these days, not a few, who, as they have grown in knowledge, have been appalled in finding the very foundations of reverence and the moral life crumbling beneath their feet may find in that book a religious earnestness, a spiritual fervor, and a love for the unseen sanctities of God" (14 June 1910 [AHDS]).

40. "As to that book, the evolution of religious thought has brought a crisis to our doors. . . . I was driven practically against my will to recognize the profound religiousness of such voices of protest and appeal as Murri's in Italy, Schell's in Germany, Loisy and Turmel's in France, and Tyrrell and Dell's in England, and forced to the opinion that here, too, some word, desolating as the necessity is, should be spoken toward the same end. . . . I felt urged to say a word which, however destructive it appears on the surface, I am still convinced is constructive toward a simpler, sincerer, and happier time to come" (Sullivan to Throckmorton, 22 June 1910 [AHDS]).

41. Sullivan to Throckmorton, 7 April 1910 (AHDS).

42. William L. Sullivan, "The Need of a Liberal Catholicism in America" (unpublished essay, 1910: AHDS).

43. Sullivan to Throckmorton, 18 May 1910 (AHDS).

44. Sullivan, *Under Orders*, pp. 80, 109–11. See also idem, *The Priest: A Tale of Modernism in New England* (Boston, 1914), in which the protagonist of the novel, Ambrose Hanlon, faces a similar crisis in his priesthood.

45. Sullivan to Throckmorton, 4 April 1910 (AHDS); Ratté, *Three Modernists*, pp. 285–87, effectively pulls together from various sources all the stories told by Sullivan of troubled or hypocritical priests who continued in the priesthood despite their disbelief.

46. Sullivan, *Under Orders*, p. 137.

47. Sullivan, *Letters to His Holiness*, pp. xiv, xv.

48. Ibid.

49. Ibid., p. 134.

50. Ibid. On this point, see Houtin to Sullivan, 7 April 1911 (AHDS).

51. Sullivan, *Letters to His Holiness*, pp. 163–64.

52. Sullivan to Wendte, 4 September 1910 (AHDS).

53. Ibid.

54. William L. Sullivan, "The Final Phase of Modernism" (unpublished essay, 1910; AHDS).

55. Ratté, *Three Modernists*, p. 327; Sullivan, *Under Orders*, p. 199.

56. William L. Sullivan, "Catholicism: Advantages and Disadvantages" (unpublished sermon, no date; AHDS).

57. [John R. Slattery], "Biographie de J. R. Slattery" (MS in Papiers Houtin, *Oeuvres*, LIV, NAF 15741–42, Bibliothèque Nationale, Paris) Chapter 1, pp. 1–10. I am indebted to William Portier, who discovered this manuscript in Paris and provided me with a copy of it. The manuscript is divided into twenty-one chapters, each paginated separately. It is written as an autobiography. The biographical details from Slattery's life are also taken from a privately circulated biographical sketch written by Portier (September 1984). See also William Portier, "A Social and Economic Portrait of John R. Slattery (1859–1926)," a paper delivered at the College Theology Society spring conference (1985). On the relationship between American Catholics and the black community, see Albert J. Raboteau, "Black Catholics: A Capsule History," reprinted in the *Catholic Digest* (June 1983): 32–38, from *The Catholic Voice* (Oakland, February 1983).

58. Stephen J. Ochs, *Desegregating the Altar: The Josephites and the Struggle for Black Priests, 1871–1960* (Baton Rouge and London: Louisiana State University Press, 1990), p. 52.

59. John Slattery, "Facts and Suggestions about the Colored People," *Catholic World* 41 (April 1885): 32–42; [Slattery], "Biographie" 9: 2–3.

60. Ochs, *Desegregating the Altar*, p. 67.

61. [Bishop Francis A. Janssens], "Colored Priests for Colored People," *St. Joseph's Advocate* 1 (April 1887): 229–31.

62. Ochs, *Desegregating the Altar*, pp. 81–84.

63. John R. Slattery, "The Negroes and the Baptists," *Catholic World* 63, no. 374 (May 1896): 265.

64. Ibid., p. 266.

65. Ibid., pp. 267, 268.

66. John R. Slattery, "A Catholic College for Negro Catechists," *Catholic World* 70, no. 415 (October 1899): 11–12.

67. In 1894 Slattery supervised the implementation of new regulations governing the training of blacks in the seminary. The regulations were clearly discriminatory, but Slattery defended them as necessary to appease bishops and other clergy who maintained that blacks were not capable of observing priestly celibacy. See Ochs, *Desegregating the Altar*, pp. 92–93.

68. Slattery, "A Catholic College for Negro Catechists," p. 12.

69. Ochs, *Desegregating the Altar*, p. 109.

70. John R. Slattery, "How My Priesthood Dropped from Me," *Independent* 61, no. 3005 (July-September 1906): 565.

71. Ibid, p. 565.

72. William L. Portier, "Modernism in the United States: The Case of John R. Slattery (1851–1926)," in Ronald Burke, Gary Lease, and George

Gilmore, eds., *Varieties of Modernism* (Mobile, Ala.: Spring Hill College, 1986), p. 78.

73. Slattery, "How My Priesthood Dropped from Me," p. 565.

74. On May 4, 1890, in a sermon delivered in the first black Catholic parish church in Washington, D.C., Ireland advocated integrated seminaries and attacked racial discrimination in the church and in society. The archbishop of St. Paul also accepted one of Slattery's black protégés, John Henry Dorsey of Baltimore, into the college department of St. Thomas Aquinas Seminary in St. Paul. See "A Famous Sermon," *St. Joseph's Advocate* 2 (July 1890): 151–52; Ochs, *Desegregating the Altar*, p. 76.

75. [Slattery], "Biographie," chapter 12: 1–2, 7–14, 17–18; chapter 5: 6–9; chapter 6: 13–19; chapter 14: 9. See also Portier, "Modernism in the United States," p. 79.

76. See [Slattery], "Biographie," chapters 12–14.

77. Marvin R. O'Connell, *John Ireland and the American Catholic Church*, pp. 350–423, passim, provides the most detailed account to date of Satolli's shifting alliances at this time.

78. [Slattery], "Biographie," chapter 11.

79. [Slattery], "Biographie," chapter 11: 22–28, chapter 16: 1–14.

80. Slattery, "How My Priesthood Dropped from Me," p. 567. Turmel later published articles on patristics in the *New York Review*.

81. Slattery, "How My Priesthood Dropped from Me," p. 567.

82. Ibid.

83. Ibid., p. 568.

84. Ibid.

85. Ibid., p. 569.

86. [Slattery], "Biographie," chapter 16.

87. Described in Portier, "Modernism in the United States," pp. 82–83.

88. John R. Slattery, "Scholastic Methods, Their Advantages and Disadvantages," *American Ecclesiastical Review* 23 (November 1900): 487, 492.

89. Slattery to O'Connell, Baltimore, 7 December 1900, quoted in Portier, "Modernism in the United States," p. 83.

90. Ochs, *Desegregating the Altar*, p. 122.

91. [Slattery], "Biographie," chapter 16: 10–14.

92. Ibid., chapter 16: 17. See Also *Rev. John Henry Dorsey, A Colored Man, Was Ordained by His Eminence, Cardinal Gibbons* (Baltimore, n.d.) in John H. Dorsey file, Josephite Fathers Archives, Baltimore. Quoted in Ochs, p. 124.

93. Slattery to Alfred Loisy, Baltimore, February 24, 1903, summarized in Portier, "Modernism in the United States," pp. 87–88.

94. A Presbyter, "A Root Trouble in Catholicism," *Independent* 55 (March 1903): 664. The "Biographie," chapter 17, confirms that Slattery was the presbyter.

95. One influence on Slattery at this time was Spinoza: "Spinoza may have grasped the notion of it best. . . . Nor can I see much sign of free will in man. Over the salient parts of one's life, place of birth, country, language, religion, parents, health or unhealth of body, education, home, a man has no freedom; it is the same way with death and the manner of taking off. Man's freedom seems not much more than a bird's. How much have I inherited which follows me like mine own-shadow? Parents, society, nation, religion, heredity, all act toward the offspring as infallible popes," Slattery, "How My Priesthood Dropped from Me," p. 570.

96. Slattery, "The Workings of Modernism," *American Journal of Theology* 13 (October 1909): 556.

97. Ibid., p. 557.

98. Ibid., p. 556, quoting Loisy, *Simples Reflexions* (Paris, 1908): 275.

99. Ibid., p. 559.

100. Ibid., p. 560. To Slattery, the Curia was adept at such "diplomacy" from long practice: "Give and take, demand and refuse, back out and insist, filled the mind on both sides."

101. Ibid.

102. Ibid., p. 561, 562. On the topic of the diplomatic relations between Rome and Germany and their influence on the modernist crisis, see Gary Lease, "Bismarck, Hohenlohe, and the Vatican: The Beginnings of Modernism," in *Modernism: Origins, Parameters, Prospects*, pp. 29–45.

103. Ibid., p. 562, 564. "When from novels we pass to magazines and the daily press in which are discussed, in a loose and haphazard manner for the most part, the questions attacked in the letter on modernism, it is clear enough that the bishops will be unable to stem the tide," p. 562.

104. Ibid., p. 569.

105. Slattery's comments, p. 571, indicate that he had carefully read Hanna's articles in the *New York Review*, that he knew of Driscoll's work, and that he was quite familiar with the situation at Dunwoodie. No doubt he got the "inside scoop" on these affairs from either Keane or Ireland.

106. Albert Houtin, *L'Americanisme* (Paris: n.p., 1904).

6. THE INTERRUPTED CONVERSATION: THE ASSIMILATION OF MODERNIST THEMES

1. The first periodicals that mentioned the imminent appearance of the *New York Review* were *Catholic News* 19, no. 23 (March 25, 1906): 4, and *American Ecclesiastical Review* 2, no. 3 (March 1905): 333. Heuser's journal later reported: "We note that there is no censor mentioned in connection with the magazine such as the Index rule demands. . . . This means probably that the Archbishop of New York confides in the orthodoxy and propriety of the

utterance of the publication under the editorship of the rector of St. Joseph's Seminary," *American Ecclesiastical Review* 3, no. 6 (September 1905): 318. Other periodicals, including the *Catholic World*, and the *American Catholic Quarterly Review* welcomed the *New York Review* by public announcement in the journal or by private letters of congratulation. The same authors appear over and over again in these journals, and it was not long before the editors of the *New York Review* were attracting these columnists and influencing their thoughts in turn.

2. Robert Trisco, "The Church's History in the University's History," *Catholic Historical Review* 75, no. 4: 659–60.

3. Catholic University professors Shahan, Grannan, Pace, and O'Gorman had studied in Europe at Institute Catholique in Paris and in Rome. Shahan and O'Gorman had become familiar with the work of historical critics such as Louis Duchesne at Paris. A number of the American Catholics had been trained at Louvain, where they had come into contact with a more flexible version of Thomism then predominant in the Roman schools, and with secular sciences and thought as well.

4. See Charles M. Westcott, "The Perils of an Unauthorized Dogmatism," *Catholic World* 77 (August 1903): 670–77; Joseph McSorley, "The Unconverted World," *Catholic World* 78 (January 1904): 427–38; McSorley, "How We Abuse Religion," *Catholic World* 70 (October 1899): 81–88; and M. J. Ryan, "The Philosophy of Newman," *American Catholic Quarterly Review* 33, no. 129 (January 1908): 77–86.

5. John T. Ford, C.S.C., " 'A Centre of Light and Truth': A Century of Theology at the Catholic University of America," *Catholic Historical Review* 75, no. 4: 569–70.

6. See Ann Taves, *The Household of Faith* (Notre Dame, Ind.: University of Notre Dame Press, 1986), for a discussion of the attempted Roman control of devotions and spirituality.

7. Henry A. Poels, "History and Inspiration: Introduction," *Catholic University Bulletin* 11 no. 1 (January 1905): 19–67; "History and Inspiration: The Fathers of the Church," *Catholic University Bulletin* 11, no. 2 (April 1905): 152–94.

8. Poels, "History and Inspiration: Introduction," p. 22.

9. Ibid.

10. Ibid., p. 23.

11. Ibid., p. 24. On Poels's life, see Door J. Colsen, C.M., *Poels* (Roermond-Maaseik, J.J. Roman and Zonen, 1955). Also consult Gerald Fogarty, *American Catholic Biblical Scholarship*, pp. 78–119.

12. Poels, "History and Inspiration: Introduction," p. 26.

13. Ibid., p. 28.

14. Ibid., pp. 29–40.

15. Ibid., p. 30.

16. Ibid., p. 33.

17. Ibid., pp. 59–60.

18. Ibid., pp. 65–67, passim.

19. Henry A. Poels, "History and Inspiration: The Fathers of the Church," *Catholic University Bulletin* 11, no. 2 (April 1905): 156–57.

20. Ibid., p. 157.

21. Ibid., p. 157–58.

22. Ibid., p. 160. "Thus, then, a Christian is never justified in departing from the teaching of the Fathers in matters of faith, by appealing to the results of scientific progress in modern times," Poels concluded.

23. Ibid., p. 166.

24. Ibid., p. 175.

25. Ibid.

26. Ibid., pp. 192–93.

27. Henry A. Poels, "History and Inspiration: Saint Jerome," *Catholic University Bulletin* 12, no. 2 (April 1906): 216.

28. Colman J. Barry, O.S.B., *The Catholic University of America, 1903–1909: The Rectorship of Denis J. O'Connell* (Washington, D.C.: The Catholic University of America Press, 1950), p. 231 n.

29. John Tracy Ellis, *The Life of James Cardinal Gibbons, Archbishop of Baltimore, 1834–1921*, 2 vols. (Milwaukee: Bruce, 1952), 2: 171–82.

30. Merry del Val to James Cardinal Gibbons, 17 July 1909, Archives of the Archdiocese of Baltimore (AAB), James Cardinal Gibbons to Merry del Val, 19 November 1909 (AAB).

31. Gibbons to Merry del Val, 19 November 1909 (AAB).

32. On this development, see R. Scott Appleby, "*Catholic University Bulletin*," in Charles Lippy, ed., *Religious Periodicals of the United States* (Westport, Conn.: Greenwood Press, 1986), pp. 100–103.

33. James F. Fox, D.D., "Scotus Redivivus."

34. James F. Fox, D.D., "The Relations of Church and State I," *Catholic World* 84 (January 1907): 523–35.

35. Ibid., p. 526.

36. Ibid., p. 530.

37. Ibid.

38. Ibid., p. 531.

39. Ibid., pp. 534–35.

40. William J. Kerby, "Aims in Socialism," *Catholic World* 85 (July 1907): 500 n.

41. Ibid., p. 501.

42. Ibid. See also Kerby, "Catholicity and Socialism," *American Catholic Quarterly Review* 30, no. 118 (April 1905): 225–43.

43. William J. Kerby, "Reinforcement of the Bond of Faith," *Catholic World* 84 (January 1907): 508.

44. Ibid., p. 516.

45. Ibid., p. 603, quoted in *Catholic World* 84 (December 1906): 345. Newman's words were as follows; "What I desiderate in Catholics is the gift of *bringing (out)* what they are, what their religion is. . . I want a laity, not arrogant, not rash in speech, not disputations, but men who know their religion, who enter into it."

46. On Keane's selection of Shahan, see "Criterions of Catholic Truth," *Catholic World* 52 (October 1890): 123.

47. Chapter 2 of this study chronicles the problems John Zahm encountered with Bishop Sebastian Messmer when he appointed O'Gorman and Pace to lecture at the Columbian Catholic Summer School. The bishop of Green Bay balked at the selection and questioned the orthodoxy of the two. Zahm rebuffed him. Gannon reported that Herman J. Heuser of the *Ecclesiastical Review* suspected Pace for studying under Wilhelm Wundt in Leipzig whom he accused of materialism. O'Gorman was consecrated Bishop of Sioux Falls in 1896. For an appraisal by his contemporaries, see "Review," *American Catholic Quarterly Review* 21 (January 1896): 220–21.

48. George M. Sauvage, C.S.C, "The New Philosophy in France," *Catholic University Bulletin* 12, no. 2 (April 1906): 149.

49. Ibid., p. 158.

50. Ibid., p. 149ff.

51. Furthermore, the work of American Catholic modernists we have studied was reviewed in these periodicals. See, for example, "Book Reviews: *General Introduction to the Study of Holy Scriptures* by Rev. Francis E. Gigot," *American Catholic Quarterly Review* 29, no. 116 (October 1904): 812–13. The reviewer noted that this was a third edition because the others were so well-received, and concluded, "There is need of a book of this kind, and if it is the means of spreading the study of Holy Scriptures, as it should be, it will have done a good work."

52. The *American Catholic Quarterly Review* was founded in 1876 as an apologetic journal. In 1889 Archbishop Patrick John Ryan succeeded Andrew Corcoran as editor, and pledged to continue the mission to "higher intellects." He served as editor until 1912 and the journal enjoyed a period of prosperity under his progressive leadership. See R. Scott Appleby, "*American Catholic Quarterly Review*," in Charles Lippy, ed., *Religious Periodicals in the United States* (Westport, Conn.: Greenwood Press, 1986), pp. 18–21.

53. Thomas J. Gerrard, "The New Apologetic," *American Catholic Quarterly Review* 29, no. 116 (October 1904): 655.

54. Ibid., p. 656.

55. Ibid., p. 657–58, passim.

56. Ibid., p. 659.

57. Ibid., p. 661.

58. F. Aveling, "The Neo-Scholastic Movement," *American Catholic Quarterly Review* 31, no. 121 (January 1906): 28–29.

59. Ibid., pp. 30–31.

60. W.H. Kent, O.S.C., "Hegel and the Schoolmen," *American Catholic Quarterly Review* 28, no. 112 (October 1903): 720–21.

61. George M. Searle, C.S.P., "Dr. Mivart's Last Utterance," *Catholic World* 71 (June 1900): 358.

62. Quoted in Searle, p. 354. For a careful and detailed treatment of this question, see John D, Root, "The Final Apostasy of St. George Jackson Mivart," *Catholic Historical Review* 71, no. 1 (January 1985): 1–25.

63. Searle, "Dr. Mivart's Last Utterance," pp. 363–64.

64. On Darwinism as covered by these periodicals, consult Edwin V. O'Hara, "The Latest Defence of Darwinism," *Catholic World* 80 (March 1905): 719, and S. Fitzsimons, "Lest We Forget," *American Catholic Quarterly Review* 28, no. 111 (July 1903): 490–512.

65. "Fogazzaro and His Trilogy," *Catholic World* 84 (January 1907): 462–76.

66. William L. Sullivan, "The Latest Word of Theology on Inspiration," *Catholic World* 84 (November 1906): 219.

67. George Tyrrell, S.J., "The Limits of the Development Theory," *Catholic World* 81, (September 1905): 730–44.

68. Ibid., pp. 743.

69. Ibid., p. 730.

70. On the nature, for example, of Sullivan's commitment to modernism, due to its respect for the individual's conscience, see Warren E. Duclos, "Crisis of an American Catholic Modernist: Toward the Moral Absolutism of William L. Sullivan," *Church History* 41, no. 3 (1972): 369–84.

71. Colman J. Barry, *The Catholic University of America, 1903–1909*, p. 177.

72. William Turner, "A Contemporary French School of Pragmatism," *New York Review* 2, no. 1 (July-August 1906): 36.

73. William Turner, "The Philosophical Bases of Modernism," *Catholic University Bulletin* 14, no. 5 (May 1908): 443.

74. Ibid., pp. 453–54.

75. "The Encyclical Pascendi Dominici Gregis," *Catholic University Bulletin* 14, no. 1 (January 1908): 3.

76. Charles Johnston, "The Catholic Reformation and the Authority of the Vatican," *North American Review* 186 (December 1907): 581–82.

77. George M. Searle, C.S.P., "Mr. Charles Johnston on Modernism," *The Catholic World* 86 (February 1908): 636–37.

78. Reprinted in *Catholic World* 86 (January 1908): 506–18.

79. Thomas Burke, C. S. P., "The Errors Condemned," *Catholic World* 86 (January 1908): 525.

80. Joseph F. Mooney, "The Rights of the Supreme Pontiff," reprinted in *Catholic World* 86 (January 1908): 520.

81. Joseph W. Daily, "The Causes of Modernism," *The Catholic World*, 86, no. 514 (January, 1908): 647.

82. John T. Murphy, C.S.Sp., "The Pope's Encyclical on Modernism," *American Catholic Quarterly Review* 33, no. 129 (January 1908): 134.

83. Ibid., p. 133.

CONCLUSION: ON THE SIGNIFICANCE
OF AMERICAN CATHOLIC MODERNISM

1. There were dozens of articles published in the *American Catholic Quarterly Review*, the *Catholic University Bulletin*, the *New York Review*, and the *Catholic World* that have not been mentioned above, many of which were quite technical. The articles also ranged widely in topic. A few examples: Thomas J. Gerrard, "The Function of the Will in Religious Assent," *Catholic World* 87, no. 518 (May 1908): 145–54; John A. Ryan, D.D., "Is the Modern Spirit Religious?" *Catholic World* 85, no. 506 (May 1907): 183–93; and James J. Fox, D.D., "The Catholic Encyclopedia," *Catholic World* 85, no. 506 (May 1907): 522–28.

2. Sullivan also apparently published in the *Revue moderniste internationale*. He mentioned to Throckmorton that after leaving the Catholic Church he had agreed to "contribute and send an occasional article or batch of news" to the *Revue*. Sullivan to Throckmorton, January 17, 1910, AHDS. See "Le catholicisme aux Etats-Unis" in *Revue moderniste internationale* 2 (1911): 347ff.

3. Angelo Roncalli's file in the Holy Office contained the accusation that he was a modernist; as Pope John XXIII he had the reference expunged. Reported in Meriol Trevor, *Pope John* (New York: Macmillan, 1967), p. 132n.

4. For a fair and accurate representation of the positions of both sides of the controversy between Charles Curran and the Congregation for the Doctrine of the Faith (and Catholic University of America) and reprints of the relevant documents generated, see Charles Curran, *Faithful Dissent* (Kansas City, Mo.: Sheed and Ward, 1986).

5. For an example of this mode of comparative history, see Gerald Fogarty, "Dissent at Catholic University: The Case of Henry Poels," *America* 155 (October 11, 1986): pp. 180–84.

6. Kurtz defines elective affinities as "the dialectical relationship between ideas and belief systems on the one hand, and the interests of various groups, classes and strata on the other," *The Politics of Modernism*, p. 2.

7. The closest approximation of such a fellowship at the turn of the century was the International Catholic Congress. On the contemporary situation,

see John Apczynski, ed., *Theology and the University* [The Annual Publication of the College Theology Society, Vol. 33] (Lanham, Md.: University Press of America, 1990).

8. "The Rev. Charles Curran, for many years professor of moral theology at the Catholic University of America in Washington, D.C., is now teaching at Auburn University in Alabama as a distinguished visiting professor. In itself this is not suprising. In the last three years Fr. Curran has done similar teaching stints at other secular institutions. . . . Fr. Curran's presence at such universities as Auburn, however, reflects the fact that he is not welcome at Catholic institutions of higher learning. Indeed, in every case where efforts have been made at departmental levels to settle Fr. Curran in a Catholic institution, he has been positively excluded by upper administration. We regard this exclusion as a continuing complicity in the original injustice done to Fr. Curran and as harmful, not only to him, but also to Catholic higher education in this country and to the church," Richard A. McCormick, S.J., and Richard P. McBrien, "L'Affaire Curran II," *America* 163, no. 6 (September 8–15, 1990): 127. Shortly after McCormick and McBrien wrote these words, Curran moved to Southern Methodist University.

9. David Tracy, *The Analogical Imagination: Christian Theology and the Culture of Pluralism* (New York: Crossroad, 1981), p. 26.

10. Descriptions of such conversion experiences may be found, for example in Sullivan, *Letters to His Holiness*; Tyrrell, *Christianity at the Crossroads*; Loisy, *My Duel with the Vatican*; and [Slattery], "Biographie." "Not only in theology but in natural science, a new model of understanding demands something like a *conversion*, which cannot be extorted in a purely rational way," Hans Küng, "Paradigm Change in Theology: A Proposal for Discussion," in Hans Küng and David Tracy, eds., *Paradigm Change in Theology* (New York: Crossroad, 1989), p. 25.

11. Quoted in Joseph A. Komonchak, "Newman's Infallible Instincts: The Argument for Elbowroom," *Commonweal*, 10 August 1990: 445–46. Also see Mary Jo Weaver, ed., *Newman and the Modernists* (Lanham, Md.: University Press of America, 1985).

12. "If anything seems to be proved in contradiction to the dogmas of faith, the believer is sure that that point will eventually turn out, first not to be proved, or secondly, not contradictory, or thirdly not contradictory to anything really revealed, but to something which has been confused with revelation. . . . His cardinal maxim is that truth cannot be contrary to truth; his second is that truth often seems contrary to truth; and his third is that the practical conclusion, that we must be patient with such appearances and not be hasty to pronounce them to be really of a more formidable character," Newman, *The Via Media of the Anglican Church*, quoted in Komonchak, "Newman's Infallible Instincts," p. 447.

13. On this point, see the essays in Küng and Tracy, eds., *Paradigm Change in Theology*, pp. 27, 154–55, 206–08, 439–40.

14. See William D. Dinges, "Roman Catholic Traditionalism," in Martin E. Marty and R. Scott Appleby, eds., *Fundamentalisms Observed* (Chicago: University of Chicago Press, 1991).

15. Richard P. McBrien has described "a quasi-official party line" developed by American bishops in the late 1980s. One central tenet of the party line, according to McBrien, is that "The academic freedom of the Catholic theologian is limited by revelation and the teaching authority of the church." "If a given Bishop's *understanding* of a particular Catholic theologian's writings conflicts with the bishop's own *understanding* of Catholic doctrine (solely derived perhaps from his seminary courses 30 to 40 years ago), the bishop may declare the theologian's work unsound or even heretical, ban his or her works from diocesan programs and seminary reading lists and prohibit him or her from lecturing in the diocese," Richard P. McBrien, "Academic Freedom in Catholic Universities: The Emergence of a Party Line," *America* 159, no. 17 (December 3, 1988): 454, 456.

16. See the discussion in William M. Halsey, *The Survival of American Innocence: Catholicism in an Age of Disillusionment, 1920–1940* (Notre Dame, Ind.: University of Notre Dame Press, 1980). The fact that Pius X, the pope who condemned modernism in 1907, ardently and successfully promoted the eucharistic piety at the heart of the twentieth-century celebration of the Tridentine illustrates the surprising continuities beneath the surface of conflict: the renewal of eucharistic piety inspired the liturgical reform movement that eventually was the foundation for a reexamination of the historical context of the earliest Christian eucharists that were in turn retrieved as the model for worship in the vernacular.

17. McBrien contends that "[Contemporary] critics of academic freedom tend to homogenize everything, so that there is no real or meaningful distinction between what truly arises from revelation (Tradition) and what arises only from custom or from a particular school of theology (traditions), between the Word of God and fallible interpretations of that Word, between definitive (infallible) teachings of the church and non-definitive (fallible) teachings." He finds that "it is not surprising that the operative understanding of theology in this emerging party line is neo-Scholastic. That was the only kind of theology these bishops studied in their pre-Vatican II seminary days and in the Roman universities. And so that is the only theological method with which they are directly and personally familiar. What is suprising is that they would not have discovered by now how classically *Protestant* their notion of theology is." Richard P. McBrien, "Academic Freedom in Catholic Universities," pp. 455–457.

INDEX